THE POLITICAL THOUGHT OF
ROGER WILLIAMS

THE POLITICAL THOUGHT OF ROGER WILLIAMS

BY

JAMES E. ERNST

KENNIKAT PRESS, INC./PORT WASHINGTON, N. Y.

Originally published in 1929
Reissued in 1966 by Kennikat Press

Library of Congress Catalog Card No: 66-25909

CONTENTS

THE POLITICAL THOUGHT OF
ROGER WILLIAMS

I

ROGER WILLIAMS

PART 1

A SURVEY OF HIS LIFE

In 1636, there was founded "a small new society in Rhode Island"—writes a distinguished European scholar and statesman— "upon the principles of entire liberty of conscience, and the uncontrolled power of the majority in secular concerns. The theories of freedom in Church and State, taught in the schools of philosophy in Europe, were here brought into practice in the government of a small community. It was prophesied that the democratic attempts to obtain universal suffrage, a general elective franchise, annual parliaments, entire religious freedom, and the Miltonic schism, would be of short duration. But these institutions have not only maintained themselves here, but have spread over the whole union. They have superseded the autocratic commencements of Carolina and of New York, the high church party of Virginia, the theocracy in Massachusetts, and the monarchy throughout America; they have given laws to one quarter of the globe, and, dreaded for their moral influence, they stand in the background of every democratic struggle in Europe."[1] The man who established this "small new society" was Roger Williams.

The beginning and the end of Roger Williams' life are shrouded in mystery. The date of his birth is unknown. There is evidence, however, that he was born about 1603, in the parish of St. Sepulchres, without Newgate, London,[2] probably in the Williams home in Cow Lane, as the street is still called, and that he spent his boyhood playing about the suburbs of London, within

---

[1] *Narragansett Club Publications,* Vol. I, Introd. p. 3; Quoted from Gervinus: *Introduction to the History of the Nineteenth Century,* p. 65. [Hereafter this series will be referred to as N C P.]

[2] Because the records of St. Sepulchres, without Newgate, were burnt, no record of Williams' baptism is left. His age is approximated from numerous sources: *Letters,* N C P., Vol. VI, *To Winthrop* (1632); *Testimony of Roger Williams* (1679), p. 399. *Rhode Island Historical Society Publications,* Vol. VIII. [Hereafter this will be listed as R I H S P.] *Ibid, Testimony of Roger Williams,* p. 156. Richman: *Rhode Island: Its Making and Its Meaning,* Vol. II, p. 157; and *Rhode Island: A Study in Separatism,* p. 13.

and without Newgate, on Snowhill, and at Smithfield.[3] His father, James Williams of London, citizen and merchant tailor, died in 1621, leaving bequests for his wife, Alice (Pemberton), and four children: Sydrach, Robert, Roger and Catherine, wife of Ralph Wightman, and also several bequests to charity. The earliest contemporary reference to Roger Williams, that has yet been found, is that in 1617 in the form of a legacy of twenty shillings from Margery Pate, the parish of St. Sepulchres. As a youth in London, he took up the study of shorthand and acquired enough skill as a stenographer to take shorthand notes of sermons and speeches in the Star Chamber. These he transcribed into longhand and presented to Sir Edward Coke, who decided to complete the education of "so hopeful a youth."[4]

Through the influence of Coke, Roger Williams was elected a scholar to Sutton's Hospital, as the Charter House School was then called, June 25, 1621. This school was not far from Williams' home. He continued his studies there until 1623. How he met Sir Edward is not definitely known; but, since it appears that Williams and Sir Edward were members of the same church, the acquaintance may have begun in that way. On June 29, 1623, Williams was registered at Pembroke College, Cambridge, receiving his annual sixteen pounds per year "pension" from Sutton's Hospital while at college. He matriculated on July 7, 1624, signed the Subscription Book in 1626, and received the degree of B.A. in January, 1626/27. For two more years he continued as a graduate student at Cambridge, presumably preparing for the ministry.

After leaving Cambridge in 1628, Roger Williams became Chaplain to Sir Edward Masham at Otes, in Essex. As far as is known, this was his first office in the ministry. Two letters

---

[3] Recent research has added considerable data to our knowledge of Williams' early life and of his ancestry. The various sources containing this data are: Oscar Straus: *Roger Williams*. Waters: *Genealogical Gleanings in England*. R I H S P: *Manuscript Abstracts* by G. Andrew Moriarity, Jr.; and *Williams vs Williams Suit in Chancery*, 1644, by Walter Angell. *Rhode Island Historical Society Collections*, Vol. VI, p. 302, Morgan Edwards: *History of the Baptists*. [Hereafter this will be listed as R I H S C.] *Letters of Roger Williams to Lady Barrington* printed in Carpenter: *Roger Williams;* photostats in R I H S Library; also in *New England Historical and Genealogical Register*, Vol. XLIII, pp. 315-320. [Hereafter this will be listed as N E H & G R.] R I H S C., Vols. XI, p. 122, XIII, p. 103, and XV, p. 64: N C P, Vols. IV, p. 65, and VI, p. 239.

[4] Letter: *To Mrs. Sadlier*, N C P., Vol. VI, p. 252.

of Williams addressed to Lady Barrington,[5] who was a daughter of Sir Henry Cromwell, and an aunt of the Protector, furnish valuable corroborative evidence for the identity of the Roger Williams of history and serve to inform us about his residence in May, 1629, two years after his graduation from Cambridge.   In these letters, he alludes to his aged mother, his pecuniary circumstances and prospects, his library, his tender conscience, his having been kept back from honor and preferment, a call to New England and several other proffers to "livings" for 100 pounds, and his love for a member of the lady's family.   While chaplain at Otes, he met Jane Walley, Lady Masham's cousin.   He seems to have fallen deeply in love with her, and made frequent visits to Hatfield Priory, where Jane lived with her aunt and guardian, Lady Barrington.   Although he had won the heart of the maiden to whom he aspired, his love affair was not prosperous.   Neighborhood gossip seems to have caused Lady Barrington to request him to cease calling at the Priory.   He complied, but sent a "paper deputie" asking for her niece's hand in marriage.   Lady Barrington frowned upon his passion and replied that he was a match altogether unsuitable for one of her family.   In despair he wrote to the obdurate lady on May 2, 1629, "We [Jane and Roger] hope to live together in the heavens though ye Lord have denied that union on earth."[6]   However, it would appear that he soon gave up all thought of Jane and transferred his affections elsewhere.   Mary Barnard, lady in waiting to Jane's cousin, "Jug" Althem, Lady Masham's eldest daughter, then attracted the disappointed lover.   The engagement of Mary and Roger is mentioned in a letter by Lady Masham in the autumn of 1629.   They were married on December 15, 1629, at High Laver, Essex.   In the records Williams is styled as "clarke," a clergyman.

At Otes, Roger Williams became acquainted with Lady Masham's family, many of whom were destined to play a vital part in the affairs of England in later years.   Oliver Cromwell, "Ship-

---

[5] N E H & G R., Vol. XLIII, pp. 315-320. The first of these two letters is undated.   The second, written, beyond a doubt, soon after the first, bears the date of May 2, 1629. Carpenter: *Roger Williams,* pp. 16-21.

[6] *Ibid.*   The sequel to the unfortunate love affair is interesting.   Jane Whalley later married the Rev. William Hooke, a Puritan clergyman, and came to Taunton, Massachusetts Bay Colony, where he was pastor from 1639 to 1644.

money" John Hampden, and Edward Whalley, then all enterprising young men, were Lady Masham's cousins. Whalley's daughter, Frances, later became the wife of William Goffe, the regicide. Lady Masham's husband and her brother, Sir Thomas Barrington, a decade and a half later, signed the famous letter giving Roger Williams free passage through Massachusetts. The friendships which, as a young clergyman, he made with these members of the gentry, men who were to shape England's future, proved later of great benefit to Roger Williams and his infant colony in its struggle with the imperialistic ideas of its more powerful neighbors—the colonies of Massachusetts Bay, Plymouth, and Connecticut.

When Williams gave up his chaplaincy at Otes is not certain, but probably shortly after May, 1629. The acerbity of tone of Williams' second letter to Lady Barrington, in which, among other pertinent things, he, in no uncertain manner, predicts for her an unhappy hereafter unless she repent, would necessitate his removal from Otes shortly thereafter. He doubtless obtained a small parish church elsewhere in Essex. In the first of these letters, Williams mentions that, "For my own part it is well known (though I would gladly conceal my self) how a gracious God and tender conscience (as Balak said to Balaam) hath kept me back from offers and preferment. Besides many former offers and that late New England call, I have since had two several livings proffered to me, each of them 100 pounds per annum." High Laver, in Essex, at which place he was married on December 15, 1629, is not more than a dozen miles from Chelmsford, where lived and preached the Rev. Thomas Hooker, in later years the founder of the colony at Hartford. That Williams and Hooker were neighbors and friends, Williams intimates to us in his numerous letters, and especially when he records a memorable ride which the two worthies took with the Rev. John Cotton of Boston, England, discussing and arguing by the way concerning the use of the Book of Common Prayer. "Possibly Master *Cotton* may call to minde" he writes "that the *discusser* (riding with himselfe and one other person of precious memory (Master *Hooker*) to and from Sempringham) presented his *Arguments* from *Scripture* why he durst not joyne with them in their use of *Common Pray-*

er."[7] His residence in Essex continued at least long enough to gain him the reputation among his neighbors of being divinely mad. In his history of New England, Rev. William Hubbard, the Ipswich minister, says of Roger Williams: "In this manner did overheated zeal vent itself in the said Mr. Williams, of whom they were wont to say *in Essex, where he lived,* that he was divinely mad."[8] Because of the lack of definite evidence, two different conclusions have been arrived at by the previous studies of Williams' life, each of which is substantiated with rather meager evidence; the one, that it is quite likely that Williams obtained a parish church in Lincolnshire, near Boston and Sempringham; the other, that after leaving Otes sometime after May 2, 1629, until his departure from Bristol for New England, late in 1630, Williams lived and preached for the most part in and around Essex, England.

Some time between his entrance into Sutton's Hospital and the latter part of 1630, Roger Williams came in contact with radical religious and political ideas which shaped his later career. The atmosphere of Cambridge was permeated and agitated with ecclesiastical and political liberalism[9] during the first half of the seventeenth century, and Williams was not the kind of youth to keep out of such discussions. His studies in history and theology brought him in contact with the popular sovereignty ideas of the philosophers and theologians from St. Paul down to those of his own day. Christianity itself as taught by Christ was a populist and individualistic movement. His mentor, Sir Edward Coke, was the leading advocate of the sovereignty of the common law, and the author of the Bill of Rights forced upon Charles I, in 1628. But this was not all, for: "Cambridge, where he attended college, was in Cambridgeshire, one of those eastern counties of England into which there had long been migrating from Holland Anabaptists and Mennonites imbued with the idea of severance

---

[7] N C P., Vol. VI, p. 65. N E H & G R., Vol. XLIII, pp. 315 ff. R I H S., Vol. XVI, pp. 81 ff. Biographies of Roger Williams by Straus, Carpenter, and Hall. Also Arnold's *History of Rhode Island,* Vol. I. The only certainty about this period of Williams' life is that the greater part of it was spent somewhere in Eastern England.

[8] Hubbard: *A General History of New England.*

[9] Mansbridge: *The Older Universities of England,* pp. xvii, 38; chapters IV and V. Masson: *Life of Milton,* especially, pp. 531-608. Of the seventeen leading men in New England about 1640, fifteen were educated at Cambridge and two at Oxford. Carpenter: *Roger Williams,* 29.

of Church and State. With this idea, Williams himself had become impressed; so much so, indeed, that he had thought it not unimportant to acquire a knowledge of the Dutch tongue."[10]   The other leaders in New England, undoubtedly, had the same opportunities for imbiding the radical ideas for which they condemned Williams, but their failure to do so is all too evident. Roger Williams, on the other hand, because of his receptive, sympathetic, and inquiring mind not only accepted the new principles but proclaimed them publicly in his native land. For this he was driven out of England by the persecutions of Bishop Laud.

Late in the year 1630, Roger Williams, accompanied by his wife, went to Bristol, and on December 1 sailed for New England on the ship Lyon, Captain Pierce. After a stormy voyage of sixty-five days, the Lyon anchored at Nantasket in Boston Harbor on February 5, 1630/1. Williams was a young man about twenty-eight years old, whom Bradford characterizes as "a young minister, godly and zealous, having precious parts." He is also mentioned by Hubbard as "of good account in England for a godly and zealous preacher." And he is one of the few persons whose arrival in Massachusetts Governor Winthrop considered of enough importance to mention in his diary.

The year 1631, in which Williams landed at Boston, was notable in both New and Old England. Charles I had decided on autocratic rule, and the clergy were encouraged to preach prerogative principles from the pulpit. Doctrines subversive of popular rights were taught, and sermons containing them were published at the command of the king. Laud had become as autocratic in the ecclesiastical office as the king in the civil. With unscrupulous zeal and severity he sought to blot out all sectarianism from the church. Calvinistic[11] and Lutheran[12] interpretations of the Articles were fanatically condemned. Laud, in his Arminian zeal, punished sectarians by physical torture and disfigurement, as well as by fines, imprisonment, and whipping. Drastic measures were taken by both church and state in the attempt to stem the tide of religious liberalism in Old England. It was from such a coun-

---

[10] Richman: *Rhode Island: A Study in Separatism,* p. 15.

[11] The Puritans were extreme Calvinists.

[12] The Anabaptists, Mennonites, and Independents were largely under the direct influence of Luther's writings.

try and from such conditions that Williams fled to the New World.[13]

He escaped from this tyranny of religious thought and civil authority, only to find similar outrages inflicted upon conscience and human rights in New England by men who, like him, had suffered in Old England. The surprise that he must have manifested upon this discovery, was followed by an indignation which his impulsiveness and impatience forced into expression. Winthrop notes that Williams no sooner landed than he declared "the magistrates might not punish a breach of the Sabbath nor any other offense," if it was a breach of the First Table; and that he also refused to hold church communion with any group favorable to the Anglican impurities. Because the church in Boston from which, upon his arrival, he had received a call, kept parishes and its members, when in England, held communion with the Anglican church, Williams refused to join the Boston church, but quitted Boston a few weeks after his arrival and united with the church in Salem.

Upon his arrival in New England, the new basic ideas about church and state were, however, only vague and general theories. Neither did there seem to be any immediate prospect of putting them into practice. The man who was later to found Rhode Island was still to be made. He was not yet tried and tempered. With the appearance of Master Hooker and Master Cotton at Boston during the latter part of the year, the final process of purification of the radical principles was to begin in real earnest. Williams, by his impulsiveness, his love of argument, and his vigorous opposition to the theocratic principles of state, had the faculty of arousing the government into activity against him, no matter what he undertook. His entrance into New England, resulting in his conflict with Cotton, Hooker and the civil authorities, was the last step needed to prepare him to put his theory into successful practice. In the next few years his ideas were to become crystallized. His life and work and mental anguish amidst bigotry and stern intolerance on the wild shores of a new world were indeed a fitting preparation for a man who was to put into practice the "noblest political conception ever propounded."

---

[13] Letter: *To Mrs. Sadlier*, N C P., Vol. VI, p. 237 (1652) London: "And truly it was as bitter as death to me when Bishop Laud pursued me out of this land" etc. Mrs. Sadlier was the daughter of Sir Edward Coke. Masson: *Life of Milton*, Vol II, pp. 560 f. Hall: *Roger Williams*, chapter II. Straus: *Roger Williams*, pp. 14, 67, 128. R I H S C., Vol. XI.

His short career at Salem was a stormy one. He began his ministry in April, 1631, and on April 31 the General Court of the Bay colony sent its disapproval and asked the church to forbear accepting him. As a congregational and independent community, Salem had the right to select him for their pastor. It was one of the church's most sacred privileges. This right the General Court flagrantly violated, and thereby laid the foundation for future conflicts. Again, soon after he landed, Williams entered his name to become a freeman. On May 12, he was made a freeman—and on that very day the Court made a new ruling that "only church members within the limits of the colony are in the future to be admitted as freemen of the Body Politic." Thus the theocracy was established on a working basis, May 12, 1631. The purpose of the ruling was partly to avoid admission of men like Williams to the body politic, and partly to establish the principle that the government belonged only to the saints. By this law, Williams claimed "magistracy was shut against natural and unregenerate men though excellently fitted for the civil offices, but also against the best servants of God, except they entered into the church state" of the Bay colony. Williams fancifully called this ruling "Moses' Church Constitution."

Due, however, to the growing opposition from Boston, Williams left Salem in September, 1631, for Plymouth, where he was pastor for over two years. Bradford says about Roger Williams' sojourn at Plymouth, "he was freely entertained, according to our poor ability and excercised his gifts among us: and after some time was admitted a member of the church and his teaching well approved, for the benefit whereof I still bless God, and am thankful to him for his sharpest admonitions and reproofs so far as they agree with the truth. He this year fell into some strange opinions, and from opinions to practice, which caused some controversy between the church and him, and in the end some discontent on his part, by the occasion whereof he left somewhat abruptly." He received his dismissal from Plymouth in 1634. Salem received him with sincere and great pleasure, "and not a few people followed him thither from Plimouth."

Two weeks after Williams had gone to Salem, on September 3, 1631, Master Cotton, the destined protagonist in the strife against the liberty championed by Williams, landed in Boston in company with Thomas Hooker and Mr. Stone—"the glorious triumvirate coming together." Upon reaching Boston, Cotton was immediately called upon to give advice and to arrange the ecclesiastical and civil affairs of the colony. He personally fixed the church polity in its regular form, so that the civil laws could be adjusted to the polity of the church and so that, while nominally distinct, they actually supported each other. And for nineteen years John Cotton was the clever master of the fierce theocracy in Massachusetts—"The unmitred pope of a pope-hating commonwealth." With the appearance of Master Cotton upon the scene, Roger Williams' tenure in Salem was to be a very short one.

The conservative forces of New England were gradually closing in on the headstrong and unruly Williams. The pastor of Salem died in August, 1634. Williams was made pastor of the Salem church over the protests of Massachusetts Bay, for Salem was again asserting its undoubted right as a congregation. Complaint was soon found against him for preaching publicly against the King's Patent, the use of the cross of St. George on the English flag, the free rights of the colony to the Indian lands, the theocratic form of government, and concerning the church of Antichrist. He received his first summons to Court on November 17, 1634. On April 30, 1635, a new accusation was served upon him: that he taught publicly against oaths of unregenerate men. He was called before the ministers and confuted, so they claimed —but Williams remained of the same opinion still. In July, 1635, he was served with new and dangerous charges—that he taught that magistrates ought not to punish the breach of the First Tables; that he ought not to tender an oath to an unregenerate man; that a man ought not to pray with such, though wife and child; that men ought not to give thanks after sacraments or after meals; and that the church of Salem persisted in calling him against the advise of the Court. For this latter fault, Salem was punished by the Court by the refusal of certain lands which belonged to her legally. Williams and the Salem congregation now wrote letters of admonition to the other churches, asking them to oppose the action of the Court. As a result, Endicot, his friend, was imprisoned for justifying the letter, and the majority of the people forsook Williams and his principles for the sake of a strip of land. Williams now threatened to withdraw from all the churches of the Bay, and shortly thereafter renounced church communion with Salem and the churches of the

Bay. This decision was hastened by a summons from the Court. His letters against various practices were read "which he justified and maintained all his opinions." Even the famous Hooker, laments Winthrop in his *Journal* for November, 1635, could not "reduce him from the error of his way." Morton, in the *New England Memorial* writes, "Hooker, Cotton and others tried to convince him of his error; not even the Court could do anything with him, but he grew more violent and assertive."

Chief Justic Durfee, in his admirable anniversary discourse, gives a vivid picture of Williams' last stand against the theocracy of the Bay:

"The future of Rhode Island, to some extent the future of the world, hangs suspended on the issue. Will he, like his church, worn out and desperate, blenching before the unknown, lose heart and yield? Never. He stands unshaken in the 'rockie strength' of his convictions. He is ready 'not only to be bound and banished, but to die for them.' So hour after hour he argues unsubdued, till the sun sinks low and the weary court adjourns. On the morrow (Friday, October 9, 1635) still persisting in his glorious 'contumacy,' he is sentenced, the clergy, all save one, advising to be banished, or to adopt the apologetic and felicitous euphemism of his great adversary, John Cotton, 'enlarged' out of Massachusetts."[14]

The clash between Roger Williams and the Massachusetts Commonwealth resulted in an order on September 3, 1635, that he was to depart within six weeks out of the jurisdiction of the Bay.[15] He was convicted for both religious and civil misdemeanors according to the order of the Court: "Whereas Mr. Roger Williams, one of the elders of the church of Salem, hath broached & dyvulged dyvers newe & dangerous opinions, against the authority of Magistrates, as also with ltres of defamacon, both of the magistrates & churches here, & that before any con-

---

[14] Durfee: *Two Hundred and Fiftieth Anniversary of the Planting of Providence*, June 24, 1886. Straus: *Roger Williams*, p. 57. The date of October 9 is incorrect. The Sentence of Banishment was pronounced neither on October 9, nor on November 3, 1635, but on September 3, instead of November 3, as stated by all his early biographers and Arnold in his *History of Rhode Island*, Vol. I, p. 37. For correct date see Palfrey: *History of New England*, Vol. I, p. 412; *Massachusetts Colonial Records*, Vol. I, p. 160. [Hereafter this will be listed as M C R.] Records of the General Court at Newe Towne, September 2, 1635; and N C P., Vol. II, pp. 18, Note 4, and 30, Note 13. Compare Winthrop: *Journal*, Vol. I, pp. 154-173.

[15] For the facts of the later life of Roger Williams, see: N C P., Vol. VI, *Letters*. Richman: *Rhode Island: A Study in Separatism*. Biographies of Roger Williams by Straus, Hall, and Carpenter.

vicôn, it is therefore ordered, that the said Mr. Williams shall dêpte out of this jurisdiction within sixe weekes nowe next ensueing."[16] According to Winthrop, the final proceedings were not based on those charges simply, but upon the whole antecedent action of the Court in its relation to Williams, beginning with May 12, 1631.[17] Later the sentence was modified to permit him to remain until spring. But when he continued privately "to draw others unto his opinions," it was decided in January, 1635/36, to send him to England. Governor Winthrop, probably out of sympathy, warned Williams in time to enable him to escape arrest by Captain John Underhill. With his servant Thomas Angell, Williams fled from Salem in the dead of winter and sought protection and shelter with his friend Massasoit, the sachem of the Wampamoags. In the spring of 1636, Williams broke ground at Seekonk, on the east bank of the Seekonk River. Here he was joined by three companions, among whom was William Harris. When warned that they were upon territory claimed by the Plymouth colony, the party moved to Mooshassuc, doubtless in the early summer, and founded Providence. The founding of Providence in the spring or early summer of 1636 marks the beginning of the constructive period of Roger Williams' life.

With the exception of two journeys to England in the interest of the colony—the first in 1643 and the second in 1652—Roger Williams spent the remainder of his life in Rhode Island. Both of these journeys were undertaken primarily to secure charter rights as a legal protection against the encroachments of the neighboring colonies, and secondarily to look after legal and trade affairs of the various members of the colony. These thirty-eight years were dedicated to the task of establishing the political structure of Rhode Island on the new and dangerous principles for which he had been persecuted out of his native England and later banished from Massachusetts Bay. That he was not an unimportant figure in the political life of his times can be gathered from the fact that he numbered among his friends and associates the great men of New and Old England of the mid-seventeenth century. Besides Sir Edward Coke, his patron, were Cromwell, Milton, Sir Henry Vane the younger, Major-General Harrison, Lord President Lawrence, the leading members of the

---

[16] M C R., Vol. I, p. 160.
[17] Winthrop: *Journal,* Vol. I, for the year 1635.

Long Parliament, Hugh Peters, the two Winthrops, father and son, and numerous others prominent in England and America. In addition to taking a leading part in the political affairs of the colony, Williams spent the later years of his life in supporting a family by farming and trade, helping unfortunates, preaching to the Indians, and acting as interpreter and peace-maker between the Indians and the other colonies of New England.

Roger Williams died between January 16 and March 15, 1682-3. The last deed known to have been executed by Williams is dated January 16, 1682-3, and the earliest reference to his death so far located is that of William Adams on March 15, 1682-3, "Mr. Williams of Providence is lately deceased."[18] His death, like his birth, caused no more "than the slightest ripple on the surface of the life of the community." Although he had ample opportunity for acquiring wealth, "he gave away" said his son Daniel "his lands and other estates to them that he thought were most in want, until he had nothing to help himself;" but "I judge" said the same son, who probably supported Roger Williams and his wife during their last years, "they wanted nothing that was convenient for ancient people."[19] The people of Rhode Island and New England had no conception of his real greatness. It remained for the future to appreciate him and his work.

---

[18] Mr. Earnest Flagg in his *Genealogical Notes,* 1926, p. 244, prints an item which shows that Williams had died before March 15, 1683. The item is as follows: "In the *Winthrop Manuscripts* (unpublished), Vol. 10, page 4, in the custody of the Massachusetts Historical Society, is a letter from William Adams to J. Richards, dated March 15, 1682/3, which contains this sentence: 'Mr. Williams of Providence is lately deceased'." A photostat copy has been placed in R I H S C., Vol. XV, p. 421. Other references to Williams' death and burial will be found in *Book Notes,* VII, p. 46; X, p. 289; XXIV, p. 57; XXIX, p. 148. R I H S C., Vol. XIV, p. 130. "Report on the Burial place of Roger Williams," R I H S P., 1884-5, p. 47.

[19] Hall: *Roger Williams,* p. 203.

PART 2

HIS POLITICAL CONTROVERSY

Roger Williams was banished from Massachusetts Bay colony because of his political opinions and his attitude towards the theocratic state. The course of Cotton and the Bay was consistent with their theory of government—and if the sentence was ill-judged and narrow according to the standards of later centuries, the fault was as much in the times as in the leaders. The assertion made by numerous writers that the reason for his exile was largely religious is both misleading and inaccurate. A close scrutiny of the statements by Winthrop, Cotton, Williams, and other contemporaries should eradicate such a false notion.[20] Neither Williams nor the leaders of the Bay considered it a religious banishment; instead their records stoutly maintain it a sentence given by a theocratic government. The actual statements of the leading figures in the "drama" and those of the contemporaries will here be accepted as the more authoritative, although some allowance must be made for the controversial aspect of these statements. Roger Williams agreed that the four particular grounds for his sentence were rightly summed up by one of the most eminent magistrates, as: "First. That we have not our Land by Patent from the King, but that the Natives are the true owners of it, and that we ought to repent of such receiving it by Patent. Secondly. That it is not lawfull to call a wicked person to Sweare, to Pray, as being actions of Gods Worship. Thirdly. That it is not lawfull to heare any of the Ministers of the Parish Assemblies in *England*. Fourthly. That Civill Magistrates power extends only to the Bodies, and Goods and outward

---

[20] In addition to the evidence presented by Winthrop, Cotton, Williams, and the records of the General Court, there are the statements of contemporaries like Samuel Gorton: *Simplicities Defence Against Seven-Headed Policy*, etc.; Governor Winslow: *Hypocrasie Unmasked*, etc.; Thomas Edwards: *Antapologia;* Robert Baillie: *Dissvasive from the Errour of the Times;* Nathaniel Morton: *New England's Memorial;* William Hubbard: *A General History of New England;* Joshua Scottow: *A Narrative of the Plantation of the Massachusetts Colony,* etc.; Cotton Mather: *Magnalia Christi Americana.* Dexter, in his *As To Roger Williams,* pp. 64 ff, quotes in his footnotes numerous historians, among whom are Governor Thomas Hutchinson, Neal, Callender, Douglass, Backus, Morse and Parish, Graham, Baylies, Bancroft, Bradford, Hildreth, Felt, Barry, Oliver, Elliot, and Palfrey, a majority of whom emphasize the religious and minimize the political aspect of the banishment.

state of men, etc."[21]   This account Cotton terms a "fraudulent expression of particulars;" for each one of these four opinions, he affirms, was known to be held by many who were still "tolerated to enjoy both Civil, and Church-liberties amongst us." It was not for the mere holding of opinions contrary to the tenets of the Commonwealth, but for the turbulent assertion of them, that he was banished. According to Cotton's "best observation and remembrance," the sentence of banishment was caused by two things: first, his violent and tumultuous carriage against the Patent; and secondly, his vehement opposition to the Oath of Fidelity. The sentence was, however, hastened by the action of Williams in inducing the Salem church to join with him in remonstrating against the action of the magistrates, and by his renouncing church communion with Salem and the Bay.[22]

All the parties are essentially in agreement on the reasons for his sentence and exile. Of the five main charges enumerated by Winthrop, the first two and the last deal with problems of civil affairs, while the third and fourth points refer to spiritual affairs of interest to the Bay colony. The Order of the Court emphasizes divers new and dangerous opinions against the authority of the magistrates and letters of defamation of both magistrates and churches.[23] Cotton stresses the opposition to civil government, but concedes that Williams' attitude towards the church was influential in hastening the sentence. The statements agree substantially with the four grounds accepted and given by Williams. In all of them, his opposition to civil government receives the more prominent position. It is true, as Cotton mentioned, that there is a difference in the emphasis placed upon particulars in the charges; but that difference is due largely to individual outlook and interests. The essential fact is that because Williams persisted in asserting new opinions dangerous to the church and civil state, the Court with the advice of the ministers passed the order of banishment. Williams had been a disquieting religious and civil influence in New England ever since his arrival in 1631. Winthrop and Cotton agree that to the charges preferred against Williams in September, 1635, must be added the whole antecedent action of the Court for over four years in order to appreciate

---

[21] *Master Cottons Letter Examined*, N C P., Vol. I, p. 40.
[22] *Master Cottons Answer*, N C P., Vol. II, p. 44.
[23] Winthrop: *Journal*, Vol. I, pp. 154 ff, July, 1635, etc.; *Ante* pp. 9-12.

fully the real basis for the sentence.[24]   This removes the apparent discrepancy between the statements of Winthrop, Cotton, the general Court, and Williams.

In his controversy with Williams, Cotton deliberately "begged the question." While Roger Williams was discussing the religious and civil significance of the "new society" for which he contended in opposition to the theocratic and despotic state, Cotton refused to discuss civil matters, and presumably remained in the sphere of the church. "It was not my intent in that Letter which he examineth, to discuss the Grounds of his Civill Banishment at all, neither did I discusse one or the other of them. And it is a preposterous shifting of the State of the Question, to put it upon me to give account of the causes of his banishment, who neither did banish him, nor provoke the Court to banish him out of the Countrey. The Magistrates and Deputies of the Common-wealth (who were then the Members of that Court) are all of them of age, and able themselves to give account of their own actions."[25] Cotton here ignores that fact that his pulpit utterances directly influenced acts of the general Court.[26]   As Master Cotton deliberately evaded any lengthy discussion of the political aspect of the controversy, the two seldom clash directly on any civil issue. But this one point Cotton does make, that Williams was sentenced to exile because he expressed his opinions openly and publicly, and threatened thereby the stability of "the society of the Commonwealth."

Because the religious and civil principles enunciated by Roger Williams "subverted," as Cotton stated, "the fundamentall State, and the Government of the Countrey" and "tended to unsettle the Kingdoms, and Common-wealths of Europe," he was banished and outlawed. This was the real and primary cause for his banishment. Williams asserted as much. Winthrop so recorded it in his *Journal*. John Cotton emphasized it in all his writings against Williams: "My express words are, '*he has banished himselfe from the society of all the Churches of this Countrey.*' The

---

[24] M C R., Vol. I, p. 160. Winthrop: *Journal,* Vol. I, pp. 154 ff. *Master Cottons Answer,* N C P., Vol. II, pp. 40 ff.

[25] *Master Cottons Answer,* N C P., Vol. II, p. 40 f.

[26] Hubbard: *A History of New England,* p. 182, in his appreciative delineation of John Cotton says, "Whatever he delivered in the pulpit was soon put into an Order of the Court, if of a Civil, or set up as a practice in the Church, if of an ecclesiastical concernment."

society of the Church is one thing, the society of the Commonwealth is another.   And the Grounds upon which he built his
Separation, were not the causes of his banishment, but of his with-
drawing from the society of the Churches."[27]   Two things are
brought out here by Cotton: he denies that the church and state
are united, for he is striving to keep the controversy within the
sphere of purely spiritual matters in spite of Williams' claim that
there is a Civil aspect.   His second point is that Williams was
banished for civil and political reasons primarily; this position
is modified by his previous explanation that the religious issues
hastened the action of the theocratic commonwealth.

John Cotton has clearly pointed out the causes, as he understood them, for the exile of Williams.   The part played by spiritual and civil issues in the controversy as presented by him needs
little comment:

"To come therefore to particulars: Two things there were, which (to
my best observation, and remembrance) caused the Sentence of his Banishment: and two other fell in, that hastened it.

"1. His violent and tumultuous carriage against the Patent.

"By the Patent it is, that we received allowance from the King to
depart his Kingdome, and to carry our goods with us, without offence to
his Officers, and without paying custome to himselfe.

"By the Patent certain select men (as Magistrates, and Freemen)
have power to make Lawes, and the Magistrates to execute Justice, and
Judgement amongst the People, according to such Lawes.

"By the Patent we have power to erect such a Government of the
Church, as is most agreeable to the word, to the estate of the People,
and to the gaining of Natives (in Gods time) first to Civility, and then
to Christianity.

"To this Authoritie established by the Pattent, English-men doe readily submit themselves: and *foraine* Plantations (the *French,* the *Dutch,*
and *Swedish*) doe willingly transact their Negotiations with us, as with
a Colony established by the Royall Authority of the State of England.

"This Patent, Mr. Williams publickly, and vehemently preached
against, as containing matter of falsehood and injustice: . . . It was
answered to him. . . . But these Answers not satisfying him, this was
still pressed by him as a Nationall sinne, to hold to the Patent, yea, and
a Nationall duty to renounce a Patent: which to have done, had subverted
the fundamentall State, and Government of the Countrey.

"2. . . . . The Magistrates, and other members of the General Court
upon Intelligence of some Episcopall, and malignant practices against
the Countrey, they made an order of Court to take tryall of the fidelitie of
the People, (not imposing upon them, but) by offering to them an Oath

---

[27] *Master Cottons Answer,* N C P., Vol. II, p. 53.

of Fidelitie: that in case any should refuse to take it, they might not betrust them with place of public charge, and Command. This Oath when it came abroad, he vehemently withstood it and diswaded sundry from it, partly because it was, as he said, Christs Prerogative, to have his Office established by Oath, partly because an Oath was a part of Gods worship . . . So by his Tenent . . . the Oath . . . was the establishment . . . of mortall men in the office. . . . So that the Court was forced to desist from that proceeding; which practice of his was held to be the more dangerous, because it tended to unsettle the Kingdomes, and Common-wealths of Europe."[28]

Two other things, says Cotton, fell in upon these that hastened the sentence: the first,

"Mr. Williams took occasion to stirr up the Church to joyne with him in writing Letters of Admonition unto all the Churches where of those Magistrates were members," against the Court depriving the Church of Salem of a parcel of land because they insisted on calling Williams in spite of the opposition of the magistrates. The second: because he "renounced communion with the Church of *Salem* . . . and the Churches in the Bay. . . . This gave the Magistrates the more cause to observe the heady unruleliness of his spirit, and the incorrigiblenesse thereof by any Church-way, all the Churches in the Countrey being then renounced by him." These two occasions "hastened the Sentence of his Banishment, upon the former Grounds."[29]

Later on he remarks:

"I know his civill Banishment was not merely his own act, I know also that he might be banished from the Commonwealth, and yet have retained (as some others have done) Fellowship with some Churches, if not with all the Churches in the Countrey."[30]

"Mere religious whimsies" remarks Masson, "they might have borne with so far in Williams, including even his Individualism, or excess of Separatism; but here were attacks on law, property, social order:"[31]. The circumstances underlying his sentence were complicated for his disagreement with Cotton and the Bay colony was both religious and civil: religious in that he held the oath a form of worship unsuitable for civil uses, condemned the attending of parish worship in England by those visiting from New England, and opposed vehemently the support of the church

---

[28] *Ibid.* pp. 44-49.
[29] *Ibid.* pp. 50-51.
[30] *Ibid.* p. 57. John Cotton maintains that he argues merely ecclesiastical problems with Williams and not civil problems, and that to discuss the affairs of state as Williams has done was beside the issue.
[31] Masson: *Life of Milton*, Vol. II, p. 561.

by the state in taxes, persecution for heresy, and legislation; civil, by his publicly denouncing the authority of the Patent and the adminstering of the oath by civil officers, and maintaining that the civil authority extends only over the bodies, goods, and outward state of men, or the complete separation of church and state. The order of banishment was accelerated by his openly voicing his principles and by his success as a leader. The ideas of the separation of church and state and individual civil rights which make his experiment in the building of a state so significant and so influential among the nations, and which he embodied in the founding of Providence, had already been partially formulated, but can "scarcely be shown to have been involved in this dispute."[32] For it is plain that Williams alone made a cogent distinction between the religious and civil activities within a state, and that Cotton engrafted on the old system in the form of the Patent a theocratic control of the state. The theocracy of the Bay undertook to rid itself of the unruly headstrong Williams; and, because he would not be convinced, the Bay convicted him and pronounced upon him a civil banishment.[33]

---

[32] Palfrey: *History of New England,* Vol. I, p. 413.
[33] Arnold: *History of Rhode Island,* Vol. I, p. 27. Arnold here suggests, after examining the evidence, that the leaders of the Bay Colony used Williams to cover up their own political activities. See also p. 41.

HIS RELIGIOUS LIBERALISM

In his religious views Roger Williams also went far astray from the "fold" into which he was born. Up to December of 1629, he was still a recognized clergyman in the Church of England. But when he arrived in New England, he was a staunch and uncompromising Independent and Separatist. When, and how, this change in his religion occurred is still unknown. That Williams was an adherent to the Puritan tenets for a short time is borne out by his own analysis of the logical transition from Anglicanism to Separatism. "Again, I believe that there hardlv hath ever been a conscientious Separatist, who was not first a Puritan: for (as Mr. *Can* hath unanswerably proved) the grounds and principles of the Puritans against Bishops and Ceremonies and prophanes of people professing Christ, and the necessitie of Christs flock and discipline, must necessarily, if truly followed, lead on to, and inforce a separation from such wayes, worships, and Worshippers, to seek out the true wayes of God's worship according to Christ Jesus."[34] Like a true non-conformist, he held that the Anglican church was anti-Christian, its rites were to be avoided, its ministry forsaken, and its communion abjured. In contrast to him, the Puritans of Boston believed that the Church of England was corrupt and needed purification by reform; but they loved its stately service, governmental patronage, common prayers, and parish assemblies. Williams had, in his search for truth, come in contact with another principle of civil government than that held by the Puritans, a principle not generally adhered to by the Independents, that of the complete separation of Church and State. Because of the fundamental differences between his views and those of the Boston Puritans, Williams refused the call as teacher extended to him upon his arrival. Instead, he accepted a call from the more liberal Plymouth Colony, which was semi-Separatist in its tenets.

While a teacher in the Plymouth church, Williams, according to Bradford, showed evidences of Anabaptist influences. Williams may have come under the influence of this sect, either while a student at Cambridge or while in active parish work. That he was intimately acquainted with Luther's treatise *On Civil Liberty,* which set forth the same ideas and had previously formed the basis for the Anabaptist principles, is shown by his frequent references to Luther and his ideas. However that contact was

[34] *Cottons Letter,* N C P., Vol. I, p. 97.

formed, he was an advocate in 1635 of one of their two most characteristic principles of church life—the absolute and complete separation of church and state, and full liberty of conscience. Except for their untiring insistence upon liberty of conscience and adult baptism (both sprinkling and immersion were in practice at this period), the Anabaptists were substantially at one with the Congregationalists and Independents. Later Williams became a Baptist, and was re-baptized into that faith in March, 1639.

But shortly after his re-baptism, Roger Williams left the Baptist faith and became a Seeker.[35] "One Mr. Williams," writes Baillie, June 7, 1644, " has drawn a great number after him to a singular Independency, denying any true church in the world. . . . This man has made a great and bitter schism lately among the Independents." Again, on July 23, Baillie writes, "My good acquaintance, Mr. Williams, says there is no church, no sacraments, no pastors, no church-officers or ordinances, in the world, nor has been since a few years after the Apostles." First an Anglican, then an intense Separatist or Independent, than a Baptist and excommunicated on that account from his former friends in New England, and now in the solitude of the wilderness having outgrown even the Baptist faith, he goes "in quest after the unattainable truth," for which he or others invented the name Seekerism. "In short," observes Masson "the arch-representative of this new religion of Seekerism on both sides of the Atlantic was no other than our friend Roger Williams," the advocate of liberty in all things. "In the poor small span of my life," remarks Williams on one occasion, "I desired to have been a diligent and constant observer." To Mrs. Sadlier, the daughter of Sir Edward Coke, he writes against blindly accepting tradition and authority, "I am far from wondering at it, for all this have I done myself, until the Father of Spirits mercifully persuaded mine to swallow down no longer without chewing; to chew no longer without tasting; to tast no longer without begging the holy Spirit of God to enlighten and enliven mine against the fear of men, tradition of fathers, or the favor or custom of any man or times."[36] To the end of his days Williams, certain that the Holy Spirit of God· by the return of Christ Jesus would newly reveal to man the divine "truths" lost a few years after the Apostles, remained a diligent and constant Seeker.

---

[35] Masson: *Life of Milton*, Vol. III, pp. 153 ff., for quotations on Seekerism.
[36] Letter: *To Mrs. Sadlier*, N C P., Vol. VI, p. 254.

PART 4

A POLITICAL PIONEER

The monument erected in Geneva which includes Roger Williams as one of the five foremost leaders of the Reformation appropriately signalizes his relative place in the world's history. But, since no record of Williams' physical appearance has been left to posterity, the statue of him is merely an ideal figure of the dauntless pioneer of religious and civil liberty. "Of his personal traits" says Straus in his life of Roger Williams, "it is difficult to form any conception. We do not know whether he was tall or short of stature, stout or spare in frame. He must have been of vigorous and robust health, otherwise he could not have endured the many hardships he had to undergo as an exile, a pioneer, and while among the Indians. He received the benefits of a university education, and we know that he was versed in five languages besides his own. . . He was ardent, impulsive, combative, and restless; but he was kind, benevolent, sincere, and forgiving; no feeling of malice, revenge or enmity ever embittered his magnanimous heart. He may have lacked some of the graces in word and manner of the cultured Puritan ministers of his times, but we have yet to find his equal in that unwavering devotion to truth, justice, and welfare of others which characterized his life from beginning to end.

"We call those great who have devoted their lives to some noble cause, and have thereby influenced for better the course of events. Measured by that standard, Roger Williams deserves a high niche in the temple of fame, alongside of the greatest reformers who mark epochs in the world's history. He was not the first to discover the principles of religious liberty, but he was the first to proclaim them in all their plenitude, and to found and build up a political community with those principles as the basis of its organization. The influence and effect of his 'lively experiment' of religious liberty and democratic government upon the political system of our country, and throughout the civilized world"[37] have been powerful enough to change public opinion and revolutionize the structure of society.

---

[37] Straus: *Roger Williams,* pp. 231, 233.

It is the purpose of this study to examine and evaluate the political ideas of Roger Williams, to show their relation to previous and contemporary conceptions of state, and to suggest their influence upon the governmental principles of the American nation and upon all representative governments. The study will progress by the consideration of the various theoretic aspects of the state, which, since the time of Bodin's *De la République,* has been generally accepted as the proper technical approach. Since Roger Williams and the other political thinkers of the seventeenth century understood the use and significance of the terminology of the publicists and political theorists, my arrangement of the study of Williams' theory of state seems to be justifiable. The order of the chapters of this study has been chiefly influenced by two things: first, the logical sequence of the fundamental conceptions of the state, as presented in chapter II, "The Origin, Nature and Necessity of the State," and followed by chapters III and IV, containing a discussion of the internal and external authority; secondly, by the fact that Williams subordinated the state to service to the individual citizen, and consequently the most significant sequence would be an analysis of the purpose of the state in chapter V, preparing for the discussion of the activities of the state in achieving that purpose in VI, and concluding with VII by discussing the limits of the state's activities with regard to individual rights.

II

WILLIAMS' CONCEPT OF THE STATE, ITS ORIGIN AND NATURE

PART 1
HIS RELATION TO THEORY

Roger Williams built his own theory of the state partly on records that the past had preserved in the form of history and philosophical speculation, and partly on ideas and practices which had become clarified by or had grown out of the pioneer life in the American wilderness. The ideas and experiences of the past which he accepted as germane to his purpose, he interpreted and applied in the light of contemporary experiences and the special circumstances in which he chanced to be placed. It may safely be stated that his theory contained much that had previously been either practiced or speculated on. In it can be found principles gathered from the Greeks, the Romans, the teachings of Jesus, the Middle Ages and the Reformation. How he came upon them may perhaps never be definitely known. But a careful study of his works gives unmistakable evidence that he combined principles of the ancient and post-Reformation absolutism with principles of Christian and Teutonic individualism, and by such combination plus his pioneer experiences laid the foundation for an "actually free state" not yet fully realized. The former is the basis for his demand that the state, as he conceived it, be the entire and competent authority in civil things; the latter justified him in making the welfare of the individual in society the chief end and object of the state.

The popular sovereignty ideas of the past that had been put forth in defense of party interests were sifted of what he considered the dross; some of the grains of "truth" that remained after the winnowing were used as the basic principles of the new structure of society that he endeavored to establish. These principles were often rather rudimentary in presentation and application, yet their bearing upon modern thought and society is incalculable. He was not the only man of his century who advocated many of these principles; John Cotton admits that many others held similar views.   But he was one of the foremost advocates of them, and no other man of his century sets forth the popular sovereignty ideas in the combination which we today recognize as peculiar to Roger Williams.   He is, moreover, undeniably the only man who founded a state with these ideas as its fundamental principles.

The significance of Roger Williams' theory lies not only in the ideas of the past which he accepted, but quite as much in those which he rejected.   He denied, both in theory and practice, the generally accepted idea of the state as a thing apart from and above the people; the principle of sovereignty as an arbitrary and irresponsible power; the doctrine of the union of church and state; the social contract as an agreement between individuals in a state of nature, between man and man as irresponsible individuals in society, or creating a permanent third but irresponsible party as sovereign, or between the ruled and ruler; the object of the state as being independent of the body of individuals who constitute it; the powers of the state as only those of war, police, and justice; the state as having no internal limits except for incapacity; and that the states in respect to each other are in a state of nature, and therefore can act arbitrarily, making war inevitable.   He repudiated these ideas as fictions invented by men in order to maintain and justify group-interests in church and state.   In place of these discarded theories and fictions, he proposed a social structure based on a combination of realistic and idealistic political principles and practices centered around the rights and liberties of the individual man in the social group.

In 1636, Roger Williams deliberately set out to demonstrate the constructive features of his political ideas.   After his second escape from the forces of intolerance—this time from Massachusetts Bay—he founded a colony for which he, in company with Sir Henry Vane and others, had only partially completed the plans during the preceding year.[1]   His five years of bitter controversy with the Bay theocracy prepared him to put into practice in the Narragansett wilderness the principles that had become clarified through conflict and suffering.   The assumption

---

[1] R I H S C., Vols. XIII-XIV; Vol. III, p. 144, in *Providence Proprietors and Freeholders.* Staples: *Annals,* p. 16. Winthrop: *Journal,* for the years 1634-1636, Vol. I.   *Cottons Answer,* p. 8, in Staples: *Annals,* p. 20. *Testimony of Roger Williams,* N C P., Vol. VI, p. 305.

made by practically all students of Williams, that his theory of state grew out of his principles of religious liberty and was a mere incidental by-product of it, must be put aside. His theory of religious liberty came, instead, out of his unique theory of the individual and the state. In order, then, to understand fully his political ideas, the political structure and activities of Rhode Island, as well as his letters and treatises, must be studied with care and discrimination. Such a comprehensive study will reveal his ideas of the state, its sovereignty, object, functions and limits. Frequent recourse must, therefore, be had to the constitutions and government of the colony, for the reason that his political ideas found expression in its several institutions[2] The result of such a study will never evoke the question of whether he was "inconsistent and impractical"—usually the attitude of the *bourgeoisie* and those who do not understand—, but it will instead establish him as one of the foremost and most daring of the seventeenth century political thinkers and statesmen.

In setting forth Roger Williams' political thought and practices, by means of which he hoped to establish the equitable civil rights and liberties of the individual in the new society, numerous difficulties are encountered. Since his opponents were steeped in ideas of theocracy, divine rights, and absolutism, his method of attack in his treatises took the form of religio-politico examination of the causes of the religious and social unrest of the seventeenth century. His own ardently religious nature preferred arguments from Scripture whenever possible. To demolish the religious biases in statesmanship, he was forced to emphasize the evils of the theocratic encroachments. But, at the same time, he also presented the constructive political principles that would work for equity and peace in the new social structure. While his treatises took on a religious and political aspect, his letters show his concern to have been almost entirely political. In fact, after 1636, and, especially, after 1640, his best efforts and thoughts were given not to theology, the clergymen commentators to the contrary notwithstanding, but to politics—to the rebuilding of society and the founding of a democratic federal state. Since Williams never systematized his ideas, it is the aim of this study to put them into a more systematic form, and to show that, contrary to the repeated assertions of numerous clerically-minded

---

[2] Sherger: *The Evolution of Modern Liberty,* p. 170. Staples: *Annals.*

biographers and historians[3] who have commented on his achievement as being merely that of an apostle of religious liberty, Roger Williams worked out a definite theory of the nature and functions of the state that has been found to be consistent, practicable, and constructive.

To draw any conclusions regarding the comparative merits of his political ideas and those of his contemporaries, or of any succeeding school of political thought, is not within the scope of this work. Nor is any attempt made to discredit or defend any of his principles or practices. No direct influences of Roger Williams on the ideas of the American Revolution have been pointed out, although certain indirect influences are occasionally suggested. Still less was it possible to work out in detail the suggestions made by Dunning in *Political Theories: Luther to Montesquieu,* that the Agreement of the Army of 1647 was based on the political theories derived from Roger Williams, or the suggestions of Jellinek in his *Declaration of Rights of Man and Citizens,* Gervinus in the *Introduction to the History of the Nineteenth Century,* and Richman in *Rhode Island,* Vol. I, that the source of the democratic doctrines which came to underlie both the American War of Independence and the French Revolution was none other than Roger Williams. One thing, however, is certain: that an understanding of the achievement of Roger Williams is essential to a correct interpretation of the ideas dominant in American political life and letters, for he was the most original thinker of colonial America and a pioneer of American thought.

The search for a new basis for society is the key to the political thought of the seventeenth century.[4] It was above all else an age of political discussion. Thinkers and statesmen from Bacon to Halifax earnestly devoted their best energies to working out a new basis for human association in place of the feudal and ecclesiastical principles which had been shattered by the Reformation and had disappeared as a vital force in life. Among these writers and thinkers were Bodin, Grotius, Suarez, Hobbes,

---

[3] I need append only a few of the many titles: Knowles: *Memoirs of Roger Williams;* Edwards: *History of the Baptists of Rhode Island;* Felt: *The Ecclesiastical History of New England;* Dexter: *As To Roger Williams;* Eddy: *Roger Williams and the Baptists;* Gammel: *Roger Williams.*

[4] Gooch: *Political Thought from Bacon to Halifax.*

Milton, Pufendorf, Spinoza, Locke, Sir Edward Coke, and James I of England, all of whom set forth what they believed to be the basic principle of a new social life within the state. Alongside of these and in colorful contrast to them stands the much neglected political thinker and founder of the "first modern state," Roger Williams.

With the exception of a few thinkers like Coke and James I, the political writers of the seventeenth century accepted the social compact as an explanation of the origin of the state. In the hypotheses of Hobbes and Locke, this theory was set forth in its most representative forms. For the basis and origin of the state, Hobbes postulated the Social Contract. The Contract was necessary because man is purely egoistic in his emotions, *"bellum omnium contra omnes,"* and human life is "solitary, poor, nasty, brutish and short."[5] Hobbes was distinctly utilitarian in his interpretation of the state, authority, law, and the actions of man. In his treatment of the law of nature, he held that natural right is the liberty possessed by all men of doing what is necessary for the preservation of life, as distinct from natural law which is a rule discovered by reason forbidding anything unfavorable to such preservation. This natural law is established by a general compact. The compact, Hobbes held, is an agreement between the people creating a third party, the ruler, who never relinquishes his natural rights and therefore can do no wrong.

With certain slight modifications of the law of nature and the compact, Locke agrees substantially with Hobbes. To him the original state of nature was one in which peace and reason prevailed. But it was a state of anarchy. Reason, Locke declared "teaches all mankind, who will but consult, that being equal and independent, no one ought to harm another in his life, health, liberty or possessions." But in the state of anarchy, reason did not always prevail; consequently, the intolerable uncertainties resulting from a lack of laws and the inability of the individual to maintain his natural rights, led to the formation of the body politic for self-preservation by means of a social contract. The contract, conceived by Locke, is specified and limited, in that the individual surrenders certain natural rights to the community as a whole in return for a guarantee of his life, liberty, and estates—all comprehended in the word property. The majority

---

[5] *The Leviathan.*

rules and may use force if necessary; the consent of the individual may be expressed or tacit. The civil society or state, according to Locke, is the direct product of the agreement to incorporate and act as a body.[6]

Spinoza founded the rights of the *de facto* government to rule upon its power to maintain itself against force from any quarter whatsoever. Hobbes' idea of the social contract entered into by the different members of society was one of complete submission. Locke allowed for revolution in the state. James I held that kings are as Gods, and may rule arbitrarily because of divine sanction. Of the eighteenth century political writers, Blackstone maintained that men hold together in society because they cannot help it. Rousseau's theory of the contract was that each person puts himself under the direction of the will of the community, yet remains free as before. His contract is not between man and a ruler, but between man and man, each and all retaining equal rights politically.[7]

Intellectually, Roger Williams grew up in the midst of the political turmoil of the early seventeenth century. His university life brought him into contact with the political ideas of the past, as well as those of his own day. The studies of theology, politics, philosophy, and history were still almost inextricably interwoven, and a student in theology, alive to contemporary thought and life, would almost invariably become as well acquainted with political philosophy as with pure dogmatic theology. Williams was powerfully influenced by the political ideas of his day; and under that stress of the common despotism, he developed distinctly radical political views. His place in the history of political ideas can best be understood when his *Bloudy Tenent* is viewed in relation to the treatises of certain contemporary writers. In 1625 Grotius published his epoch-making treatise *De Jure Belli ac Pacis Libri Tres;* and in 1628 Charles I was forced to grant the Petition of Rights requested by Parliament and drafted by Sir Edward Coke. Hooker's *Eccliastical Polity*, 1594, was fa-

---

[6] *On Civil Government.* Parts I and II.

[7] The Contract theories were merely webs of sophistries, and are now generally held to be untenable hypotheses. See the opinions of: Wilson: *The State*, pp. 8 ff; Willoughby: *The Nature of the State*, pp. 119 ff; Duguit: *Law in the Modern State;* Laski: *Foundation of Authority in the State*, pp. 120 ff; Sorel: *Le Décomposition du Marxisme;* Oppenheimer: *The State;* Russell: *Roads to Freedom.*

miliar to all Englishmen interested in either church or state. Williams' first important treatise on church and state, The *Bloudy Tenent of Persecution,* appeared in 1643. In 1649 appeared Milton's *Tenure of Kings and Magistrates;* in 1651, Hobbes' *Leviathan;* in 1656, Harrington's *Oceana;* in 1680 Filmer's *Patriarcha;* and in 1689, Locke's *Two Treatises on Civil Government.*

Roger Williams was also in search of a new basis for civil society. But he differed with the other political thinkers of his time as to the origin of the state and about certain essential details of the civil agreement or social contract. The clearest and most definitive statement, in New England, of the Social Contract theory was presented by Thomas Hooker in 1648, anticipating Locke by almost half a century. Williams, Hooker, and Locke agree in at least three essential elements of the social agreement: that men are equal, politically; that the agreement may be explicit or implicit, or both; and that the right of rebellion is inherent, although they differ in the method and form this rebellion may take.[8] The origin of the state Williams places not in the civil agreement, but in the community consciousness of a common social purpose and the desire for civil peace and welfare. The civil agreement is the formal expression of this community consciousness in an orderly assembly through the consent of the majority. This agreement creates a government which serves the individuals in the state impartially. The natural rights of the individual are now conditioned by the demands of law and order, or the civil liberties, as he calls them, the laws which are necessary to maintain for each individual his equal rights as a member of civil society. A bill of rights guarantees to each member certain rights, such as life, liberty, estates, freedom of conscience, civil equality which, as an individual, he possesses inalienably against the encroachment of the civil state. The agreement may be changed by the majority, which rules at all times, and force may be used when necessary. The law of nature, given by God to govern the universe, can be discovered by mankind through reason, observation, experience and history,[9] and teaches that all mankind is equal and independent politically and spiritual-

---

[8] Hooker: *A Survey of the Summe of Church Discipline,* 1648; Locke: *On Civil Government,* 1689; Williams: *Bloudy Tenent of Persecution,* 1643.

[9] Letter: To the Town of Warwick, 1666, R I H S C., Vol. VII, p. 147. *Bloudy Tenent. of Persecution,* N C P., Vol. III, pp. 246-257.

ly. It is an orderly, essential rule of life which, while it demands that man strive for self-preservation, forbids him to offer harm to another in any form. But since, through greed and selfishness certain men ignore the natural laws and tyrannize over the natural rights of others, the creation of a civil government is necessary for the common peace and well-being. Universal history and experience show, he argued, that "it is of binding force to engage the whole and every interest and conscience to preserve the common liberty and peace,"[10] for "security is the chief purpose back of civil authority."[11] Besides "our dangers . . . now especially, call upon us to be compact in a civil way and power."[12] In this way throughout his letters and treatises, he continually spins his argument, supported by history, nature, and necessity.

---

[10] *The Hireling Ministry*, p. 29.
[11] *Queries*, N C P., Vol. II, p. 22.
[12] Letter: *To Governor Winthrop*, 1636, N C P., Vol. VI, p. 4.

WILLIAMS' CONCEPT OF STATE

Roger Williams desired to establish a state that would assure to each man political, religious, and economic liberty.[13] His theory of the state was the product of an extensive survey of the cause, continuation, and decline of states and governments of the past. History, experience and reason, each pointed to the civil necessity of upholding the dignity of the individual man in society. Since he considered the ideal state one that guaranteed and practised complete individual liberty in every sphere of human activity, he maintained it as inevitable that the state must be highly sensitive in its administrative organs to the will of the people and the circumstances of time and place.[14] He therefore rested the power of the state in the people as a whole, limited the power of government, and held that its form must be fitted to the nature, conditions, and constitution of the people and country. This made the form of the government variable, with no more executive or judicial influence than was granted it by the people from time to time. To Roger Williams' understanding of civil society, the state and the will of the people as expressed by the majority of them were one and identical.[15]

In his letters and treatises, Williams definitely, although in scattered passages, presented his view of the origin and nature of the state. He discarded much of the obsolete and fictitious political philosophy invented in the past by the different parties contending for political and religious, and thereby economic power. In turn, he presented radical and "seldom heard of" political views that correspond in many respects with the theories of the most advanced modern publicists and jurists.[16] He recognized and accepted, however, certain elements of "truth" resident in each of the three main theories of the state's origin: the divine

---

[13] Letters: *To the Town of Warwick*, 1666, R I H S C., Vol. VIII, p. 125; *To the Town of Providence*, N C P., Vol. VI, p. 263.

[14] *Bloudy Tenent of Persecution*, N C P., Vol. III, pp. 350, 399. N C P., Vol. IV, p. 180. *Rhode Island Colonial Records*, Vol. I—Letters, Charters, and Constitutions. [Hereafter this will be listed as R I C R.]

[15] N C P., Vols. II, IV, VI. R I C R., Vol. I.

[16] Gierke: *Political Theories of the Middle Ages;* Oppenheimer: *The State.* Compare also: Duguit; Lasson; Bertrand Russell; Wilson; Laski; and Roscoe Pound.

element, the human agreement, and the historical growth; but he made them merely contributory to his own particular view that the state begins in a community consciousness.

As a theologian of no mean proportions, it was only natural for him to see divine elements at work in forming the civil state. He made free use of Biblical texts not only to justify the state and its authority, but also to establish his claim for civil obedience and civil liberty. That divine influences are back of the state he accepted on the authority of St. Paul: "Let every soul be subject unto higher powers. For there is no power but of God; the powers that be are ordained of God."[17] The state is a part of the creation of God, but it is no more divine than are all natural things. This divine origin, even according to Paul, in no way confuses the policies of the church and state. "For the rulers are not a terror to good works, but to evil . . For he [the ruler] is the minister of God to thee for good. But if thou do that which is evil, be afraid; for he beareth not the sword in vain."[18] Again, the apostle Peter admonished the Christians, "submit yourself to every ordinance of man for the Lord's sake; whether it be king, as supreme; or unto governors . . . as free, and not using your liberty for a cloke of maliciousness, but as servants of God."[19] In the teachings of the Old Testament, the Jewish state, according to Williams' interpretation, was held to have its origin immediately in an ordinance of God.[20] The religious and political life were both under the direct supervision of the divine power. But Christ and his disciples taught that the church and state are two distinct authorities, each requiring and deserving obedience within its particular sphere of influence. "Render, therefore, unto Cæsar the things which are Cæsar's; and unto God the things which are God's." To another Christ answered "Who made me a judge or divider over you?"[21] Under stress of political circumstances, St. Paul appealed to Cæsar[22] for protection, according to Williams' understanding, "from Civill violence, and slanderous accusations, about seditions, mutiny, civill obedience,

17 Romans, 13:1.
18 Ibid, 13:3, 4.
19 I Peter, 2: 13-17.
20 Genesis, 9; Exodus, 19, 20 and 21.
21 Matthew, 22:21. Luke, 12:14.
22 Acts, 25.

etc."; and "who doubts," writes Williams, "but God's people may appeal lawfully in *civill* things to *civill magistrates.*"

The Scriptures, Williams maintained, contain no instructions definitely promulgated for the guidance of the modern civil state,[23] as distinct from the theocracy of the Old Testament. Yet the New Testament, he finds, mentions four kinds of swords in discussing the relation of spiritual to civil affairs. The first is the sword of Persecution which Herod used against James; the second, the sword of God's Spirit, namely the Word of God;[24] the third, the sword of War and Destruction—the Red Horse of Revelation. The fourth is the sword referred to in *Romans* 13 as a *"Civill Sword,* called the Sword of *Civill Justice;* which being of *material civill justice,* for the *defense* of *Persons, Estates, Families, Liberties* of a *City* or *Civill State,* and the *Supressing* of *Uncivill* and injurious persons or actions by such *civill punishment.* It cannot according to its utmost reach and capacitie . . . extend to *spiritual* and *Soul-causes,* Spiritual and Soule *punishment* which belongs to the *Spiritual Sword* with the two edges."[25] The civil sword which is the "Arm of Flesh" and the "Sword of Steel" can be used only in civil causes; for the spiritual offenses the spiritual sword is sufficient at all times, either to convert and subdue or to flay and execute spiritually.[26] Yet the Christian is commanded by God to obey and pray for the ruler and magistrate, and keep the civil peace; but there are no special instructions in the Scriptures for the "Civill Magistrate" in the civil state.

In his exegesis of the words "the powers that be are ordained' of God" Roger Williams, like Manegold von Lautenbach, Suarez, and Nicolas of Cusa,[27] rejected the theory of the state's direct divine origin. Yet he agreed that divine elements are present: "Government and order in families, towns, etc. is the ordinance of the Most High, Rom. 13, for the peace and good of mankind[28] . . . . Magistracie is properly and adequately fitted by God, to preserve the Civill State in civill peace and order."[29] This divine descent of the state gives it, however, no more power in spiritual

---

[23] *Bloudy Tenent of Persecution,* N C P., Vol. III, pp. 113 f.
[24] Acts 12; Ephesians, 6; Revelation, 1; Hebrews, 4.
[25] *Bloudy Tenent of Persecution,* N C P., Vol. III, p. 160.
[26] II Corinthians, 10:4.
[27] Sullivan: *The Antecedents of the Declaration of Independence,* pp. 67-82.
[28] Letter: *To the Town Clerk Of Providence,* N C P., Vol. VI, p. 401.
[29] *Master Cottons Letter,* N C P., Vol. I, p. 51.

things whatsoever. For "That *Minister* or *Magistrate* goes be-yond his commission," Williams asserted, "who intermeddles with that which cannot be given him in commission from the people. . . Unless Master *Cotton* can prove that all the people and inhabitants of all the *Nations* in the *World* have *spiritual power, Christs power, naturally, fundamentally* and *originally* residing in them (as they are people and *inhabitants* of this *World*) to rule . . . the *church.*"[30]

The state, Williams held, is a concrete and particular thing, but only indirectly from God. It is in this sense that he always discusses it. The state is the body of people as men, "orderly assembled." "It is most true that *Magistracy* in general is of God (*Rom.* 13) for the preservation of mankind in *Civill peace* and *order.* . . . So also it is true that *Magistracy* in special for the several kindes of it is of man, I Peter, 2:13."[31] Whether or not the magistrate be a Christian has no bearing upon his author-ity, for he can receive no more than the *"Body* of *People* and *Civill State,* as *men,* betrust him with. . . . It is but flattering of *Magistrates,* it is but the accursed trusting to an *arm* of *flesh,* to persuade the *rulers* of *earth* that they are *Kings* of the *Israel* or the *Church* of *God,* who were in their *institution* and govern-ment immediately from *God.*"[32] In discussing the *de jure* power in England versus the *de facto,* Williams maintains that "the Gentile Princes, Rulers and Magistrates . . . receive their *callings, power* and *authority,* (both *Kings* and *Parliaments*) mediately [that is, mediately from God but immediately] from the people.[33] . . . The True and *living God,* is the *God* of *order, spiritual, civill* and *natural*: Natural is the same ever and perpetual; *civil* alters ac-cording to the *constitution* of *peoples* and *nations*: *spiritual* hath changed" from the National Church of Israel to the particular or congregational churches of the Protestant sects. "Tis true, that *Magistratsie* is of God, but yet no otherwise than *Mariage* is, be-ing an *estate* meerly *civill* and humane, and lawfull to all Nations of the World, that know not God. Tis true that Magistrates be of God from the light of Nature."[34]

And according to the light of nature only can the state be

---

[30] *Bloody Tenent Yet More Bloody,* N C P., Vol. IV, p. 187.
[31] *Bloudy Tenent of Persecution,* N C P., Vol. III, p. 398.
[32] *Bloody Tenent Yet More Bloody,* N C P., Vol. IV, p. 187.
[33] *Bloudy Tenent of Persecution,* N C P., Vol. III, p. 343.
[34] *Bloody Tenent Yet More Bloody,* N C P., Vol. IV, pp. 80, 282 f.

considered of divine origin[35]. . . that is, "it is *natural, civill,* and humane" and has exisited from the beginning of the world. The state is only in general from God by his order as the creator of the world. The church and the kings of Israel are immediately from God; but the modern civil state, on the contrary, receives its power and authority immediately from the people, that is mediately and indirectly from God but directly and in particular from the people as a community.[36] This position of Williams strikes at the root of the claim of the divine right of kings derived from the divine right of the state, to rule arbitrarily. "How is that heavenly charge, Touch not mine Anointed, *etc.* (*Psalm* 105) common to all *Christians* (or anointed with) *Christ* their Head, by way of *Monopoly* or privilege appropriated to *Kings* and *Princes?*" The civil state was never invested by Christ Jesus with the "power and title of Defender of the Faith," much less the King and Prince; "let any man show me such a *commission, instruction* and *promise* given by the *Son* of *God* to *Civill powers.*"[37]

During the Middle Ages the publicists were divided on the question of state and church, and the sphere of sovereignty of each. Can the state and the church exist side by side, each independent in its own sphere of influence, and yet remain true to the sacred principle of the organized Oneness of Mankind?[38] Martin Luther held that they could; that the complete separation of church and state indeed, was the first necessary step toward the solution of the political and economic unrest of the sixteenth century.[39] A century later, Roger Williams based the demand for complete separation of church and state upon his conception of English and continental corporation law. The church is merely a corporation, " a society as well as the Society of Merchants, Drapers, etc. . . .(and yet if a company of men combine themselves into a civil Society by voluntary Agreement, and voluntarily dissolve it, it is not justice to force them to continue

---

[35] Generally held in antiquity. Bluntschli: *The Theory of the State,* p. 293; Dunning: *Political Theories: Ancient and Medieval;* Gierke: *Political Theories of the Middle Ages.* Gierke contains an extensive bibliography of Medieval writers. Figgis: *From Gerson to Grotius.*
[36] *Bloudy Tenent of Persecution,* N C P., Vol. III, pp. 108 f, 343.
[37] *Ibid,* pp. 337 f, 120, 277.
[38] Gierke: *Political Theories of the Middle Ages.* Dunning: *Political Theories: Ancient and Medieval.* Gettell: *History of Political Thought.*
[39] Luther: *On Civil Magistracy; To the German Nobility.*

together) ;"[40] and therefore the church can dissolve at any time without the civil consent.

The distinction between the civil and spiritual state was clearly understood by Williams, as shown by the following passage:

"The Church or company of worshippers (whether true or false) is like unto a Body or Colledge of Physitians in a Citie; like unto a Corporation, Society, or company of East-Indie or Turkie Merchants, or any other Societie or Company in London: which Companies may hold their Courts, keep their Records, hold disputations; and in matters concerning their societie, may dissent, divide, break into Schismes and Factions, sue and implead each other at the Lawe, yea wholly break up and dissolve into pieces and nothing, and yet the peace of the Citie not be in the least measure impaired or disturbed; because the essence or being of the Citie, and so the well-being and peace thereof is essentially distinct from those particular Societies; the Citie-Courts, Citie-Lawes, Citie-punishments distinct from theirs. The Citie was before them, and stands absolute and intire, when such a Corporation or Society is taken down. For instance further, The City or Civil state of Ephesus was essentially distinct from the worship of Diana in the Citie, or of the whole city. Againe, the Church of Christ in Ephesus (which were Gods people, converted and call'd out from the worship of the City unto Christianitie or worship of God in Christ) was distinct from both.

"Now suppose that God remove the Candlestick from Ephesus, yea though the whole Worship of the Citie of Ephesus should be altered; yet (if men be true and honestly ingenuous to Citie-covenants, Combinations and Principles) all this might be without the least impeachment or infringement of the peace of the City of Ephesus.

"Thus in the City of Smirna was the Citie itself or Civill estate one thing, The Spiritual or Religious state of Smirna, another; The Church of Christ in Smirna distinct from them both; and the Synagogue of the Jewes, whether literally Jewes (as some think) or mystically, false Christians (as others). . . distinct from all these. And notwithstanding these spiritual oppositions in the point of Worship and Religion, yet heare we not the least noyse (nor need we, if Men keep but the Bond of Civility) of any Civill breach, or breach of Civil peace amongst them: and to persecute Gods people there for Religion, that only was a breach of Civilitie itself."[41]

The spiritual state has its origin in the command of Christ. In this spiritual state, "the Monarchical power" and the "power of making lawes" belong to the "Lord Jesus;" but the deputed and ministerial power in spiritual things lies in the church or congregation, delegated to the church by Him. The *"government*

---

[40] *Bloudy Tenent of Persecution,* N C P., Vol. III, p. 73.
[41] *Ibid,* pp. 73 f.

of *Christs Kingdome* or *Church"* must have "the true *commission, power* and *keyes* from *Christ*."[42] Only when the church has its immediate origin and keys from Christ, is it a true Christian church. The state religion of the world, Williams emphasized, is a politic invention of men to maintain the civil state.[43]

In his distinction between a state and a national state and the Christian church and National church of Israel, Williams was quite clear and definite. The true national state, he held, is a state in which the people are of one seed and language, and have the same spiritual, intellectual, social, and political development,[44] best exemplified in the Israel of the Old Testament. Of the modern states "few *Nations* of the *World* but are a mixed Seed, the people of *England* especially: the *Britaines, Picts, Romanes, Saxons, Danes* and *Normans,* by a wonderful providence of *God* being become one *English* people. . . . But where hath the *God* of *Heaven* in the *Gospel* separated whole *Nations* or *Kingdomes* (*English, Scotch, Irish, French, Dutch, etc.*) as a peculiar people and *antitype* of the people of *Israel*." With the coming of Christ the true national state and the true national church of which Israel was the type, was dissolved. Neither state nor church since Christ's coming can claim Israel as an antetype.[45] A national church is "opposite the very Essential and Fundamentalls of the Nature of a Civill Magistrasie, a *Civill Commonweal* or *combination* of Men, which can only respect civill things."[46]

By rejecting the direct divine origin of the state and the absolute divine right of kings on the basis of experience, Scriptural authority, the law of nature, and the light of reason, Williams cleared the ground for his new concept of the state. The divine element present in the state, he held, arises out of the nature of things—the natural order of human existence and association —and is only mediately from God through a direct human agency. And since the Christian church, or spiritual state, has its direct origin in the command of Christ, the church and civil state are essentially different in nature; and consequently each is inde-

---

[42] *Ibid.* pp. 348 ff, 357, 346.
[43] *Bloody Tenent Yet More Bloody,* N C P., Vol. IV, p. 222.
[44] *Bloudy Tenent of Persecution,* N C P., Vol. III, Chapters 82-138.
[45] *Ibid,* pp. 323 f, 416.
[46] *Queries,* N C P., Vol. II, p. 35.

pendent of the other in sovereignty, functions, and purpose, and must be kept distinct and separate.

Another contributing factor to the origin of the state is that man, by his very nature and instinct, desires a peaceful and congenial means of life and association. In his letter to the Town of Providence in 1680, Roger Williams in his defense of the civil government said that among the six things written in the hearts of all mankind was the fact "that mankind cannot keep together without some government."[47] He, moreover, frequently emphasizes the importance of man's instinctive search for some form of protection against the greed of his fellows, and that by his nature man desires companionship of other men and is willing to forego certain personal advantages to satisfy his gregarious nature. In this postulate he is upheld by the weight and authority of the Greeks and of men like Cicero and Polybius,[48] who assumed that man's instinctive and natural love of society lies at the basis of the origin of the state.

Nor did Williams feel called upon to repudiate entirely the idea that the family is historically the primal unit of the political society and the basis for the larger growth which finally evolved into civil government. *"Families* are the *foundation* of *government,* for what is a *commonweale,* but a *commonweale* of Families agreeing together for common good."[49] While the family is the fundation upon which the government is built, it is not the basis for the origin of the state. But Williams holds it a powerful influence back of the desire for civil peace and well-being. Here again Williams found plentiful support in the writings of the past and the facts of contemporary political life.

Although Williams did not agree with those who held that Force or the fear of it fully explains the origin of the state,[50] he, nevertheless, recognized that the consciousness of the force back of organized society as a protective influence impelled men to

---

[47] Letter: *To the Town Clerk of Providence,* N C P., Vol. VI, p. 410.

[48] Polybius: *Histories,* VI, 1-9. Bluntschli: *The Theory of the State.* Sullivan: *The Antecedents of the Declaration of Independence,* pp. 67 ff. See also Plato: *Republic;* Aristotle: *Politics,* 4; Aquinas: *Summa Theologica.* Aquinas attributes the origin of the state to the fall and wickedness of man.

[49] *Bloudy Tenent of Persecution,* N C P., Vol. III, p. 242. See Wilson: *The State.*

[50] Oppenheimer: *The State,* chapters I and II. Bluntschli: *The Theory of the State.* Maine: *Ancient Law,* chapter III. Willoughby: *The Nature of the State.*

seek shelter under a civil government. Force or will is inherent in his conception of the civil state—the will of the people as a body and the rule of the majority. For "the *civil state* may bring into *order*, make *orders*, preserve in *civil order* all her members . . .; against any civil mischief (though wrought *conscientiously*) the *civil state* is strongly guarded."[51] Unless the state preserve civil order and peace, the "*World* otherwise would be like the *Sea*, wherein Men, like *Fishes*, would hunt and devoure each other and the greater devoure the lesse."[52] At least the latent force and authority is necessary for the sake of peace and order; for "if the *sword* and *balances* of justice . . . be not drawn and held forth . . . that *civil state* must dissolve,"[53] and the unprotected members suffer unjustly. And so the minority, whether criminal or law-abiding, are held in subjection by the majority, or the rulers who profess to represent the voice of the majority, by a civil force or will either expressed or latent.

The ideas associated with the social agreement which Williams accepted as the formal expression of the state fixing the procedure of the body politic, were the product of centuries of political speculation.[54] Among the first to advance the doctrines resembling the social compact were Protagoras and the Sophists.[55] By Cicero's time, 106-43 B. C., three ideas of the social compact were known to the ancient world. These doctrines were the conscious institution of government by men, held by Protagoras, the Sophists, and the Epicureans; the equality of men, held by the Stoics; and the idea of natural rights, held by the Cynics, and Stoics and later greatly clarified by Cicero. The Christian doctrines of equality and brotherhood of men were further clarified by the Roman jurists of the early empire, especially by Gaius and Ulpian. Of the early church fathers, St. Augustine, 354-430, is probably the most important. So far as is known, he was the first to use the term "pactum" in the sense of a social compact. In elaborating Plato and Cicero's theory that man by his own

---

[51] *Bloody Tentent Yet More Bloody*, N C P., Vol. IV, pp. 80, 145.
[52] *Bloudy Tenent of Persecution*, N C P., Vol. III, p. 398.
[53] *Bloody Tenent Yet More Bloody*, N C P., Vol. IV, p. 222.
[54] Gettell: *History of Political Thought.* Gierke: *Political Theories of the Middle Ages.* Jenks: *Law and Politics in the Middle Ages.* Dunning: *Political Theories*, Vols. I and II.
[55] Plato: *Dialogues.* The Sophists flourished 481-411 B.C. Among the other writers who contributed to the ideas were Plato, Aristotle, the Cynics, Epicurean and Stoic schools of philosophy, Polibius and Cicero.

nature entered into society, he held that man entered into society to have peace. St. Augustine added two revolutionary theories of state to the three already held in Cicero's time: that the power of kings rests on the consent of the governed, given in the form of a compact; and that obedience need not be given to royal laws that are contrary to the laws of God—the right of rebellion.[56] Already by the beginning of the fifth century, the five fundamental doctrines of the Contract theory had been postulated: The conscious institution of government by men; the equality of men; the idea of natural rights; the theory that the power of kings rests upon the consent of the governed, given in the form of a compact; and the right of rebellion. These doctrines were, however, not made a part of practical politics until after the Reformation, but remained in the realm of philosophic speculation.

The Middle Ages clarified and developed the doctrines of the law of Nature and the Social Contract handed down by the ancients. The Romans identified the law of nature as *jus gentium* and civil law as *jus civile*. Later Ulpian made a distinction between *jus naturale* and *jus gentium*. Three kinds of laws had then come to be recognized: the law of nature, law of God, and positive law.[57] The law of nature was next combined with and subordinated to the law of God. Finally, the idea of the law of nature was considered as human reason rather than as absolute authority. Other ideas were added during this period. Manegold von Lautenbach, 1080, declared that a tyrant may not only be disobeyed but actually deposed by the people. William of Occam, among other things, taught that the right of civil government and private property was based on the consent of the governed.[58] Others like Gratian, Thomas Aquinas, Duns Scotus, John of Salisbury, Marsilius of Padua, Wyclif, Nicolas of Cusa, and Luther, did much to keep these doctrines alive and bring them more and more into practical politics. Thus by the sixteenth and seventeenth centuries, the material and intellectual conditions favored a more decisive exposition of political thought. This new expository work was begun in earnest by the continental

---

[56] Sullivan: *The Antecedents of the Declaration of Independence*, pp. 67-82.

[57] Ritchie: *Natural Rights*, chapters I and II.

[58] *Octo Quaestiones Dialogus.*

thinkers. In the writings of Bodin,[59] Suarez,[60] and Grotius,[61] European jurisprudence of the catholic and protestant thinkers was consciously marshalled to uphold natural law and rights, the social and political contract, and popular sovereignty, in opposition to despotic political pretensions in church and state.[62]

The use of the contract as the basis for establishing the body politic[63] was a widespread practice in New England.[64] The Plymouth colony was the first to employ it in the famous Mayflower Compact of 1620.[65] The political and religious oligarchy of the Bay colony— "with just what admixture of sincerity and guile it is difficult to say"—certainly did claim the trading company character as the patent or contract upon which to erect the civil government and as a sanction for their despotism. Yet the charter gave them no more legal rights than those possessed by any civil business corporation.[66] In the adoption of the "Fundamental Orders" of Connecticut, January, 1638-9[67] the contract theory as understood by the leading thinkers of New England, outside of Rhode Island, was clearly set forth: "We, the Inhabitants and Residents. . . doe associate and conjoyne ourselves to be as one Publik State and Commonwealth and doe, for ourselves and our successors and such as shall be adjoyned to use any time hereafter, enter into Combination and Confederation together to mayntayn and preserve the liberty and purity of the gospel of our Lord

---

[59] *De la République.*

[60] *Tractatus de Legibus ac Deo Legislatore.*

[61] *De Jure Belli ac Pacis.*

[62] Dunning: *Political Theories: Luther to Montesquieu.*

[63] Althougth Massachusetts Bay and Plymouth colony were merely trading companies and for a time carried on their civil affairs according to the traditional practices of English trading companies on the European continent, they are here considered as bodies politic. But no sooner had they landed than they began to evolve a civil government beyond the privileges granted by the Patent. In this discussion I accept the tradition of the American historians.

[64] The Mayflower Compact, 1620; Fundamental Orders of Connecticut, 1638/39; Providence Agreement, 1636-7, and 1638; Portsmouth Compact, 1638; Newport Declaration, 1641—the boldest democratic statement made up to this time in New England Contracts; Massachusetts Bay Agreement. These documents are found in R I C R., Vol. I,; Poore: *Constitutions and Charters*, Vol. I; Merriam: *American Political Theories.*

[65] Merriam: *American Political Theories.*, p. 16.

[66] Richman: *Rhode Island*, Vol. I, p. 5.

[67] Fiske: *Beginnings of New England*, p. 127. John Fiske calls it "the first written constitution known to history, creating a government." Fiske is slightly in error, for the "Fundamental Orders" was the creation of an established government; it created no government.

Jesus, which we profess, as also the discipline of the Churches, which according to the truth of the said gospel is new practised among us, as also in our Civil Affaires to be guided and governed according to such Lawes, Rules, Orders and decrees as shall be made, ordered and decreed as followeth."[68]   In Rhode Island, in addition to that of Providence in 1636, social contracts were also found at Portsmouth in 1638, and at Newport in 1641. The theory on which these contracts rested has its counterpart in the voluntary agreement between a number of individuals to constitute themselves a church.

Like many others of his century, Roger Williams assumed a time when men were governed by the law of instinct and nature,[69] "written in the hearts of all mankind."   Since this law was, however, not obeyed by all men, the result was a state of disorder and conflict in which men would "hunt and devour each other, and the greater devour the lesse."[70]   In order to protect themselves against the offenders and "scandalous breakers" of the civil law, the individuals of the community or territory formed a body or combination for the sake of the "common peace, order, and welfare."   By means of this combination the offenders could be judged and punished by the majority who fixed the standards of civil right and wrong in the civil state.   "The *civill state* must judge and punish the *offenders*, else the *civill state* cannot stand, but must return to *barbarism*. . . which is a *wilderness* of *life* and *manners*."   "Natural Order or Law," he held is the "same ever and perpetual;"[71] it is also civil and moral in its manifestations, for it is "true, the second *Table* [of the Ten Commandments] containes the Law of Nature, the Law Morall and Civill."[72] So indelibly impressed on man is the natural need of some form of government among men who associate, that not even robbers, pirates and rebels themselves can hold together "but by some law among themselves and government."[73]

---

[68] *Connecticut Colonial Records*, Vol. I, pp. 21, 524.   [Hereafter this will be listed as C C R.]

[69] Maine: *Ancient Law*, Chapter III; Hooker: *Ecclesiastical Polity*, Book I, X; Sullivan: *The Antecedents of the Declaration of Independence*, pp. 67 ff.

[70] *Bloudy Tenent of Persecution*, N C P., Vol. III, p. 398.

[71] *Bloudy Tenent Yet More Bloody*, N C P., Vol. IV, pp. 148, 222, 80.

[72] *Bloudy Tenent of Persecution*, N C P., Vol. III, p. 358.

[73] Letter: *To the Town Clerk of Providence*, (1680), N C P., Vol. VI, p. 401.

Mankind holds together against dangers, ambitions, greed, and offenders of the common welfare by means of a "Compact in a civil way and power;" this compact is both political and social to secure political, religious, and economic liberty. Unlike the social compact of Hobbes and Locke, it is an agreement made neither between ruler and ruled nor between independent individuals of a community. But it is a variable agreement between individual men in an unorganized society, "orderly managed."[74]

Roger Williams' conception of the civil agreement as a basis for the visible state is clearly demonstrated in the founding of his colony. In 1636, he proposed in a civil compact for Providence colony that "we. . . do with free and joint consent promise each unto other, for our common peace and welfare we will. . . subject ourselves in active and passive obedience to such orders and agreements" made by the "greater number of the present householders."[75] This agreement was not made between men as unrelated independent individuals but as a "Combination of Men which can respect only *civil* things."[76] The points of difference between Williams' agreement and the compact of Hobbes and Locke is shown in the words: *we, joint consent,* and *greater number of present householders;* that is, we as individuals within the community consciousness and interests. He repudiates the fictitious state invented during the Middle Ages, and instead identifies the state with the people as a body or combination of men.[77]

The state originates subjectively at that indeterminate moment when the people are conscious of a common purpose and end. It begins as an objective thing when the people agree to make laws and erect a government. In fact, the people, as a body or community, possess in a latent or active form the supreme, original and basic civil power to create a body politic, which in turn may erect the government. For "the very *Common-weales,*

---

[74] Letter: *To Governor Winthrop,* 1636-37, N C P., Vol. VI, pp. 4-12.

[75] *Ibid.* He also writes in the same letter; "I have not yet mentioned these things to my neighbors," p. 6. Williams very seldom uses the term "compact." He seems purposely to avoid its use.

[76] N C P., Vol. II, *Queries,* p. 35; Vol. III, pp. 214, 249, 366; Vol. IV, p. 491.

[77] *Queries,* N C P., Vol. II, p. 35. Gierke: *Political Theories of the Middle Ages;* Oppenheimer: *The State.*

Bodies of People . . . have fundamentally in themselves the *Root* and *Power*, to set up what *Government* and *Governors* they shall agree upon."[78] The government and civil magistrates thus set up, "whether succeeding or elected," are "the Minister or servant of the people[79]. . . . Derivatives and Agents . . . immediately employed for the good of the whole," and they are, therefore, but the "eyes and hands and instruments" of the people.[80]

The agents of the state "have not the least inch of Civill power, but what is measured out to them from the free consent of the Whole. . . this civil power belonging to their [the people's] goods and bodies."[81] It is evident that "such *Governments* as are by them erected and established have no more power, nor for a longer time than the *civil power* or people consenting and agreeing shall betrust them with. This is clear not only in *Reason,* but in the experience of all *Commonweales,* where the people are not deprived of their *naturall freedom* by the power of *Tyrants.*" And so he grants to the people the right to change their government, to rebel, when it no longer serves the end and best interests of the majority. This rebellion or change of government in no way affects the essential character of the state itself, because the state is the people who have the final voice in selecting the kind of civil machinery which most effectively carries out their purpose. The civil officer, Williams held, retains all his civil rights while serving the state, but he does not acquire any additional civil rights by virtue of his office—he acquires many additional duties and services as the official of a corporation.[82] In all matters of the state, the last appeal is to "the Bar of the People or Commonweal, where all personally meet, as in some Commonweales of small number, or in greater by their representatives"[83] Williams in this sweeping statement presents an evolu-

---

[78] N C P., Vol. III, pp. 249 ff, 214, 366; Vol. IV, pp. 187, 80. R I C R., Vol. I, *Letters, Proceedings, Charters and Constitutions.*

[79] *Bloody Tenent Yet More Bloody,* N C P., Vol. IV, p. 187.

[80] *Bloudy Tenent of Persecution,* N C P., Vol. III, p. 378.

[81] N C P., Vol. III, pp. 366, 249, 418; Vol. IV, pp. 491, 187.

[82] *Bloudy Tenent of Persecution,* N C P., Vol. III, pp. 248 ff, 445. "Some Papists and some Protestants agree in deposing of Magistrates."

[83] *Ibid,* p. 356.

tionary theory of state, accepts a representative government, and fixes the source of all civil power in the people in assembly.

Since Roger Williams refused to accept the "fiction" of the state as something apart from and unrelated to the people themselves and supreme in itself with unquestionable power over them, he naturally felt the need of clearly distinguishing between the power or will of the people and its administrative organs through which the civil power obtains an external expression. This external expression may take different forms, so that "true *Republickes & Commonweales*" are possible "without *Kings*."[84] Since the people may erect and establish whatever form of civil government best meets their immediate needs, no one has ultimately a right to "question the *lawfulness* of other *formes* of *Government, Laws* and punishments which differ" from that of their own particular state. Whether that form is monarchical, aristocratic, democratic, or what-not, is of little consequence so long as it serves[85] its citizens. For, since the government is immediately created and employed by the people as the public servant, the civil states can make their own "severall lawes and Agreements (as is most probable, according to their severall Natures, Dispositions and Constitutions and their Common peace and Welfare."[86] The government, then, is the servant and agent of the civil state, the people, and not the master.

The state is natural and necessary. By its nature, the state is humane and civil; its attributes are force and service. "The civill state . . . being in a naturall state[87] . . . is none else but a part of the world, and so (since every part more or lesse in degree follows the nature of the whole) it is but naturall."[88] The "very nature and essence of a Civill Magistrate . . . [is] the same in all parts of the world, where ever people live upon the face of the Earth (agreeing together in *Townes, Cities, Provinces, Kingdomes*: I say the same *essentially Civill*" both in its origin in "the peoples *choice* and *free consent* and in its object, the safety of their bodies and goods.[89] It is true that "honestie and Innocence, Reason and Scriptures are Infinitely Excellent in their

[84] *Bloody Tenent Yet More Bloody*, N C P., Vol. IV, p. 488.
[85] *Bloudy Tenent of Persecution*, N C P., Vol. III, pp. 249, 364, 343.
[86] *Bloody Tenent Yet More Bloody*, N C P., Vol. IV, p. 487.
[87] *Bloudy Tenent of Persecution*, N C P., Vol. III, pp. 398, 160, 125.
[88] *Bloody Tenent Yet More Bloody*, N C P., Vol. IV, p. 180.
[89] *Bloudy Tenent of Persecution*, N C P., Vol. III, p. 354.

way, but are they sufficient to Charm?"[90] For that the power of
the state is necessary. "Concerning justice," he asserted, "that
if the *sword* and *balances* of *justice* (in a sort or measure)" are
not held forth as an active or latent force against "*scandulous offenders* against the *Civil state*, that *civil state* must dissolve by
little and little from civility to barbarism. The first object of
civil justice, he sets forth, is that of preserving the civil rights
of every citizen; "and the *Rights of Civil Society ought* to be
preserved by a *Civil State.*"[91]

In the new society conceived by Roger Williams, the "state"
is a body of people or combination of men, as men free and
equal in all civil things,[92] who have a common will and purpose,
and who desire common and civil order, peace, welfare and good,
possessing potentially the sovereign, original and essential source
of all civil power and service.[93] This state is prior to the ideas
of sovereignty, definite territory, organization and permanency.[94]
In its origin it is natural and necessary, divine, partly the product
of force, with the family as its original type of formal expression
and its actual formal expression in the social and civil agreement or constitution. Its outward manifestation is a "com-

---

[90] Letter:*To the Town of Warwick,* R I H S P., Vol. VIII, p. 152.

[91] *Bloody Tenent Yet More Bloody,* N C P., Vol. IV, pp. 222, 80.

[92] *Bloudy Tenent of Persecution,* N C P., Vol. III, pp. 355, 35; Letter:
To the Town of Warwick, 1666, R I H S P., Vol. VIII, p. 153.

[93] *Ibid.* Chapters 6 and 7, pp. 92-138.

[94] No generally accepted definition of the state has yet been formulated, because many political thinkers do not distinguish state from government. The nationalists and those on the "right" consider the state as
a visible unit. Woodrow Wilson in *The State,* page 8, has given the
best summary definition of this group: "A State is a people organized
for law within a definite territory." For further discussion of this view
see, Bluntschli: *The Theory of the State,* p. 23 f; Woolsey: *Political Science,* Vol. I, p. 140 f; Burgess: *Political Science and Constitutional Law,*
Vol. I, p. 51; Lasson: *System der Rechtsphilosophie,* p. 283 f. Many
publicists and jurists who maintain that the state and government are
one and the same thing, hold that the "state" as prevalently understood
is a fiction and that the state or government is a public service corporation divested of unity, definite territory, sovereignty, or an organized people. The only state they can find is the government controlled either by
a powerful individual or by class groups struggling for control of the political and economic means. See Wilson: *The State,* p. 8; Laski: *Foundations of Authority in the State,* p. 109; Duguit: *Law in the Modern State;*
Machiavelli: *The Prince;* also the writings of Oppenheimer, Karl Marx,
Sorel, Bertrand Russell, Arthur Bentley and Roscoe Pound. To avoid
confusion, the state and government must be clearly distinguished, declare such writers as Willoughby in *The American Constitutional System,* p. 24, and Garner: in his *Introduction to Political Science,* pp. 262 ff.

munity of men," a common and general will. The civil government, and not the state, is created not by the individuals in a
state of nature, but by the people "by all or a major part of them"
orderly assembled by means of a civil constitution, for the state
has already originated in the community consciousness.[95]   Whenever the government refuses to conform to the commission, literal
and explicit, given in the constitution, the people as creators may
rise up against it and change it.   This state manifests itself botn
subjectively and objectively: "The peace of a *civil State* is *civil,
internal* in the mindes of men, *external* in the administration and
observance of it."[96]   The civil state *internal* is the *state,* and the
civil state *external* is the government.   In its origin, nature, functions and purpose, this state is absolutely and completely uncon-
cerned with purely spiritual matters.

---

[95] N C P., Vols. II, IV and VI; R I C R., Vol. I, p. 145.
[96] *Bloody Tenent Yet More Bloody,* N C P., Vol. IV, p. 72.

PART 3

EXAMINATION OF WILLIAMS' THEORY OF STATE

Such a theory of state was too broad and too significant for general comprehension in the seventeenth century. And to many of the leading men of his day and since, both in Europe and America, it has seemed pregnant of destructive license—a conclusion not dispelled by the tendence toward Rhode Island of such persons who found themselves uncomfortable in neighboring states.[97] To Williams these political and religious refugees were not merely men, but individuals with the courage of their convictions. His shrewd, observant, logical, and independent mind saw in these individuals who were seeking an escape from political and economic bondage, material with which to found a state that guaranteed to each citizen "such peace, such security, such liberties for Soule and Body as were never enjoyed by any English men, nor any in the world that I have heard of."[98]

In his theory Roger Williams incorporated the two most vital contributions of the Reformation to social and civil life, the right of individual inquiry, and the equality of all men in civil and spiritual matters. The age with its theological, social, and political unrest did muct to stimulate his fertile mind to seek a solution for his fellow men. The princes of Europe had seized upon nationalism, the immediate political and social product of the Reformation, as the regulative principle of church and state within their respective territories. No room was left by them for the chief principles of social life emphasized by the Reformation, comprehended in the right of private judgment. And this vital concept of liberty, Roger Williams maintained, must be one of the chief foundation stones of the new civil society. His whole environment accepted it, not in reality, but as sound philosophical speculation. It was for this principle that he was willing to be banished or even die if necessary. As a disciple of Coke, though not slavishly so, as a student of Cambridge, the hot-bed of liberalism, and as a zealous adherent of the most radical branch of the numerous religious sects, the Independents, he continually found himself in the very midst of the intellectual ferment of the cen-

---

[97] Scott: *Development of Constitutional Liberty,* p. 114.
[98] Letter: *To the Town of Warwick,* 1666, R I H S P., Vol. VIII p. 153.

tury. His active, inquiring mind soon penetrated beneath some of the fictions and pretensions, and discovered an avenue to a more liberal and tolerant social structure. The courage of his convictions and the ardency of his temperament led him to proclaim his principles with such effectiveness that he soon became *persona non grata* in his native land. And it was through his conflict with the theocratic state both in England and the Bay colony that he finally arrived at his conception of the relation that the church, civil government and the individual should bear to one another.

Since the time of Plato many publicists and thinkers, especially the extreme liberals and the adherents to the idea of popular rights, have been unable to accept the political fictitious concept of the state as something unrelated to its citizens and subjects with arbitrary power over them. Williams refused to accept the "fiction" of the state prevalent up to his day. By making the state a body of people, men as men in assembly, in whom resides the original sovereign power to set up and tear down the civil machinery which serves them in a civil state, Williams made the individual man the dominant influence in social life. The state was no longer a super-imposed authority which could bend man to all its needs and desires, with an end distinct from the men who composed it. The new social order for which Williams strove and planned was to restore the abstract individual invented by medieval philosophers to his rightful place in civil society on the principle of consent. This broke the historical continuity in Europe, and laid the basis for future revolutions and social upheavals. On its destructive side it was sane and reasonable; but the disintegration also carried with it unpleasant consequences, and something of value of the ancient culture may have disappeared. But on its constructive side something of value appeared in the creation of a new culture and society in which a not insignificant part was taken by Roger Williams. Perhaps the briefest way of stating the result is to say that it made America inevitable.

The medieval culture as it appeared to the contemporaries of Aquinas and Dante lived in a dream of eternity with the visible and spiritual world a unity, definite and secure. The attempts to disrupt the civil and spiritual unity in the Middle Ages in the form of serf and peasant revolts and church reforms did little outwardly to cause any concern to the kings and religious leaders.

But the Investiture Controversy and the intellectual movements throughout Europe, together with the failure of medieval thought to dominate and direct social life and absorb contemporary experience, all cntributed in the final disruption of the ancient culture in the Reformation, when, one by one, the dreams of oneness and eternity began to dissolve. With the founding of Rhode Island, the unity accepted by the Middle Ages had disappeared. Church and state were now torn apart, and each forced to an independent status. Even the state as they had conceived it was discarded, and in its place was a state whose source lay in the descendants of the serfs and peasants whom the medieval culture considered mere chattel. Furthermore, the new state lost its eternal and stable aspect and became a variable and evolutionary concept, ever as changeable as the majority of individuals composing it. Then, too, the government became a representative organism, deprived of its national and absolute character, and required to conform to the particular "Nature, Conditions and circumstances of the peoples" which it represented. And finally, the individual man could claim for himself the right of rebellion against an unjust and despotic state and the deposition of the tyrant. The definiteness and security of medieval culture was exchanged in the new society founded by Williams for a flexibility and changeableness and seeming insecurity designated to provide for the common peace and well-being of the individual man.

With the ideas of the law of nature and the social contract as they had been shaped and modified by the abstract philosophies of Suarez, Bodin, Grotius, John of Salisbury, Hooker and Sir Edward Coke, Williams had some acquaintance. He understood that by the contract the legitimacy of existing governments was determined, the title of the rulers established as valid, and the origin of the state explained. He undertook to apply the abstract theories, under thorough modifications, to practical government. He applied the social agreement idea not to the origin of the state, but to the formal expression of the guiding principles of the body politic.[99] The natural "law" and rights of the individual were either modified and limited by civil rights and liberties or guaranteed by a bill of rights, by a constitution which was explicit and literal in its exposition. And he maintained that the

---

[99] *Ante* pp. 46 f.

origin of the state was natural but not independent of man whose choice was to enter largely in the shaping and modifying of the governmental machinery. The grounds and origin of society are accordingly the acceptance of conditions which come into existence by man's inherent sociability and are developed by man's spontaneous search after convenience, order and peace, while the civil institutions originate and develop by deliberate human effort under the influence of conditions fixed by human nature and the external world of activity.

To Roger Williams the state is neither an abstract idea or concept, a formal expression of the common consciousness of the community in the form of a contract, nor the whole and aggregate civil machinery of organized society. The state postulated by him is an unorganized society working consciously through experience, honesty, justice, reason and potential power, to obtain and maintain for the individual political, religious, and economic liberty. The state, furthermore, is not an end in itself, but a means; the chief purpose of its existence is the well-being of all the members of society. History, experience and reason demonstrated to Williams that as a people and a society, the state is irresistibly but surely groping its way to complete individual liberty.

The state creates through an orderly assembly a machinery of administration[100]—the government or magistrate. This government, then, has the following elements, usually attributed to the state by publicists: organization, a definite territory, granted civil powers, a certain degree of permanency, and laws.[101] The government does not exist primarily by force; but it subsists chiefly by making proselytes to sound reason and by compromise and arbitration among its members,[102] thereby securing harmony between the majority and the minority. And only when the civil peace of society as a whole is at stake may the power of the government compel the individual. On this basis of law and reason, individual liberty is secured and license minimized. Such a government, coinciding with the modern use of the term state, is a civil power and a public service,[103] serving for the good of

---

[100] R I C R., Vol. I, for the years from 1636 to 1663.
[101] N C P., Vol. III, pp. 249, 297 ff Vol. IV, pp. 80, 145.
[102] N C P., Letters, Vol. VI; Vol. IV, Chapters V and VI.
[103] *Bloudy Tenent of Persecution*, N C P., Vol. III, pp. 164 f.

the whole—the servant and agent. For this state, therefore, the utmost flexibility in its civil machinery is necessary to meet the common needs; and the state will be ever variable as the will of the body of people.[104] To achieve this flexibility and to make the civil polity entirely amenable to the requirements of the people, Williams found it necessary to posit the supreme power and authority of the state originally and perpetually in the hands of the people who created, it.

---

[104] N C P., Vol. III, pp. 398, 355; Vol. IV, pp. 80, 187, and Chapter VI.

III
THE SOVEREIGNTY OF STATE

PART 1
CONTEMPORARIES OF WILLIAMS ON SOVEREIGNTY

Whenever the political thinkers and statesman of the seventeenth century postulated a new basis for society,[1] they were confronted with the problem of finding or inventing some supreme power or authority that would stabilize the social structure. The state could not hope to exist, they all agreed, without some power that could compel obedience to its orders and laws. This supreme power they named the sovereignty of the state. In defining the nature and essence, as well as in seeking the location of the supreme power, they differed widely. But in spite of such differences, the political writers of the century may be roughly grouped into either the absolutist or the popular sovereignty class. The former held that sovereignty is absolute and indivisible, and may be arbitrary; the latter held that sovereignty is absolute and indivisible, but that it rests permanently either in the people or the will of society, and therefore may not be arbitrary.

Among the members of the absolutist school were not only those who advocated the Divine Right of Kings, but some of those who postulated the origin of the state in the Social Contract. Bodin in his theory declared that sovereignty is absolute, indivisible, and independent.[2] Hobbes refined and elaborated the theory of absolutism with a subtlety and an ingenuity that put him far ahead of the ancient Sophists. The sovereign or king himself, he held, is above the law; and sovereignty is unlimited, indefeasible, impeccable, irresponsible, irrevocable, and inalienable, although based on a social compact between the ruled and the ruler.[3] Like Pufendorf, Hobbes formulated a political union in order to make government authority absolute.[4] At the other extreme of the social contract theory as the source of the sover-

---

[1] Gooch: *Political Thought from Bacon to Halifax,* Chapter I.

[2] *De la République.* 1: 6, 8; Bodin is considered the first to use sovereignty as a technical term in political theory.

[3] *The Leviathan.* (1651).

[4] *De Jure et Gentium.* Written 1658; published 1675. See also Dunning: *Political Theories, Luther to Montesquieu.* pp.335 ff.

eign power, was the theory of Divine Right of Kings, likewise absolutist in principle, championed by James I, of England. Monarchy, asserted James, as a divinely ordained, hereditary right, is indefeasible; kings are accountable to God alone, and resistance to lawful kings is sin. "It is presumption and high contempt in a subject to . . . say that a king cannot do this or that . . . Kings are justly called Gods."[5] Both groups of absolutists were formulating systems to combat the rising tide of republicanism.

The supporters of the idea of popular sovereignty concurred in the idea that sovereignty is the result of an agreement either among individuals or a body of people. The fundamental political principle of Milton was that ultimate political power inheres in the people.[6] His theory of liberty as the "birth-right" of men and nations, places him with Luther and Williams as one of the earliest prophets of modern individualism. Harrington, one of the earliest interpreters of the economic basis of history and political structure, maintained that a law fixing the maximum amount of property a person could possess, would place the authority in the hands of the majority, secure political stability, and make the commonwealth the proper form of government.[7] In order to establish limitations upon government authority, Locke ascribed sovereignty to the collective body created by the social compact. He avoided the term itself and granted no unrestricted power to any human hands. In the last resort, it is the public will of society, according to Locke, "to which the members owe obedience." The public "Will of Society" is declared "in its laws."[8] "The essence and union of the society" consists, he maintained, "in having one will."[9] In these passages he foreshadows Rousseau's famous doctrine of *volonté generale*: "Though power may be divided, will cannot."[10] Like absolutism, popular sovereignty is also held to be absolute, indivisible, and permanent; but it may not at any time be arbitrary. In the denial of the right of the supreme power to be arbitary is found the

---

[5] *True Law of Free Monarchies, or the Mutual Duty betwixt free King and his Subjects.* Figgis: *The Divine Right of Kings*, Chapter 9, pp. 219 ff. Laski: *Foundations of Sovereignty*, pp. 293 ff.

[6] *Tenure of Kings and Magistrates.* (1649).

[7] *The Commonwealth of Oceana.* (1656).

[8] *On Civil Government.* Sections 121, 122, 127, (1689). See Dunning: *Political Theories: Luther to Montesquieu*, pp. 335 ff.

[9] *Ibid.* Sections 151, 212.

[10] *Social Contract.*

basis for the justification of revolution and the right of rebellion against the unjust and despotic state.

In the following section, this study will set forth the concept and nature of the supreme power of the state which Roger Williams ascribed to the body of people, assembled in an orderly manner. In this respect he belonged to the popular sovereignty group of political thinkers. Like his contemporaries, he considered the supreme power as absolute and indivisible. But unlike most of them, he never lost sight of the individual's right to civil liberty; consequently, he held that sovereignty could and did limit itself within a certain sphere of rightful action by means of laws and a constitution. The expression of the supreme power in a civil state, Roger Williams limits to the civil government through the civil agreement. But the people never relinquish their ultimate sovereign power. They merely delegate it to an agent. As a result whenever the agent goes beyond the limits fixed by the people at various times, they may rightly disobey, and even rebel. His theory of the power and authority of the state can best be understood by studying Rhode Island as a natural social growth from a group of unorganized men into a federal commonwealth.

PART 2

WILLIAMS' THEORY OF SOVEREIGNTY

The growth of the Providence government from 1636 to 1650 clearly demonstrates how a state and a government develop among a group of persons in a given place. Even granting that the determining cause of political union between two or more communities has always been force or the fear of it from one or another power,[11] yet this fact should not detract from our appreciation of how a simple society can develop into a representative democracy and still remain true to the fundamental democratic principles.[12] Like all natural births, this was not effected without much travail. Every member of the group was an individual with strong and stubborn individual convictions. Among these turbulent spirits, the ideas of state ranged from an ultra-conservatism that wanted a theocracy to an anarchism that desired "a better government then the country hath yet, and lets not particularize, by a general governor, etc.," which would raze "the fundamentall liberties of the country."[13] Yet in spite of all the diversity of opinion, Williams prevailed in founding a state on the principles of religious liberty and "liberty and equality, both in land and government."[14]

One of the first instances of "Squatter Sovereignty" in the new world appears with the founding of Providence, a situation forced upon the settlers by the despotic rule of Massachusetts Bay.[15] The only *de jure* title to the land in the new world recognized by the settlers of Rhode Island was that of purchase from the Indians, the actual owners. But this title was not recognized by England; the colony was trespassing on her unoccupied territory. Yet true to his principles of state, Williams formed a government, after purchasing land from the Indians, to carry out the will of the social group as the final authority, without sanction from the assumed authority of England. It was only when Massachusetts threatened to annex the Narragansett

---

[11] Jenks: *Government of Victoria*, p. 373. Oppenheimer: *The State.*
[12] Sherger: *The Evolution of Modern Liberty*, p. 175.
[13] Letter: *To Mr. Governor of Massachusetts*, 1637, N C P., Vol. VI, p. 23.
[14] Letter: *To the Town of Providence*, 1654, N C P., Vol. VI, p. 263.
[15] R I H S P., Vol. III, p. 146.

country, that the Providence colony decided to obtain a charter from England as a legal recognition of its political existence and as a protection against illegal encroachment.[16]

That some kind of authority and agreement existed between the settlers in the summer of 1636, masters of families, is apparent from the available records of that year. Under the date "16 die 4th month" appears the following: "It was agreed by the Towne that after warning given to come to the town meeting, etc."[17] From this record two things are evident: that the town had been incorporated, and that the form of government was a direct democracy. Expediency further aided Williams in his plans for popular sovereignty: "these 25 acre men encreasing the purchasers calld upon them to doe service as well as themselves to the Towns and Country they did so, and thereby came the priviledge of equall ordering of all Towne Affaires, and equally paid (to a peny) to the later purchase."[18] Local interests, desire for security, expediency in their social life, rampant individualism, each in its turn aided and justified Williams in his development of a new social structure centered around the individual man. Greater complexity of social life and increase of population demanded changes in the form of government to meet the new needs, so that by 1650 the colony had become in its institutions a representative democracy.[19]

That the political theory for the structure of the new state was furnished by Roger Williams is clear from a letter by him to Winthrop in the fall of 1636.[20] "I have therefore had thoughts of propounding to my neighbors a double subscription. . . We whose names are hereunder written. . . do with free and joint consent promise each unto the other, that, for the common peace and welfare . . . we will from time to time subject ourselves in active and passive obedience to such orders and agreements, as shall be made by the greater number of the present householders,

---

[16] Letter: *To Major Mason*, 1670, N C P., Vol. VI, pp. 333 ff.

[17] R I C R., Vol. I, pp. 12 f. For the discussion of the date of this particular letter see footnote on page 12; also, Staples: *Annals*, p. 38 f; Winthrop: *Journal;* Letter: *To Governour Winthrop*, N C P., Vol. VI, pp. 3 f.

[18] Letter: *To Thomas Hinckley*, 1678, R I H S., Vol. 8, p. 158.

[19] R I C R., Vol. I, pp. 228 ff. N C P., Vol. VI, pp. 187, 478; III, pp. 41, 343.

[20] N C P., Vol. VI, Note, pp. 3 f, by the editor, based on Winthrop's *Journal*, pp. 231-3, and Drake's *History of Boston*, p. 201. The letter was written probably in August or September, 1636.

and such as shall hereafter be admitted by their consent into the
same privilege and covenant." This gives the gist of Williams'
social and political agreement. It is not rigid but variable. He
adds later, "I have not yet mentioned these things to my neighbors."[21] Williams purposely ignored any mention of the church
in this agreement, because he considered the church merely one of
the many civil corporations within the state. The new-comers,
however, added as a precaution, no doubt, "only in civil things."
This brief form of political agreement is pregnant with ultimate
significance. It is a "free and joint consent" as individuals, but
individuals in a community; they promise "from time to time
[to] subject" themselves; they never lose individual identity and
rights in the state, which has a variable form of government and
variable fundamental laws. They submit "in active and passive
obedience"—this is an absolute necessity to the minority even in
a majority rule. Finally, they will obey all orders made by the
present members "in our ordinary meeting and such as shall
hereafter be admitted"—the basic principle that a foreigner possesses no state privileges until naturalized. Here in small compass are presented all the dynamic elements necessary for Williams' new civil society.

Since the colonists believed a state is in large measure capable
of deliberate direction, much thought and planning went to the
shaping of the new structure. "Agreed, that after many Considerations and Consultations of our owne State and alsoe of
States abroad in way of government, we apprehend no way so
suitable to our Condition as government by way of arbitration.
But if men agree themselves by arbitration no State we know
of disallows that, neither doe we."[22] The Proposals for a Form
of Government in 1640 show a significant step in the conception
of state machinery and the necessary sovereignty to meet the
needs of a later social order more complex than that of 1636. Its
principles are, however, in perfect harmony with Williams' conception of the state. The Proposals conclude with an emphatic
statement of the absolute sovereignty of the state within the
limits prescribed by its own laws. The significant ideas in this
constitution are: arbitration of differences; respect for private

---

[21] Letter: *To John Winthrop*, 1636, N C P., Vol. VI, pp. 3-6; R I C
R., Vol. I, pp. 13-15.
[22] R I C R., Vol. I, pp. 8 f, Section III.

property; liberty of conscience, religious and secular; government by arbitration as most suitable for the colony; common humanity between man and man as the basis of government; power of the majority to compel obedience; and an authority in the state that has "absolute determination, laying ourselves down subject to it."[23] Here the man is never lost in the state, nor may the state be entirely absorbed by the individual. The interest of each is identical, but the relation is reciprocal. The state, like the men who compose it, is capable of a natural growth. And, since the state is always the body of people, it is capable of growing with the development of the people. Roger Williams believed that men in society are conscious of their corporate existence and can, by taking thought, control to a considerable degree the direction of their progress.[24]

The authority of the state Williams located inalienably in the body of people. The two legal instruments of the colony, the Charter and the Constitution, were drawn up in strict conformity with the principles promulgated by him in his treatises and letters. The location of the sovereignty is in the "voluntary consent of all, or the greater Part of them. . . lawfully met and orderly managed."[25] "The *Soveraign, originall,* and *foundation of civill power,*" declared Williams, "lies in the people, (whom they must needs mean by the civill power distinct from the *Government* set up.") This "*Soveraign power* of all *Civill Authority* is founded in the *Consent* of the people," who alone possess it "radically, and fundamentally." These "Bodies of People" have fundamentally in themselves the "*Root* of *Power,* to set up what *Government* and *Governors* they shall agree upon" as "most meete for their *civill condition.*"[26] The governments and governors "Whether *Monarchicall, Aristocraticall,* or *Democraticall.* . . receive their calling, power and authority (both Kings and Parliaments) mediately[27] from the people." This original, sovereign civil power re-

---

[23] *Ibid.* pp. 27-31.
[24] Letters: N C P., Vol. VI, *To the Town of Providence,* (1648) p. 149, (1653) p. 262, (1655) p. 278; *To the Town of Warwick,* R I H S P., Vol. VIII, pp. 147 ff; *To the General Court of Massachusetts,* N C P., Vol. VI, (1651) p. 231, (1654) p. 269, (1655) p. 293.
[25] R I C R., Vol. I, pp. 147, 157.
[26] *Bloudy Tenent of Persecution,* N C.P., Vol. III, pp. 249, 214, 366.
[27] Mediately—this term according to the context means that it is not directly from God, but indirectly, since he is the ruler of the world. The people are his media for forming the state, which is consequently immediately from them.

mains permanently in the body of people, and is only temporarily deputed: "It is evident that such Governments as are by them erected and established, have no more power, nor for longer time then the civill power or people consenting and agreeing shall betrust them with."[28]

In locating the supreme power of the state in the body of people, Williams had ample authority and precedents. The Charter granted by England allowed the colony "full power and authority" to form a government with laws according to "the Nature and Condition of the time and place."[29] And this charter was granted on terms that were congenial to Williams' ideas of civil rights and powers. Until eventually Williams became a Seeker, he ranked with Thomas Hooker and Sir Henry Vane, Jr., as one of the foremost American Independents. With them he also ranks as one of the three foremost colonial democrats of the seventeenth century.[30] The Independents, a radical religious sect, rested their religious activity on a twofold basis: the independence of each congregation, and the sovereignty of its members.[31] In the Middle Ages the theory of sovereignty was based on the rules of corporation law, which held that the majority of the corporation had the right and power to represent the whole. The medieval advocates declared at the outset that in all cases it was "collectively" and not "distributely"[32] that the corporation, or community as a corporation, was entitled to exercise supreme power. Williams, in this case, not only put the theory of corporation into practice successfully, but he is more explicit and more radical in his position than any of the medieval writers had been. The people collectively are originally and fundamentally sovereign —"absolute determinate." Furthermore, they retain this power perpetually. To administer this authority to their common interest and well-being, they appoint agents and delegate certain specific powers to them only for the time being—not perpetually. To Roger Williams the civil government is but a corporate agency created by the people. It has no inherent powers and can do

---

28 *Bloudy Tenent of Persecution*, N C P., Vol. III, pp. 343, 249.
29 *Charter and Constitution of Providence Plantation*, 1647. R I C R., Vol. I, pp. 143-228.
30 Gooch: *History of Democratic Ideas*, p. 76.
31 Sherger: *The Evolution of Modern Liberty*, pp. 122 ff. Robinson: *Justification of Separation: A Just and Necessary Apology*, 1625, in the *Hanbury Memorial of the Independents*, Vol. I; Brown: *A Book Whiche Sheweth*. Def. 35; *True and Short Declarations;* Neal: *History of the Puritans*. Vol. II.
32 Gierke: *Political Theories of the Middle Ages*. pp. 62 ff, 4, etc.

only what it is authorized to do by the provisions and limitations established by the people.[33]

The founding of Providence marks the transition of popular sovereignty and sovereignty of the people from theory into political practice.[34]

Both in theory and in practice Williams made a clear-cut distinction between the political and legal authority of the state. The legal authority comes into existence only with the formation or acceptance of the fundamental laws designating what powers the body politic is willing to transfer for the time being to its administrative organs. It is only upon the formation of the agreement that the state becomes a subject of public law.[35]   The people in assembly, together with a flexible agreement as a guide for the government, Williams considers as the only *de jure* sovereign. This he makes clear by the use of an historical event: "To these famous practices of *Josiah* I shall parallel the practices of Englands Kings: and first *de jure,* and a word or two to their right: then *de facto,* discusse what hath been done. First *de jure. . .* the Gentile Princes, Rulers, and Magistrates," no matter what the form of civil government "receive their *callings, power* and *authority*" from the bodies of the people directly. This "*calling, power,* and *authority*" is "measured out to them by free consent of the whole" as "*commission*" or "*instruction*" in the form of "*Civil Lawes* and *Constitutions.*" These laws and constitutions are the legal or *de jure* sovereign, containing the delegated portion of the state's sovereignty.[36]   Such legal sovereign, although supreme and absolute within its own sphere, is, nevertheless, always subject to the will of the people in assembly. This agreement in turn fixes the legal activities of the political ma-

---

[33] *Bloody Tenent Yet More Bloody,* N C P., Vol. IV, Chapters VI and VII.

[34] Popular sovereignty is the authority of the state existing in the mass of its citizens; sovereignty of the people is the will of the people expressed by voting, speeches, press, or in innumerable other ways. M'Kechnie: *The State and the Individual,* p. 132.

[35] Holcombe: *The Modern Commonwealth,* p. 55. Burgess: *Political Science and Constitutional Law,* p. 49.

[36] *Bloudy Tenent of Persecution,* N C P., Vol. III, pp. 253, 297, 349, 254, 366, 418. *De Jure*: in this instance neither the Kings of England since Henry VII nor the Parliament had *de jure* supreme authority in the state which had become theocratic in aspect, but took it *de facto.* N C P., Vol. III, p. 343. Williams uses such synomyms for the *de jure* sovereignty: combination of men; powers granted them; civil constitution; instructions; commissions; callings; compact; power measured out, etc.

chinery; for Williams held that every lawful civil government, whether hereditary or elective is "the Minister or servant of the people," and that government and magistrate "goes beyond his commission, who intermeddles with that which cannot be given him in commission from the people."[37]

De jure authority, however, is limited, for "the people" cannot give anyone authority over liberty of conscience and civil liberty.[38] Yet this does not prevent an unlawful and usurping sovereignty from tyrannizing over a people *de facto*. Williams' emphasis on this aspect of civil life is evident by his frequent return to the principle that *"In civil things nothing is lawful (de jure) but what is according to law and order."*[39] The fundamental Liberties" of the state make it imperative that certain laws must be obeyed by the citizens. Otherwise there could be no civil peace, no common welfare, no civil liberty. "It is, gentlemen, in the power of the body [assembly] to require the help of any of her members," and "in extraordinary cases. . . extraordinary means for common safety may be used."[40] In the legal sovereign, then, is located that authority which has the power to issue the final command.[41] To it is attributed the right of laying down the laws of the state. In the United States the legal sovereign is said to be the Constitution; in England, the Parliament. In the Providence Plantations it resided in the bodies of people, expressed in the constitution as created by and continually subject to such bodies.[42]

In the first part of the constitution of 1647 a Bill of Rights limits the legal sovereign:

"That no person, in this Colonie, shall be taken or imprisoned, or be disseized of his Lands or Liberties, or be Exiled, or any otherwise molested or destroyed, but by the Lawfull judgement of his Peeres, or by

---

[37] *Bloody Tenent Yet More Bloody*, N C P., Vol. IV, p. 187.

[38] N C P., Vols. I-VI; Letter: *To the Town of Warwick*, 1666, R I H S P., Vol. 8, pp. 147 ff, on civil liberty. Conscience, when used by Williams, means more than merely a religious conscience—usually he means the knowing part of man, reason, inmost thought or sense.

[39] *Cottons Letter Examined and Answered*, N C P., Vol. I, p. 48.

[40] Letter: *To the Town of Providence*, N C P., Vol. VI, pp. 149 ff.

[41] Compare Williams' position with Bodin: *De la République*, 1: 6, 8; Hobbes: *The Leviathan;* Austin: *Lectures on Jurisprudence*, Vol. I, p. 117; Burgess: *Political Science and Constitutional Law*, Vol. I, p. 50; Bluntschli: *The Theory of the State*, pp. 492 ff.

[42] N C P., Vol. III, pp. 214, 249, 366; Vol. IV, pp. 149 ff..

some known Law, and according to the Letter of it, Ratified by the major part of the Generall Assembly lawfully met and orderly managed."[43]

The conclusion to the main body of the constitution further limits it:

"These are the Lawes that concern all men, and these are the Penalties for the transgression thereof, which by common consent are Ratified and Established throwout this whole Colonie; And otherwise then thus what is forbidden, all men may walk as their conscience perswade them, every man in the name of his God."[44]

The political supreme authority expressed by the body of people, Williams recognized as the source of all government. But he was not, however, blind to the fact that the political sovereign may be viewed as either legal, or actual but illegal. *De jure,* the kings of England were not the head of the church of England, but merely *de facto,* as appears by the Act of Parliament establishing Henry VIII the supreme head of the church. "But neither Pope nor King can ever prove such power from Christ derived to either of them."[45] Yet they were the actual political and legal sovereigns, each in his time and place. Actually, therefore, the sovereign powers may exist by usurpation. *"Subjection* may be either to lawful *governors,* or but to *pretenders* and *usurpers.* Again *subjection* to *lawful rulers* may be in cases pertaining to their cognizance, or in cases which belong to neither, but another *court* or *tribunal,* which undue proceeding is not tolerable in all well ordered States. . . we used to say, that *subjection* is either active or passive."[46] The latter form of subjection, the result of usurpation, does not in any way affect the principle that the political sovereignty lies in the people as their unorganized will. Might usually establishes the standard of right prevalent in the community, but might never can change ultimate principles. And so, in spite of any unlawfully assumed control, these civil powers remain permanently and essentially in the people, or the state, as distinguished from the government.

Williams was in substantial agreement with the authors of the Model[47] when they maintained that the civil power is the combined influences that lie behind the government and law; that it

---

[43] R I C R., Vol. I, p. 157.
[44] *Ibid,* p. 190.
[45] *Bloudy Tenent of Persecution,* N C P., Vol. III, p. 344 f.
[46] *Bloody Tenent Yet More Bloody,* N C P., Vol. IV, p. 267.
[47] *A Model of Church and Civil Power. By New England Ministers,* quoted in N C P., Vol. III, pp. 247 ff

can gain its ends only by political means; and that these political means are the power to establish a government suitable to the people, to formulate civil laws and constitutions, to provide for elections, to execute the laws, to maintain internal civil peace, and to prepare against external aggression. But he could not follow the authors in uniting the civil and spiritual governments. Original civil power, Williams held, is political, and only political:

"Whereas they say, that the Civill Power may erect and establish what *forme* of *civill Government* may seem in *Wisdome* most meet, I acknowledge the *Proposition* to be most true. . . But from this *Grant* I infer, (as before hath been touched) that the *Soveraign, original,* and *foundation* of *Civill power* lies in the *People,* (whom they must needs mean by the *civill power* distinct from the Government set up.) And if so, that a People may erect and establish what *forme* of *Government* seemes to them most meete for their civill condition: It is evident that such *Governments* as are by them erected and established, have no more *power,* nor for no longer time, then the *civill power* or people consenting and agreeing shall betrust them with. This is cleere not only in *Reason,* but in the experience of all *commonweales,* where the people are not deprived of their naturall freedom by the power of the tyrants."[48]

The political sovereignty is distinct from the legal, and may be prior as well as subsequent to it. Fundamentally it resides in the people, but actually it may be usurped by tyrants.

Now, with the political authority clearly distinguished from the legal, he allows his inevitably logical mind to follow up the line of reasoning to the unavoidable conclusion. As a result he launches a prophetic *coup de grace:* "Besides (as I elsewhere observed) what if the people will have no *Kings, governours,* etc., nay no *Parliment,* no *general Court,* but leave vast *interregnums, Ruptures* of *Government,* yea conclude upon frequent *changes,*"[49] could they not so conclude since they possess the original sovereign civil power? William Harris had come to the same conclusions.[50] Only his *lèse majesté* rested in the fact that he attempted to carry out this principle against the will of the majority. Williams opposed him because the majority had, for the time being, concluded differently. Is Williams in this instance inferring that a

---

[48] *Bloudy Tenent of Persecution,* N C P., Vol. III, pp. 249 f.
[49] *Bloudy Tenent Yet More Bloudy,* N C P., Vol. IV, p. 171.
[50] R I C R., Vol. I, pp. 361, 3 f. Williams in this case acted as the President of the colony. As such, his theory required him to carry out his commission from the people. His action against Harris was supported by a verdict from the assembly. On several other occasions he supported Harris in opposition to the other leaders.

condition of social life without government machinery, or anarchy, would be preferable?[51] Or is he merely postulating the possibility of absence of government machinery, and suggesting instead a rule by either public opinion, society, or the common will of the people? Would such a rule be tyranny or the nearest possible approach to a condition of true liberty?

That the sovereignty can be neither divided nor alienated was clearly indicated by Williams throughout his writings, although he never used the technical terms of "indivisible" or "sovereignty." He seems to have purposely avoided using them. In his attitude toward the divisibility of the supreme powers, he was in agreement with the political thinkers of his century.[52] But he differed from them in the location and permanent possession of sovereignty. He held that all forms of government whatsoever, if lawful, receive their power directly from the people.[53] But the original civil power remains in them perpetually, and may be limited or even withheld whenever they so desire. In locating and placing sovereignty inalienably in the people, he may have been partly influenced by medieval theory. Certain medieval writers held that sovereignty is divisible into the head and body. The *whole* is not the mere body of the state as sovereign, but the body, as conceived by the thinkers of the Middle Ages, consisted only of the "active Burghers" not as individuals but "collectively" as a social factor of the community.[54] Williams held that sovereignty is not only indivisible but also inalienable, because the whole is represented by the people assembled as individuals in a community. The supreme authority is the will of the major portion of the individuals assembled who possess universal, natural, civil, and humane rights. This civil power remains in the original body, whole, complete, and competent; "the Citie" he contends, "stands absolute and intire."[55]

Because of a definite distinction made between state and government, Williams did not fall into the error of postulating a

[51] Williams' principle here referred to is diametrically opposite the position of certain modern anarchists who wish by physical force to establish a minority opinion.

[52] Such as: James I, Hobbes, Bacon, Milton, Harrington, Sidney, Filmore, Locke, and Halifax.

[53] N C P., Vol. III, pp. 343, 214, 249; Vol. IV, p. 3. R I C R., Vol. I, pp. 145, 157.

[54] Geirke: *Political Theories of the Middle Ages,* p. 63 ff.

[55] *Bloudy Tenent of Persecution,* N C P., Vol. III, pp. 398, 73.

dual civil sovereignty. The "civil power lies in the people," and is "distinct from the government set up." States, governments, governors, laws, punishments and weapons, he exclaimed at another time, are "all of a civill nature." The civil magistrates, kings, parliaments, general courts, and assemblies have their various civil powers granted them by the people in the form of commissions.[56] The units of a state possess their powers only by grants from this sovereignty through the constitution. Williams, therefore, understood that these units of granted civil powers are not a division or alienation of the sovereignty of the state.

The question of the divisibility of sovereignty came to the front with the appearance of the modern federal state. How can a supreme authority be split into numerous parts and still remain sovereign? If sovereign power implies unity, a division of it implies disunion, weakness, paralysis. The federal union of the United States consists of three grades of powers—the constitution, the federal government, and the individual states—each supreme in its own sphere. But the indivisibility of its sovereignty is not affected by this federal system. A federal union makes one complete state and only one, with a single sovereign.[57] After the adoption of the Constitution in 1789, the doctrine of "divided sovereignty" aroused much discussion. Hamilton and Madison in the *Federalist*[58] held that the United States is sovereign as to powers conferred, and the "states" as to powers reserved.[59] This doctrine was later made a part of the law of the land by the decisions of the Supreme Court.[60] Webster defended the doctrine proposed by Judge Story that the United States is sovereign as a state.[61] This is the doctrine of our present national state. A third group, best represented by Calhoun, declared that sovereignty is lodged exclusively in the several states.[62] He repudiated the social contract and maintained the indivisibility of sovereignty, declaring that it "is an entire thing," that to 'divide it, is . . . to

---

[56] *Ibid.* pp. 108, 116, 249 ff, 297 ff.

[57] Gilchrist: *Principles of Political Science,* p. 111.

[58] Nos. 4, 9, 31, 39.

[59] See De Tocqueville: *Democracy in America;* Chipman: *Principles of Government,* 1833; on page 273 he writes, "Experience has shown it capable of division."

[60] *Chisholm* vs *Georgia,* 1792, 2 Dallas, p. 435, etc.

[61] Webster: *Works.* Story: *Commentaries on the Constitution.* 1833.

[62] Calhoun: *Disquisitions on Government.* Works, Vol. I, p. 146. Compare Tucker: *Commentaries on Blackstone,* 1833. A Virginia jurist.

destroy it. . . . We might just as well speak of half a square or half a triangle as of half a sovereignty."[63] Although Calhoun held the several states of the United States as sovereign, each as a state in itself, he nevertheless considered that sovereign not capable of division. Unanimity of opinion will probably never be reached; but most of the later publicists and jurists hold that Calhoun was right and that sovereignty, as such, is indivisible.

The notion of a divided or dual supreme authority arises from the failure to distinguish state from government. The constitution of any federation grants supreme powers to various organs or units of the government. This division of civil powers is not the same as the division of the sovereignty of the state.[64] The difficulty lies largely in discovering the political or *de facto* sovereign.[65] If it lies with the people, how can they express this authority under a complicated national machinery except through actual civil rebellion? Yet ultimately the final command does lie with the people by the sheer force of numbers, as shown in recent European upheavals. But, since the people of the United States, as purposely designed by the framers of the constitution, have difficulty in expressing their will through the laws because of the intricate system of checks and balances, who and what is the real acting sovereign in our national state?[66] Whose *will* is the actual authority in the polity of state? But such a question is a departure from theory into the realm of practice. Theoretically, then, there is only one sovereign of the federal state, which in its *de jure* aspect issues into the various powers of the government. Ultimately, it is said to be in the organized will of the people, because they can rise in their might and make whatever new arrangements they desire. "Analysis, therefore, is driven to say that with us sovereignty rests in its entirety with the not very determinate body of persons, the people of the United

---

[63] *Works*, Vol. I, p. 146.

[64] Patrick Henry was corrected when he maintained with reference to the *Virginia and Kentucky Resolutions*, 1798-9, that Virginia as a member of the United States had no more sovereignty than did the county of Charlotte as a part of the state of Virginia—that is, the several states were each merely administrative organs *de facto*.

[65] *The Federalist;* John Adams: *Works*, Vol. VI, p. 476, the letter to John Taylor; Madison: *Notes on Jonathan's Debates*, Vol. V.

[66] Holcombe: *The Modern Commonwealth*. Laski: *Authority in the Modern State*.

States, the *powers* of sovereignty resting with the state and federal authorities by delegation from the people."[67]

The individual towns of the Providence Plantations, corresponding to members of the federal state, were mere corporate bodies of the civil government. As such they had corporation rights, free and absolute, subject to the final disposal of the "General Assemblie power and Authority" and the constitution. Neither legal nor political sovereignty was granted them in essence, effect, or fact. Williams and his followers, thereby avoided the evident fiction of the Swiss and United States constitutions. In this he had as clear and logical a grasp of the *de jure* and *de facto* sovereignty of the federal state and its significance as a central, absolute, and undivided authority, as did Patrick Henry and Thomas Jefferson.[68] As Moderator of Providence, May 18, 1647, Roger Williams drafted the instructions for the Committee of Ten who were to represent the Town in drawing up a constitution and organizing the government of the Plantations. This document gives his view of the place the town should have in the new government. "We all voluntarily assenting, do hereby give you full power and authority as followeth: First. To act and vote for us respectively and otherwise, as if we ourselves were in person. . . Secondly. To act and vote for us, as aforesaid, in the choice of all general officers as need shall require. . . . Thirdly. We desire to have exact and orderly way open for appeals unto General Courts. . . That each town should have a charter of civil incorporation, apart, for the transaction of particular affairs; if the Court shall proceed so far as to agitate and order the same, we give you full power, etc."[69] These significant phrases definitely indicate the "absolute and intire" authority of the state. The town requests "granted powers" from the state, but does not order the state to grant it powers.

The majority of the colony agreed with this view of the "intire" sovereignty of the state. This fact is stressed by the charter of incorporation granted to the town of Providence. "Upon the

---

[67] Wilson: *The State*, p. 92; *An Old Master and Other Essays*, pp. 93 f. Goodnow: *Principles of Constitutional Government*.

[68] See the *Virginia and Kentucky Resolutions*, 1798-9; also the utterances of these two men in defense of the Resolutions.

[69] *Instructions from the Town of Providence*, May 18, 1647, R I C R., Vol. I, pp. 42-44. Roger Williams was a member of this committee, for which he drafted the instructions.

petition and humble request of the freeman of the Town of Providence, exhibited unto this present session of the General Assembly, wherein they desire freedome and libertie to incorporate themselves into a body politicke, and we the said Assembly, having duly weighed and seriously considered the premises, and being willing and ready to provide for the ease and liberty of the people, have thought fit and by the authority aforesaid, and by these presents, do give, grant, and confirm, etc. . . . Provided . . . always reserving to the aforesaid Generall Assemblie power and authority so to dispose the generall government of that plantation as it stands in reference to the rest of the plantations, as they shall conceive, from time to time, most conducing to the generall good of the said plantations."[70] The various conditional phrases make it sufficiently clear that the town was a mere territorial unit of adminstration within the civil state.[71] The local unit received full power to transact all its local affairs in harmony with the laws of the state. But the local unit possessed only delegated civil powers which could be recalled at any time. Yet the dilemma of a bureaucratic national state was wisely avoided, by frequent elections, joint and individual initiative of civil laws, referendum and recall[72] by popular vote of all civil laws and the constitution, and a single legislative body, which enabled the people to retain their original sovereignty in fact. By this form of government a condition of decentralized sovereign powers actually resulted without a division of the sovereignty of the state.

The principles of civil liberty and self-government dictate that the government must be conducted on a definite understanding between it and the people. The right of the individual must be defined and guaranteed by specific safeguards. The authority and functions of those who are to rule must be limited and determined by unmistakable custom or explicit fundamental laws, and they must be held responsible directly to the people.[73] But a gov-

---

[70] *Charter of Providence*, 1649, R I C R., Vol. 1, pp. 214-16. Like grants were made to Newport and Portsmouth.

[71] R I C R., Vol. I, p. 209. "If any town refuse (to select six men to the Assembly) the Court shall chose them for them." Liberty and local self-government were reciprocal only when the latter was based on law and order in harmony with the state and the commonwealth.

[72] Channing: *History of the United States,* Vol. I, p. 395. Hart: *Actual Government*, pp. 78 ff. Compare this liberalism with the Swiss and American governments on "optional referendum" in local affairs.

[73] Wilson: *Problems of Modern Democracy*, p. 65.

ernment cannot be directly responsible to the people nor can it meet the changing conditions of national life, when it is the organ of a rigid and unvarying fundamental law. By declaring that the constitution is neither sacred nor rigid in the American sense, Williams was able to guarantee both liberty and internal peace. Yet he was in harmony with the American fundamental principle of the division of the political powers.[74] He, however, adds another safeguard to civil liberty, by declaring that the fundamental laws of the state can be interpreted by no one but those who made them—the people or the assembly.[75]

Because the power conferred by the Charter of 1643 was sufficiently vague, Rhode Island was able to make its own civil laws.[76] No form of government was prescribed by it, making possible a liberal form of government. The fundamental laws were continually amended or sliced down, whenever inadequate to meet a present emergency. The constitution was merely a commission to the governors and government, as agents of the people[77] to whom the government was directly responsible. This was in accord with Williams' theory of governmental responsibility: "I stand accountable," wrote he as president of the colony, "to our General Court."[78] The Court, or assembly, elected by the citizens just prior to the session, could, with their approval, change the laws and the government to meet new or unusual civil conditions. For the only law, both equitable and just, is such as "indeed concern Life and Manner, according to the Nature and Constitution of the Severall Nations and Peoples of the World."[79] Ultimately and in practice, the citizens of Rhode Island retained the undivided sovereignty in civil affairs.

The division of the political powers granted by the constitu-

---

[74] Compare Bourgeaud: *The Rise of Modern Democracy*, (1891).

[75] R I C R., Vol. I, p. 210. This is the only guarantee of civil liberty. The legislature interpreted its own laws. The legal and political check fixed upon the people of the United States by the power of interpretation granted to the Supreme Court has its origin in England's attempt to regulate and review colonial legislation during the latter part of the seventeenth and the eighteenth centuries.

[76] Staples: *Annals*, p. 56.

[77] Channing: *History of the United States*, Vol. I, p. 394. N C P., Vol. III, pp. 249 f, 388 ff. Compare the present British political theory and practice.

[78] Letter: *To John Endicott*, 1656, R I H S P., Vol. 8, p. 146.

[79] Letter: *To the Town of Warwick*, R I H S P., Vol. 8, pp. 147 ff. Bill of Rights in the Constitution of 1647, R I C R., Vol. I, p. 157. N C P., Vol. IV, p. 485.

tion of Rhode Island, it is evident then, did not affect the principle of indivisible and inalienable sovereignty. Of all the colonial federative systems, this was the most nearly perfect and the most influential. Furthermore, the continual change in the form of civil machinery and fundamental laws affected neither Williams' principle of sovereignty nor any other of his political ideas.[80] Rather it upheld them. For, since the civil state is natural and humane, it must consequently be capable of infinite growth, and never rest *in statu*. The colony exemplified this. If this is so, it is impossible to escape the fact that a rigid constitution and form of government must of necessity, then, be tyrannical. For how can it adjust itself to the changing conditions of social life?

With true democratic instinct, Williams distinctly anticipated later liberalism. The federal constitution contained a Bill of Rights, granted religious liberty, and limited governmental powers. The legislative body consisted of one house, the members of which were elected by the people just prior to the opening of the session. This guaranteed attention to present needs. The president was elected directly by the people, was forced to serve or pay a fine, and was responsible directly to them.[81] He could be deposed and replaced at any time, if he refused to conform to the "Instructions." Annual election of all officers, with a joint compulsory initiative and referendum, kept the legal sovereignty in absolute subjection to the majority of the people.[82]

The whole structure of the civil machinery was so arranged that the government with its three departments, although not distinct like those of modern states, was no longer the master of men imposing its sovereign will on its subjects. It no longer issued commands. Instead it strove to conciliate. To pacify the minority, who would have to submit to the supreme authority, Williams advocated the use of the compromise, frequent elections, and referendum and recall. And in his own colony harmony between the minority and majority was continually gained by the means of arbitration. This principle was repeatedly urged and

---

[80] *Bloudy Tenent of Persecution,* N C P., Vol. III, p. 48; IV, pp. 80, 219.

[81] N C P., Vol. III, pp. 356, 161, 249, 297, 398; II, p. 259. Compare Laski: *Foundations of Modern Sovereignty,* chapter on the *Responsibility of the State.*

[82] R I C R., Vol. I, covers the years from 1636 to 1663.

practiced by Williams himself.[83] The election was influenced not by irresponsible political parties, but by present issues and principles. The court of justice was merely a "Court of Tryall," and could in no way form or interpret constitutional law. The power to interpret the fundamental law was explicitly retained by the people, or their direct representatives. The government became simply the manager of the common business. Hence the state of Rhode Island was nothing so much as a "great public service corporation."[84] By means of checks and balances, the people made the colonial state the servant and agent.[85] Sovereignty, here, was neither alienated nor divided. And above all, a liberal government was successfully established on principles of liberty far in advance of any other state before or since his time.

In the new society founded by Williams, the sovereignty of the civil state and that of the spiritual state were given two distinct spheres of political and juristic activity.[86] The civil state has power only over the bodies and goods of men; the spiritual is limited in its authority to the spiritual life and religious conscience.

This idea of the different natures of civil and spiritual sovereignty grew out of Williams' theory of state and his concept of man.[87] Man is an individual having a material body and an immaterial conscience or subjective self. The civil state, an external thing, can have authority only over the material civil part of man. The conscience and mind are free from civil power, so long as no civil disorder results. The spiritual state has control over the spiritual life of man only as he is a particular member of a particular religious group. Otherwise that conscience or mind is unfettered.[88] This is indeed a truly mystical conception of sovereignty.[89] The distinct nature of the two states,

---

[83] *Ibid*, pp. 32, 249, 352, 377. N C P., Vol. VI, pp. 90, 150, 265, 267. R I H S P., Vol. 8, p. 160. This later was advocated by Locke and by Rousseau.

[84] R I C R., Vol. I, the period from 1636 to 1663. Compare Duguit: *Law in the Modern State,* pp. 51 ff. Duguit here makes clear the idea of the government as a public-service corporation.

[85] *Bloudy Tenent of Persecution,* N C P., Vol. III, pp. 356, 398.

[86] *Bloudy Tenent Yet More Bloudy,* N C P., Vol. IV, p. 199.

[87] See Scott: *Development of Constitutional Liberty,* p. 114.

[88] N C P., Vols. I-VI. Only a careful study of Williams' complete works will make this distinction clear.

[89] Compare Carlyle: *French Revolution,* II, p. 2. "It is most true that all available authority is Mystic in its conditions."

he makes clear in this manner: "As the *Apple-tree* among the *Trees* of the *Forrest*. . . so great a difference is there between the *Church* in a Citie or country, and the civill State, a City or country, in which it is. . . The power of the *Civill Magistrate* is superior to the *Church policie* in *place, honours, dignity, earthly power* in the *World;* And the *Church* superior to him, being a member of the *Church, Ecclesiastically*. . . so that all the *power* the *Magistrate* hath over the *Church* is *temporall* not *spirituall*, and all the *power* the *Church* hath over the *Magistrate* is *spirituall* not *temporall*."[90] This separateness of the essential civil powers is the same "all the world over."[91]

The state is non-religious. The civil power of the magistrate is not increased or diminished by his being Christian or pagan. This is true, because in a civil state, the "*Power, Might, or Authority,* is not *Religious, Christian, etc.* but natural, humane, civill." It can show no "*commission, instruction,* or *promise* given them by the Son of God." Although the civil state and the spiritual are independent, they "are not inconsistent" but "may stand together."[92] The civil state should, however, countenance and protect the persons of the church from violence and disturbances in body and goods. "Civil violence," Williams explains, "is breaking bounds and orders of the citie, town or court," and comes under the jurisdiction of the civil state. The church, on the other hand, helps the peace and prosperity of the commonwealth by prayers and obedience. Soul judgments are not a right of the state; "such a *sentence* no *Civill Judge* may passe, such a Death no *Civill Sword* can inflct."[93] That the civil and spiritual state, the church and commonweal, are "like *Hippocrates Twinnes*: born together, grow up together, laugh together, weep together, sicken and die together," he declared is "yet a most dangerous *Fiction* of the *Father* of *Lies*."[94]

---

[90] *Bloudy Tenent of Persecution*, N C P., Vol. III, pp. 94, 226.

[91] *Bloody Tenent Yet More Bloody*, N C P., Vol. IV, p. 80.

[92] *Bloudy Tenent of Persecution*, N C P., Vol. III, pp. 355, 398, 277, 224; also IV, p. 174. All previous writers have erroneously claimed that Roger Williams established a Christian state and society. He himself definitely denies it.

[93] *Ibid*, pp. 280, 303, 225, 125; IV, p. 71. But he holds the state has no right to collect the church tax. He also emphatically denies the validity of the Geneva plan.

[94] *Ibid.* p. 333. He declares this wrong in five particulars.

That Williams considers sovereignty by nature absolute, competent, and determinate, is fitly illustrated in his "Parable of the Ship of State":

"There goes many a ship to sea, with many hundred souls in one ship, whose weal and woe is common, and is a true picture of a commonwealth, or a human combination or society. It hath fallen out sometimes, that both papists and protestants, Jews and Turks, may be embarked in one ship; upon which proposal I affirm, that all the liberty of conscience, that ever I pleaded for, turns upon these two hinges— that none of the papists, protestants, Jews, or Turks, be forced to come to the ship's prayers and worship, nor compelled from their own particular prayers or worship, if they practice any. I further add, that I never denied, that notwithstanding this liberty, the commander of this ship ought to command the ship's course, yea, and also command that justice, peace and sobriety be kept and practiced, both among the seamen and all the passengers. If any of the seamen refuse to perform their services, or passengers to pay their freight; if any refuse to help, in person or purse, toward the common charges or defence; if any refuse to obey the common laws and orders of the ship, concerning their common peace and preservation; if any shall mutiny and rise up against their commanders and officers; if any should preach or write that there ought to be no commanders or officers, nor corrections nor punishments, no laws nor orders, I never denied, but in such cases, whatever is pretended, the commander or commanders may judge, resist, compel and punish such transgressors, according to their deserts and merits."[95]

An almost similar aspect of absolute and uncontrolled sovereignty is presented in a letter to the town of Providence in 1680. The letter presents, in addition, his theory of state and government, and a word on the nature and instincts of man:

"1. Government and order in families, towns, etc., is the ordinance of the Most High, Rom. 13, for the peace and good of mankind. 2. Six things are written in the hearts of all mankind, yea, even in pagans: 1st. That there is a Deity; 2d. That some actions are nought; 3rd. That the Deity will punish; 4th. That there is another life; 5th. That marriage is honorable; 6th. That mankind cannot keep together without some government. 3. There is no Englishman in his Majesty's dominions or elsewhere, who is not forced to submit to government. 4. That there is no man in the world, except robbers, pirates and rebels, but doth submit to government. 5. Even robbers, pirates and rebels themselves cannot hold together, but by some law among themselves and government. 6. One of these two great laws of the world must prevail, either that of judges and justices of peace in courts of peace, or law of arms, the sword and blood. 7. If it comes from the courts of trials and peace, to the trial of sword and blood, the conquered is forced to

---

[95] Letter: *To the Town of Providence,* N C P., Vol. VI, pp. 278 f.

seek law and government. 8. Till matters come to a settled government no man is ordinarily sure of his house, goods, lands, cattle, wife, children, life. 9. Hence is that ancient maxim, *It is better to live under a tyrant in peace, than under the sword, or where every man is a tyrant* . . . . 10. No government is maintained without tribute, custom, rates, taxes, etc. . . . 13. Our charter excels all in New England, or, *in the world, as to the souls of men.* . . . 15. Our rates are the least, by far, of any colony in New England. 16. There is no man that hath a vote in town or colony, but he *hath a hand in making the rates by himself or his deputies.* 17. In our colony the General Assembly, Governor, magistrates, deputies, towns, town clerks, raters, constables, etc., have done their duties, the failing lies upon particular persons. 18. It is but folly to resist (one or more, and if one, why not more?) God hath stirred up the spirit of the Governor, magistrates and officers, driven to it by necessity, to be unanimously resolved to see the matter finished; and it is the duty of every man to maintain, encourage, and strength the hand of authority."[96]

Here we have testimony to his keen interest in problems of the state and government. Although this letter was written at about the age of seventy-seven and after innumerable bitter disappointments, Williams still held substantially the same theory of state that he presented almost half a century before in his *Bloudy Tenent,* and that he upheld in 1655 in his Parable of the Ship of State.

Sovereignty as conceived by Williams is the absolute authority of the state over all its members, including the minority who are opposed to certain particular policies. This minority does not necessarily include the same individuals each time, and in his colony it seldom did.[97] No powers within the state, whether federal or otherwise, are superior to this authority. Yet it is more than the constitution, government, and separate towns taken together. It is that which gives vitality to the state. It appears as power and force only in case of necessity. More often it manifests itself as cause for obedience through reason and will.[98]

But the theoretical sovereign, Williams maintained, is also the actual sovereign. This sovereign, original, fundamental power lies in the major part of the people orderly assembled. And in the colony, the major portion of the people controlled and regulated the civil relations between man and the state, and between man

---

[96] *Ibid.* pp. 401 ff. (1681 Jan.)

[97] Roger Williams on several occasions defended his bitterest enemies; he found himself with the minority on numerous occasions in economic disputes, and then contended for compromise.

[98] N C P., Vol. III, pp. 299, 397 ff, 257, 302, 247 ff ; IV, 145, 222, etc.

and man. Williams' actual and theoretical sovereignty, furthermore, is unlimited except by the nature, conditions and circumstances of peoples and nations.   To all intents and purposes,
therefore, it is unlimited internally.   Externally it is limited by
the rights and might of other states.[99]   During the periods of
internal peace, this final authority is merely a latent power or
force.   And since this sovereignty is the will of the major part
of the people, perpetually, it cannot be considered in essence
either despotic or tyrannical.[100]   For Williams never conceived
of it as a technically arbitrary power of the state.

The supreme power and authority of the state, as Williams
set it forth in theory and practice, is independent, competent, perpetual as the state, uncontrolled, universal, absolute and entire,
inalienable, and indivisible.[101]   His idea of the nature of authority
differed from that of the other political thinkers of the seventeenth century both in England and on the Continent.   They
could think of sovereignty only as an objective thing.   Williams
held it to be by nature both subjective and objective.   The civil
state is *"civil, internal* in the mindes of men, and *external* in the
administration and conversation of it."[102]

In theory and practice Williams maintained that the constitution, government, laws, and rulers must conform to the demands of the sovereignty of the state.   But man, he held, nevertheless, remains an individual within the corporate whole.   His
final and most startlingly revolutionary idea is that he allows for
a variable expression of this sovereignty in accordance with the
nature and circumstances of time and place.   In actual colonial
practice the fundamental law could be and was changed annually,
and even at times semi-annually.   The whole structure of the
state Williams considered variable because state and sovereignty
are as variable as the body of the people.   He definitely opposed
King James' idea of state, that "Kings are justly called Gods,"
with this answer: "Grant the *Magistrates* to be as *Gods,* or strong

---

[99] Letter: *To Major Mason,* N C P., Vol. VI, pp. 342 ff.   Man and
nations have certain rights to freedom.

[100] This does not mean that in actual practice sovereignty has ever
attained such an ideal.   To the minority, or at least to certain individuals,
it appears despotic at all times.

[100] This does not mean that in actual practice sovereignty has ever
III, pp. 73, 72, 343, 398.

[102] N C P., Vol. IV, pp. 72 f.

ones in a *Resemblance* to *God* in all *Nations* of the *World*. Yet that is still within the compass of their calling. . . servants of the *Commonweale*."[103] Unlike James I, Hobbes, Digges, Laud, Milton, and Locke, he denied that either political sovereignty or legal authority could justly be capricious or tyrannical.[104] To Williams sovereignty is the highest political power in the state; but when lawful it is the servant and agent of the people. It is the power "to select the policy of the nation, propose, formulate and modify its laws, determine its relation with other nations, and its place of leadership in the world."

---

[103] *Bloody Tenent Yet More Bloody*, N C P., Vol. IV, pp. 277 f.
[104] Figgis: *The Divine Right of Kings*, pp. 228 ff.

PART 3
SOVEREIGNTY AND SELF-GOVERNMENT

To Roger Williams, democracy was not a particular form of government, but a stage of political development which by long discipline and political training may eventually prepare the people for complete self-rule by law. But before this freedom through law can be attained, the people must possess powerful ideals with enough initiative to translate these ideals into political practices and institutions that will serve them in their every-day life.[105] He regarded the state and government as the natural growth of the social organism. That he correctly estimated the psychological, economic, social and political aspects underlying the free state of a liberty-loving people, is fully attested by Channing in recounting the characteristics of the colony: "In Rhode Island, individualism always had its highest development . . . . Everywhere in the colony men held strong opinions, and everywhere there was extreme toleration of the ideas of others. In such a community, men of power would profoundly influence the thoughts, lives, souls, and doings of others."[106] Gooch, in his *History of Democratic Ideas,* also suggests that Williams' theory of state was mostly concerned with individual freedom: "If democracy, however, in its ultimate meaning, be held to imply not only government in which the preponderant share of power resides in the hands of the people, but a society based on the principles of political and religious freedom, Rhode Island beyond any other of the American Colonies is entitled to be called Democratic."[107]

The new politics of religious and civil freedom which grew out of the Renaissance and the Reformation emphasized the place of the individual in civil society. "The Gunpowder Plot," says Gooch, "marks the triumph of the new politics. The equivocations of Garnet were promptly extolled by Bellarmime." In this new politics Williams makes the state a non-religious body, and the church a mere corporation within the state. If the state is

---

[105] Wilson: *Address at Independence Hall,* July 4, 1914, presents this idea in a vivid manner.
[106] *History of the United States,* Vol. I, pp. 397 f.
[107] *History of Democratic Ideas,* p. 83.

natural, civil and humane, man as a member of this state has natural, civil and humane rights and duties. The subjective state is natural, humane, and civil; the objective state is merely civil. Man in this state is considered as both a subjective and an objective member. The subjective man is free and independent of the civil state. The objective man is liable to civil control by the civil state; yet he always has the claims of nature and common humanity against the state. Williams' theory of state and sovereignty, contrary to all claims made heretofore, has its basis not in religion, but in his conception of the individual man in a civil state or society.

In order to secure civil freedom to man, it was evident to Williams that some form of government must at present exist. This fact was inherent in the circumstances and necessities of man. At bottom he was united with all parties of his century in his respect for law and his anxiety to defend government;[108] but he differed with them as to the nature of both. Laws, as the expression of sovereignty, must be supreme, and social chaos must be prevented. He also recognized the inevitable conflict between the desire of the individual for complete liberty, or unrestrained individualism, and the necessity of granting to government the power to carry out its functions. In opposition to the conservative view that law is to restrain freedom,[109] he maintained the liberal view that the object of law is to enlarge freedom. Locke, Sidney, and Milton held that the original agreement is rigid, limits the form of government, and reduces the state to a mechanical instrument. In contrast to them, Williams declared that the agreement ought to be independent of and prior to the form of government, and that both were subject to growth and change without the necessary destruction of either. He agreed with both Aristotle and the supporters of the divine right theory that the state is a natural organism, a part of life. And then with life, it must change in its object and function. To facilitate this development and to avoid the usual destructive features associated

---

[108] Figgis: *The Divine Right of Kings,* p. 245.

[109] Bret: *A Defense of Liberty,* p. 139. Adams: *Three Episodes,* p. 385, makes this reference to the clearness of Williams' concept, "Human thought had not yet grasped the distinction between personal liberty where the rights of others are not involved, and license where those rights are involved."

with a change in the social organism, Williams placed the sovereignty not in tradition or a rigid constitution, but in the citizenry of the state.

The sovereignty of the state, according to Williams, resides originally, fundamentally, and perpetually in the people collectively. This supreme power is independent, uncontrolled, just, natural, absolute, entire, inalienable, and indivisible. It is the source of all government. Yet it appears as power or force only in case of extreme necessity; more often it secures obedience by appeal through reason and will. By nature it is both subjective and objective. Internally, the sovereignty is unlimited except by the nature, conditions, and circumstances of the peoples and nations; externally it is limited only by the right and might of other states. Since he considered the state non-religious, he separated the spiritual and political state in their political and juristic powers. At no time can a state acquire authority over the civil liberties and the consciences of men. The political and legal sovereignty are made two distinct aspects of the sovereignty of the state; the legal is established by the people in assembly through a flexible civil agreement. The supreme civil power is the combined influences that lie behind government and law, and can gain its ends only by such political means as formulating laws and constitutions, establishing a civil government suitable to the people, providing for elections, executing the laws, maintaining internal peace, and providing against external aggression. The civil government created by the supreme power is but a corporate agency without any inherent powers and with only such powers as have been fixed by the constitutional provisions and limitations established by the people.

The danger of postulating a dual civil authority, he avoided by making a distinction between state and government. The territorial units of the state, federal or otherwise, become mere administrative units of the central state—civil corporate bodies of the civil government with full power and authority to transact all the local affairs in harmony with the laws of the state. In this federated system of government, the local units possess only delegated sovereign powers which can be recalled at any time. The dilemma of a bureaucratic national state is avoided by the use of frequent direct elections, joint and individual initiative of all laws, compulsory referendum and recall by popular vote of civil laws and the constitution itself, and a single legislative body, thereby enabling the people to retain their original sovereignty in fact. In this manner he achieved a condition of decentralized sovereign powers without a division of the sovereignty of the state.

In the Rhode Island Constitution of 1647, Roger Williams anticipated later liberalism. The civil agreement contained a Bill of Rights, granted religious liberty, and limited the governmental powers. By centering the legislative powers in a single house, the members of which were elected by the people just prior to the opening of the session, he provided for a legislative body that would pay attention to the immediate needs of society. The president, elected directly by the people, was directly responsible to them and could be deposed or replaced at any time if he refused to conform to the constitution. By making the legislature the interpreter of the fundamental laws, and providing for annual election of all officers, and joint compulsory initiative and referendum, the legal sovereignty was kept in subjection to the people. To pacify the minority, Williams advocated frequent elections and the use of arbitration. By means of numerous checks and balances the state was made the manager of the common business. It was no longer the master of men, imposing its sovereign will on its subjects; it was now the servant and agent of the people.

It would be folly to deny that Williams was influenced by Christianity and Judaism. But the theocratic idea is not the basis for his political system, as the clergymen expositors of Williams would have it.[110]   Modern democracy and liberalism must be recognized as the "Child of the Reformation and not of the Reformers."[111]   The Reformation was born out of the enunciation of two great intellectual principles: the rightful duty of free inquiry and the priesthood of all believers.[112]   Back of the Reformation and also contemporary with it, were the influences of the Teutonic, Greek, and Hebrew estimates of man and conceptions of state.[113]   All these influences, to some extent,

---

[110] See Figgis: *The Divine Right of Kings*, p. 219. He states that Hobbes alone ignored a religious basis; but Williams did likewise.
[111] Gooch: *History of Democratic Ideas*, pp. 8 f.
[112] Luther: 95 *Theses; On Christian Liberty; To the German Nobility.*
[113] Gierke: *Political Theories of the Middle Ages.*

had their effect upon the men of the seventeenth century who were trying to find a new basis for the shattered social structure.

In the political theory of Roger Williams, Greek and Teutonic paganism and the "truth" of Hebraism met and mingled. In him experience, imagination, and revelation joined hands and formulated a new basis for human association. This new form of society received a trial in two entirely different social structures, and when strictly applied seemed to be surprisingly successful. Not only the Colony of Rhode Island, but also the English Revolution of 1647-8 embodied the political theories enunciated in the *Bloudy Tenent of Persecution*.[114] In these two instances were translated into practice the principles of government and politics already recognized by Aristotle and Protagoras. Like the earlier paganism, Roger Williams realized that "man is the measure of all things," that the individual is the unit of value in the social group, be it city, state, or nation. He demonstrated that on the self-denial of the individual depends the safety and welfare of the state. The life of the state—sovereignty—he disclosed is not of itself, but rather the result of the deliberately exercised consciousness and will of the people. Yet his democratic state derived no support from the practices of the classical states,[115] although in his concept of man he is in harmony with their leading philosophers. Masson in his life of Milton describes the civic part of Williams' achievement as "the organization of a community on the unheard of principles of absolute religious liberty combined with perfect civil democracy." As a founder of a state, writes Newman, "no less than as an advocate of a great principle, Roger Williams deserves the gratitude and respect of all lovers of religious and civil liberty."[116]

---

[114] Dunning: *Political Theories: Luther to Montesquieu*, p. 234.
[115] See Wilson: *The State*, for his discussion of the relation of modern democratic practices to practices of classical states.
[116] *Life of Roger Williams*, p. 73.

IV

THE RELATION OF STATE TO STATE

PART 1

THE NOTION OF A SOCIETY OF STATES

The Peace of Westphalia in 1648 marked the dissolution of the Roman Empire, and with it the disappearance of the old conception of a common superior.[1] The notion of a society of states at once supplanted the idea of a universal empire. But no state in this society had full legal capacity in respect to other states. What the Peace actually did, was to give each nation a qualified international status. Furthermore, it established for the states, individually, equal territorial rights, ecclesiastical and political.[2] To find an explanation and a justification for this new society of states, its members and its laws, was the special task of the statesmen and publicists of the seventeenth century.

In the new society of states, recognized by the so-called Roman Empire in the Peace of Westphalia, the interstate relations could, according to the theories of contemporary publicists, be established on the principle of equality of states. This concept of interstate relations was derived chiefly from two sources: the existent rules of diplomacy and warfare established by custom, usages and understandings; and the law of nature, a law grounded on reason and valid for all mankind, applied to the relation between separate states.[3] Since the states had no longer a common superior, they must, by an analogy to men in a state of nature, be in a state of nature in respect to each other and be controlled by natural law. The next necessary step was made when this principle of natural equality was applied to the several states in the new international society of the seventeenth century.

---

[1] Because of the incapacity of either Emperor or Pope to command universal obedience, the old theory of a common superior in church and state had decayed.

[2] Dickinson: *Equality of States*, Chapters I and VII. In the treaty of Osnabrück between the Emperor and Sweden, Art. 8 states: "All and every one of the Electors, Princes, and States of the Roman Empire are so established and confirmed in their rights, prerogatives, liberties, the free exercise of territorial rights, spiritual as well as temporal, lordship, regal rights, etc." Note, p. 231.

[3] *Ibid*, p. 32.

The external sovereignty of the state comprehends the independence of that authority of any external or foreign power, ecclesiastical or civil. Internal sovereignty is the supreme jurisdiction of the state over all persons and property within its domain; external sovereignty signifies the power to determine the nature of its relation to other states. In the traditional theory is implied the freedom of the state to make its own laws.[4] "If a state is conpelled to recognize the political sovereignty of another, it loses its sovereignty, and becomes subjected to the sovereignty of the latter."[5] Since every state is theoretically an absolute and independent unit, it naturally follows that all states are, in like manner, equal.

That states have an equal capacity for rights in the law of nations is, however, a creation of the publicists.[6] The principle had its inception in the classical theories of the law of nature.[7] By drawing an analogy between natural persons and separate states or international persons, the idea of natural equality was introduced into the law of nations.[8] The roots of the idea are found in the medieval conception of the single whole, *principium unitatis*. It was a common practice in the Middle Ages to compare every human organization to an animate body, thereby attributing to every unit of human life a personality.[9] Not until the seventeenth century, however, did the organic conception of the state develop into the legal idea of a state personality, in the principles of Hobbes[10] and Pufendorf.[11] Since the concept of natural equality in a state of nature prevailed as a common tradition, the medieval disposition led the philosophers and publicists to draw analogies between corporate and natural bodies. These analogies were applied to state theories and principles,[12] and formed the basic idea for the later developments in the principle of external sovereignty.

---

[4] Fenwick: *International Law*, pp. 163, 44. Wilson: *The State*, p. 91, "No community which is not independent can have a law of its own." M'Kechnie: *The State and the Individual*.

[5] Bluntschli: *The Theory of the State*, p. 506. Willoughby: *The Nature of the State*, p. 196.

[6] Dickinson: *The Equality of States*, p. 5.

[7] Ritchie: *Natural Rights*, pp. 21 ff.

[8] Dickinson: *The Equality of States*, pp. 29, 6.

[9] Gierke: *Political Theories of the Middle Ages*, pp. 22-30; also Notes, pp. 129-139.

[10] *Leviathan*. The opening passage.

[11] *De Jure et Gentium*, written 1658, published 1672.

[12] Dickinson: *The Equality of States*, p. 32.

Among the publicists of the seventeenth century who contributed to the development of the laws of this new international society, the names of Grotius, Hobbes, and Pufendorf stand out pre-eminently. Grotius labored to distinguish public and formal from private and informal wars. He did not attribute equal capacity for rights to the states in the international society, but, like our contemporary practice, recognized many differences of status and resulting differences in capacity.[13] Hobbes' philosophy of state was based upon the analogy between the state and natural body. By making the sovereign's judgment the law of God, the law of nature and the law of nations, he cast aside the law of nations with which Grotius endeavored to shackle the sovereign. He made the state truly absolute. Then, by declaring that states once organized, "do put on the personal properties of men"[14] and are, with respect to each other, like men in a state of nature, in a natural condition, he came to the conclusion that the law of nature and the law of nations are the same thing.

Pufendorf accepted Hobbes' anthropomorphic idea of state, but considered the state of nature as a condition of peace and equality. Like Hobbes, he conceived of the state as a "compound moral person;" yet he took his theory of sovereignty from Grotius.[15] A state could be externally limited and still retain its sovereignty—for, since the law of nature and the law of nations are the same thing, the states are equal because each is in a state of natural liberty. By a direct application of the familiar theories of natural law, the state of nature and natural equality, to separate states, Pufendorf laid the basis for the relation between the separate units in the new society of states which has been generally accepted since by publicists and statesmen.[16] To Grotius, Hobbes, and Pufendorf, then, we are accustomed to look for the most distinctive contributions made in the seventeenth century on the relation between the members of the new international

---

[13] Grotius: *De Jure Belli ac Pacis,* Parts I and II. Dickinson: *The Equality of States,* Chapter IV on Grotius. Figgis: *From Gerson to Grotius,* pp. 190, 216, 220, 242. Maine: *Ancient Law,* p. 103.

[14] *Leviathan,* Parts I and II. Compare with Grotius: *De Jure Belli ac Pacis,* I, 3, 7 and II, 6, 4. *Dominion,* XIV, 4, in *English Works,* II, 186.

[15] *De Jure Naturae et Gentium,* VIII, 4, 17. "All kingdoms are by their own nature free and independent." II, 3, 23; VII, 2, 13.

[16] Dickinson: *The Equality of States,* p. 82.

society.   But meanwhile in the American colonies of New England, a somewhat different theory of relations between independent states was being worked out, principles since then ardently advocated by the United States, by the leaders of the Union of 1643 and Roger Williams.

THE NEW ENGLAND SOCIETY OF STATES

Early colonial New England, like Western Europe of the seventeenth century, suddenly found itself confronted with the problem of establishing a system of relationships between independent communities or states. The society in New England was composed of newly founded colonies and numerous Indian tribes still in the "Stone Age" period of civilization. Consequently, the task Roger Williams set for himself in the new world, was in one respect more complicated than that which confronted the European publicists. He endeavored to establish an equal and just basis for the relations not only between independent communities of practically the same race and culture, but between the colonies and the Indians—a highly civilized group and barbarians. In his effort to maintain peace, order and justice, and to prevent wars between the several petty political units, Williams enunciated his principles of international relations. His theory of interstate affairs naturally has points in common with the most advanced theories of his century, due perhaps to his early environment and his intellectual training. But in many respects, he may be called the forerunner of the most modern speculations on the relation of states in an international society.

The colonies at this time were none too friendly toward each other. All of them were imperialistic.[17] Rhode Island was rapidly increasing her settlements; Plymouth was building trading posts in Connecticut and Maine; New Haven was erecting outposts on Long Island and closing in on the Dutch settlers on the Sound; while Connecticut purchased Saybrooke from the patentees in 1644,[18] and was rapidly extending her towns to the east and the west. "Massachusetts had long adopted the definite policy of extending her claims and control as fast and as far as possible. In the race for land and power, her numbers, resources and central position, all gave her immense advantages, to which was added the no mean one of an unscrupulous disregard for the prior rights of others."[19] The Union of 1643 offered the weaker colonies some

---

[17] Adams: *Founding of New England*, Chapters IX-X.
[18] C C R., Vol. I, pp. 266 ff.
[19] Adams: *Founding of New England*, p. 226.

protection not only from the Indians and the foreigners, but from the increasing aggressiveness of Massachusetts Bay. But, while the equal political voice of Connecticut, New Haven, and Plymouth helped to protect them against the Bay, no such protection existed for Maine and Rhode Island, which were refused admission into the Confederacy. Massachusetts refused to recognize either as true states, because to do so "would have placed awkward moral obstacles in the way of the manifest destiny of God's elect."[20] She absorbed Maine ten years later. And, in 1644, when Rhode Island applied for admission, the answer of the Confederacy, undoubtedly dictated by Massachusetts, was an "utter refusall" unless they would "absolutely and without reservacõn submitt" to either Plymouth or herself.[21]

All the colonies followed opportunist policies in colonial affairs as well as toward the government of England. The intolerance of Massachusetts Bay and her ignoble greed for property and power were an ever-present menace to the towns of Rhode Island. The real menace, however, was her possible military dominance. Nor were the colonies of Connecticut and Plymouth without selfish designs on their more liberal neighbor. The lands around Narragansett Bay had been known even before 1636 to be attractive sites for colonizing.[22] The climate, soil, and broken coastline suitable for trade and 'fishing, made it not undesirable for mercantile purposes. The Bay colony was longing for this savory morsel of country. By 1643, she had absorbed New Hampshire, and was engaged in encroaching upon the northern boundaries of Plymouth and Connecticut. As the controlling voice in the Union, she could obtain a kind of legal approval for her "illegal poachings,"[23] and at the same time nullify any adverse action by any other colony. To the south, the Bay, in concert with the other members of the Union, was slowly driving the entering wedge into Rhode Island territory through the actions of Gorton and the behaviour of the Narragansett Indians. In his attempt to prevent them from dividing and annexing this

---

[20] *Ibid,* pp. 227 f.

[21] *Acts United Colonies,* Vol. I, p. 23. [Hereafter this will be listed as A U C.]

[22] Lechford: *Plain Dealing,* p. 79. Adams: *Three Episodes,* Vol. I, p. 28.

[23] Adams: *Founding of New England,* p. 228.

country, Roger Williams advocated equity and justice as the only sound basis for the relations between independent states.

Through the Charter of 1643, the Rhode Islanders had hoped to secure toleration and respect from their neighbors to the east and west[24] of them. But Massachusetts and Plymouth viewed it as a sword rather than as an olive branch. Because of the acts of subjection by the Arnolds and the towns of Punham and Saconoca, the Bay and Plymouth claimed eastern Rhode Island and the island of Aquidneck. After many bitter controversies these claims were practically disallowed in 1665, in the fixing by the King's Commissioners of the eastern coastline of Narragansett Bay as the western limit of any possible claim by Plymouth. The whole question was finally settled by a decision of the crown in 1746-47.

Although her policy had been easily achieved in the north, Massachusetts Bay received an unexpected check from despised Rhode Island in the south.[25] The Bay had already claimed a portion of the territory, and assumed jurisdiction over some of the natives during the Gorton affair in 1643. At the same time, she was craftily planning through her agents in England to gain control over Rhode Island by means of a royal charter, which Roger Williams was meanwhile successful in securing. Through this charter the towns of Rhode Island Plantations were enabled legally to resist encroachments after 1643. After this, "the country about was more friendly," wrote Williams, "and treated us as an authorized colony only the difference of our conscience much obstructed."[26] Even though not legally granted, the pretended charter of Massachusetts for control of Rhode Island was at first used by the Bay to support her claims. The charter procured by Williams evidently failed to settle all the Plantations' vexing inter-colonial problems. Both Plymouth and the Bay continued to put forth claims to Warwick. Both sent out colonists to take possession of Gorton's land in the Narragansett country, but the Braintree people were dispersed by the Plymouth settlers in 1644. Meanwhile, Williams was informed by the Bay to desist from exercising any authority in Narragansett Bay country. But, in spite of protests by members of the Union, Warwick was admitted

[24] Richman: *Rhode Island,* p. 45.
[25] Adams: *Founding of New England.*
[26] R I C R., Vol. I, p. 458.

into the Providence Plantations in May, 1647, as an equal to the other Towns. With the return of Gorton from England bearing a permission from the Commissioners to resettle upon his lands without molestation until the title should be legally decided, the chief source of trouble at Warwick was ended.[27]

At Patuxet, a party was also busily at work in the interests of the Bay colony. In order to evade the paying of certain taxes, this party appealed to the Bay in 1651 for protection. Massachusetts, still claiming jurisdiction, warned Williams that if the colony persisted in taxing the residents of this section, Massachusetts would seek satisfaction "in such manner as God shall put into their hands."[28] The meaning of this statement is clear. Finally in 1658, the Bay resigned her claims; while, to provide against similar trouble in the future, Rhode Island, soon after, passed a law forbidding any citizen from placing his lands under the jurisdiction of another colony.[29]

But Massachusetts and Connecticut were soon to lay claim to another section of unoccupied land. Both colonies held a claim to the Pequod country by right of conquest. The Pawcatuck river was the dividing line between the Narragansetts on the east and the Pequods on the west.[30] Massachusetts, however, claimed not only a large part of the Pequod country, but tried to establish her rights to the rich lands of the Narragansetts on the east bank. To this she had no valid claim. On the other hand, Rhode Island was entitled to it under her charter.[31] Minor conflicts for control of the territory became frequent. A clash between the Rhode Island citizens at Stonington and the Bay authorities resulted in three Rhode Islanders being carried off to Boston and imprisoned. The Rhode Island government, in turn, protested and herself claimed jurisdiction over the lands of the Atherton company. But several months later the Bay colony renewed her fiction of the Narragansett patent; that by it she had a valid title to "all that tract of land, from Pequod river to Plymouth line" and ordered the Rhode Island government to cease exercising

---

[27] *Ibid*, pp. 367 ff. Winthrop: *Journal*, Vol. II, pp. 360 ff. M C R., Vol. III, pp. 95 ff.

[28] M C R., Vol. III, p. 228; Vol. IV, pt. 1, pp. 47, 333.

[29] R I C R., Vol. I, p. 401.

[30] Bowen: *Boundary Disputes of Connecticut*, pp. 33 ff. A U C., Vols. II and III. R I C R., Vol. I, pp. 451 ff; C C R., Vol. I, pp. 570 ff.

[31] R I C R., Vol. I, pp. 465 f.

authority within these lines.[32] The inter-colonial troubles were now rapidly approaching a state of war, threatening the destruction of the smallest colony and a possible quarrel over the spoils —the harbors and rich lands of Rhode Island—by Connecticut and Massachusetts. Fortunately, no doubt, for the future of America, the interference of the mother country saved the integrity of Williams' colony.

"By her policy of annexation," writes Adams, "Massachusetts had added over forty thousand square miles to her territory; while by that of nullification, she had patently shown that the bonds uniting the New England Confederacy were but ropes of sand. Confederation was a failure and imperial control impossible. The unification of New England was progressing rapidly, but it was a mere process of absorption by Massachusetts. Had there been no hindrance offered by England to the movement, the fate of the other colonies was amply foreshadowed. A single state, with its capital at Boston, guided by the reactionary ideas of its leaders, would probably have arisen, and much of the work already accomplished for the enfranchisement of the individual by Connecticut and Rhode Island, as well as the progress so far made by Massachusetts herself, might have been lost."[33] But despised little Rhode Island checked her imperial pretensions. And "in spite of the many fine qualities of the Bay colony, and the services which she rendered in the settlement of New England, it was fortunate that her career of aggrandisement was halted, for the United States could ill afford to have lost the independent contributions made to her intellectual and political life by the smaller colonies. Indeed, it may even be questioned, if any single powerful, unscrupulous, and aggressive state had come to occupy the whole of New England, and possibly the Hudson Valley, whether the United States, as a federal nation in its present form, would have come into existence at all. When one considers the possibilities involved in a wholly different balance of power among the colonies in the following century, the early career of Massachusetts and the checks she encountered take on a larger interest."[34] In this effort to check the advance of Massachusetts Bay, Williams developed his theory of international relations.

[32] A U C., Vol. II, pp. 144, 455 f.
[33] *Founding of New England*, pp. 245 f.
[34] *Ibid.*, p. 246.

PART 3

WILLIAMS ON THE RELATION OF STATES

Because of his conception of the state and its sovereignty, Williams quite naturally took the position that all states have an equal capacity for rights in international affairs. Since each state is the community consciousness and sovereignty is the "collective will," either latent or expressed,[35] the state is absolutely independent of the authority of any other power or influence, ecclesiastical or civil. That no people can lawfully authorize its government to interfere with the internal affairs of another, seems too self-evident to need discussion. Yet, because the times differed with him, he reiterated the principle that: "The *Soveraign, original,* and *foundation* of *civill power* lies in the *people*[36]. . . Every lawful Magistrate whether succeeding or elected. . . goes beyond his *commission* who intermeddles with that which cannot be given him in *commission* from the people.[37] . . . *Subjection,*" he states at another time, "may be either to lawful *governors,* or to *pretenders* and *usurpers.* . . which undue proceeding is not tolerable in all well-ordered states."[38] Even if we cast aside reason and experience, and turn to the teachings of Christ, we learn that he "leaves the *severall Nations* of the *World,* to their own *severall Lawes* and *Agreements* (as is most probable) according to their severall *Natures, Dispositions* and *Constitutions,* and their *common peace* and *welfare.*[39] . . . But no people can betrust him [the magistrate] with any . . . power" except "with a Civill power belonging to their *bodies* and *goods.*"[40] Each state, accordingly, is independent and equal in the society of states, for 'who can question the *lawfulnesse* of other formes of *Government, Lawes,* and *punishments* which differ, since civil constitutions are mens ordinances."[41]

True state-liberty demands autonomy of the state—freedom

---

[35] *Ante,* Chapters II and III.

[36] *Bloudy Tenent of Persecution,* N C P., Vol. III, p. 249.

[37] N C P., Vol. IV, p. 187; Vol. III, pp. 266, 297; Vol. II, *Queries,* p. 19.

[38] *Ibid.,* Vol. IV, p. 267; Vol. III, p. 418.

[39] *Ibid.,* Vol. IV, p. 487.

[40] *Ibid.,* Vol. III, p. 418.

[41] *Ibid.,* Vol. III, pp. 398, 364, 214, 249, 253; Vol. IV, pp. 80, 485, 487, 495; Vol. VI, pp. 295, 342 ff. R I C R., Vol. I, p. 323.

from foreign dictation. But, unlike other political thinkers of the times, Williams did not arrive at his idea of equal capacity of states by an anlogy between natural men and separate states or international persons. His principle of equal capacity for rights in the law of nations grew out of his conception of medieval corporation law and the law of nature. The state, like a corporation,[42] according to the medieval jurists, possesses rights and privileges within its own body with which no other corporation has any authority to interfere. In these rights each corporation is equally independent and sovereign.[43] The law of nature, "written in the hearts of all mankind, yea, even pagans," declares that "Mankind cannot keep together without some form of government." This government is the creation of "the Civil state. . . [which] being in a natural state. . . is no else but a part of the world, and so, since every part in more or lesse degree follows the nature of the whole, it is but natural."[45] If natural, then the state has certain natural rights and privileges which are independent of every other state, and it can demand autonomy from external interference.

But Williams was not content to rest Rhode Island's claims to freedom and equality only on corporation and natural law. "By the Charter," says Staples, "which he now brought, they had become the equals of these colonies [Massachusetts, Connecticut, and Plymouth] in rights and powers, though not in numbers and wealth. This was to them the assurance of a legal existence."[46]

"Considering, upon frequent exceptions against Providence men," writes Williams to Major Mason, "that we had no authority for civil government, I went purposely to England, and upon report and petition, the parliament granted us a charter of government."[47] A charter would give the colony a legal standing among the states of New England; and Williams considered it merely an instrument of expediency and utility for its legal existence. What principles should guide their inter-state relations he

[42] Gierke: *Political Theories of the Middle Ages*, pp. 67 ff.
[43] *Bloudy Tenent of Persecution*, N C P., Vol. III, pp. 72 ff.
[44] Letter: *To the Town Clerk of Providence*, N C P., Vol. VI, pp. 401 f.
[45] N C P., Vol. IV, p. 187; Vol. III, p. 125.
[46] Staples: *Annals*, p. 57.
[47] Letter: *To Major Mason*, N C P., Vol. VI. p. 340.

clearly pointed out in the controversy about the conflicting colonial claims to the Narragansett territory. "I answer, the Father of Mercies and God of all Consolations hath graciously discovered to me, as I believe, a remedy which. . . will preserve you both in the liberties and honors of your charters and government, without the least impeachment of yielding one to another. . . . I will not put you off to a Christian moderation or Christian humility. . . . For I design a civil, a humane, and political medicine, which, . . . you will find it effectual to all ends. . . . My receipt will not please you all."[48] Between members in the society of states, Williams held the relation to be that of civil, humane, and political equality.

Because Rhode Island was legally[49] and politically equal to every other colony in New England, Williams firmly opposed external interference with its sovereignty. And above all, he strenuously opposed an "arbitrary Government" based on the "dictates and decrees of that sudden spirit that acts them."[50] So empahatic in this was he that with the aid of his fellow-citizens a law was put on the statute books of Rhode Island, in 1658, forbidding a citizen to place his land under any foreign jurisdiction, or to seek to introduce any foreign power.[51] This legal equality of the colony, he asserted, was publicly recognized, "since it pleased first the Parliament, . . . the council of state, and lastly Lord Protector and his Council, to continue us as a distinct colony, yea, and since it hath pleased yourselves, by public letters and references to us from your public Courts, to own the authority of His Highness among us,[52] be pleased to consider how unsuitable it is for yourselves. . . to be obstructors of all orderly proceedings among us."[53] To Connecticut he complains, addressing Major Mason, "I see yourself, with others, embarked in a resolution to invade and despoil . . . your ancient friends, of

[48] *Ibid.,* pp. 349 f.
[49] Staples: *Annals,* p. 57.
[50] Letter: *To George Fox,* N C P., Vol. VI, p. 360.
[51] R I C R., Vol. I, p. 401.
[52] Letter: *To General Court of Massachusetts,* 1655, N C P., Vol. VI, p. 298. Williams writes as president of Rhode Island. During his second stay in England in 1652-3, he resided for the most part with Sir Henry Vane, Jr. He was also intimately acquainted with Milton, Cromwell, General Harrison, and the leading members of the council and Parliament. See Masson's: *Life of Milton,* Vols. I-III. Straus: *Roger Williams.*
[53] Letter: *To General Court of Massachusetts,* R I C R., Vol. I, p. 323. Here the word *obstruction* is used instead of *instruction* as found in N C P., Vol. VI, p. 295.

our temporal and soul liberties."[54]   When he applied to the Bay
colony for a permit, in 1651, to sail for England from the port
of Boston, he was not only seeking physical security against
punishment for returning from banishment but also emphasizing
the fact that as an officer of his colony he must respect the
territorial rights of another state.[55]   In his letter to the General
Court of Massachusetts, he writes on another occasion, "I humbly appeal to your own wisdom and experience, how unlikely it
is for a people to be compelled to order and common charges"[56]
when another state interferes.   And finally, an "exposition of the
word dominion" by the Lord President of England[57] argues
against one state interfering with the laws of another.   Yet he
repeatedly asserts the principle of "collective" responsibilities of
the states.   And so, throughout his writings, Williams unceasing-
ly stresses his comprehensive view of "Liberties"[58]—the right of
men and nations to freedom.

According to the international law of Europe, priority of discovery gives a nation supreme and unlimited right to the discovered territory.   Whatever may be the legal status of this theory,
there can be no question of the ethical correctness of Williams'
denial of such a right.[59]   The doctrine was established and almost universally accepted with the discovery of the American
Continent.   The discovery of Columbus aroused the attention of
the maritime states of Europe.   Here was opened an outlet for
their ambitions—love of glory, hope of gain and dominion.   First
Spain, and then England under Henry VII, laid claim to lands
unoccupied by any Christian nation, discovered by ships or fleets
flying the national flag.   The doctrine was at once accepted in
1492.   Any title to such land when founded on the right of discovery was accepted as a just and sufficient claim.   It was probably accepted as a convenient and flexible rule to regulate claims
and to prevent wars.   Furthermore, it was, indeed, a policy of
peace and repose, and perfect equality of benefit according to
effort put forth.   In 1493, Pope Alexander VI gave this prin-

[54] Letter: *To Major Mason,* 1670, N C P., Vol. VI, p. 334.
[55] *Ibid.,* p. 342. Letter: *To John Endicott,* 1656, R I H S P., Vol. VIII,
p. 144.
[56] Letter: *To the Honored General Court of Massachusetts,* 1651, N C
P., Vol. IV, p. 231; 1655, p. 296.
[57] Letter: *To John Winthrop, Jr.,* 1666, N C P., Vol. VI, p. 261.
[58] N C P., Vols. I-VI; R I C R., Vols. I-II.
[59] Straus: *Roger Williams,* p. 35.

ciple the sanction it so much needed, by issuing a Bull. Papal authority thus came as a priceless aid in the design, against Heathenism and for Catholicism.[60] Ostensibly, the Pope's purpose was spiritual; actually, it was temporal and economic. The right was now thoroughly grounded—politically, ecclesiastically, "legally."

When the principle of the Right of Discovery was once established, no subject was allowed to set up a counter title, for the title was arbitrarily held to be the exclusive right of the state alone, in its sovereign capacity.[61] The next step was almost inevitable. The state now enlarged its authority to include the right to extinguish the Indian title, establish its own dominion, and dispose of the soil at its own pleasure.[62] This claim at once became the basis of the European polity and regulated the exercise of the right of sovereignty and settlement in all the American colonies.

It is not easy upon general reasoning to establish or accept the doctrine of the Right of Discovery. Especially is this the case with land already inhabited. Nor can this doctrine be successfully vindicated, either in conformity to the law of nature or in point of justice or humanity. It can establish no right of authority over the aborigines in America.[63] The right of the Indians whether of occupation or use stands upon original principles of the law of nature, asserted Williams, and cannot be modified or abrogated without their free consent.[64]

In denying the principle of Right of Discovery and Conquest, Williams undermined the very foundation upon which rested the authority of the king's Patents.[65] This denial was a cause for his banishment. "I judge your surmise is a dangerous mistake," he writes to Mason, "for Patents, grants and charters, and such like royal favors, are not laws of England, and acts of Parliament. . . but such kinds of grants have been like high offices in England, of high honor, and ten, yea, twenty thousand pounds gain per annum, yet revocable or curtable upon pleasure,

---

[60] Story: *On the Constitution,* pp. 5, 7.
[61] Chalmers: *Annals,* pp. 676 f.
[62] Marshall's opinion on *Johnson v. McIntosh,* 8 Wheat. 543, on the right of discovery.
[63] Story: *On the Constitution,* pp. 6 ff.
[64] *Master Cottons Answer,* N C P., Vol. II, p. 44. Potter: *Narragansett,* p. 15. Story: *On the Constitution,* pp. 6 ff. See *Ante,* Chapters II and III.
[65] Winthrop: *Journal,* Covering the period from 1633 to 1636.

according to the King's better information."[66]   But we colonies "have not our land merely by right of Patent from the King, but that the natives are the true owners of all they possess, or improve."[67]   In contrast to Providence, the colonies of Plymouth and the Bay deemed it unnecessary to obtain a title from the Indians to the soil before they began their plantations, although Cotton claimed and the General Court advised that the settlers purchase from the Indians the land upon which they settle.   But they relied in the first instance either upon their own possession or on a grant from the king as sufficient.[68]   The authorities of these colonies, therefore, condemned Williams' pamphlet against the Patent in 1633, because it repudiated the accepted theory of the Right of Discovery, was disloyal to the king, and affected the basis of colonial government.[69]   The promulgation of these sentiments formed one of the principle charges against Williams.   That he was sincere about the *"sinne of the Pattents"* in New England, is evinced by the fact that he reduced his principle of the primary Indian rights to practice in Providence.[70]

In a letter to Major Mason in 1670, Williams set forth the principles that should underlie the relations between independent states:

"I crave your leave and patience to present you with some few considerations, occasioned by the late transactions between your colony and ours.   The last year you were pleased, in one of your lines to me to tell me that you longed to see my face before you died.   I embraced your love. . . .

"The occasion, I confess, is sorrowful, because I see yourself, with others, embarked in a resolution to invade and despoil your poor countrymen, in a wilderness, and your ancient friends, of our temporal and soul liberties.[71]

"It is sorrowful, also, because mine eye beholds a black and doleful train of grievous, and, I fear, bloody consequences, at the heel of this business, both to you and us. . . .

---

[66] Letter: *To Major Mason*, 1670, N C P., Vol. VI, pp. 348 f.

[67] *Master Cottons Answer*, N C P., Vol. II, p. 44.

[68] Staples: *Annals*, pp. 10 f.

[69] Winthrop: *Journal*, 1635-36.   Winthrop refers to a pamphlet against Patents which was destroyed by the order of the colony.   Cobb: *The Rise of Religious Liberty*, p. 184.

[70] *Bloody Tenant Yet More Bloody*, N C P., Vol. IV, p. 461.   Staples: *Annals*, p. 26.

[71] He refers to a question of jurisdiction over the people of Westerly and Narragansett.   Massachusetts, Connecticut, and Rhode Island made claims to the territory.   Arnold: *History of Rhode Island*, Vol. I, pp. 341-348.   R I C R., Vol. II, pp. 309, 328.

"Sir, I am not out of hopes, but that while your aged eyes and mine are yet in their orbs, and not yet sunk down into their holes of rottenness, we shall leave our friends and countrymen, our children and relations, and this land, in peace, behind us. To this end, Sir please you with a calm and steady, and a Christian hand, to hold the balance and to weigh these few considerations, in much love and due respect presented:

"First, when I was unkindly and unchristianly as I believe, driven from my house and land and wife and children, in the midst of a New England winter, now about thirty-five years past, at Salem. . . Mr. Winthrop, privately wrote to me to steer my course to Narragansett Bay and Indians, for many high and heavenly and public ends, encouraging me, from the freedom of the place from any English claims, or patents. . . .

". . . But I received a letter from my ancient friend, Mr. Winslow . . . to remove but to the other side of the water, and then, he said, I had the country free before me, and might be as free as themselves, and we should be loving neighbors together. These were the joint understandings of these two eminently wise and Chrsitian Governors and others, in their day, together with their counsel and advice as to the freedom and vacancy of this place. . . .

"Fourth. When next year after my banishment, the Lord drew the bow of the Pequod War against the country . . . I had my share of service to the whole land in that Pequod business, inferior to very few that acted. . . ."[72]

"Considering, upon frequent exceptions made against Providence men, that we had no authority for civil government, I went purposely to England, and upon my report and petition, the Parliament granted us a charter of government for these parts, so judged vacant on all hands. And upon this, the country about us was more friendly, and wrote to us, and treated us as an authorized colony; only the differences of our consciences much obstructed. The bounds of this, our first charter, I, having ocular knowledge of persons, places, and transactions, did honestly and conscientiously, as in the holy presence of God, draw up from Pawcatuck river, which I then believed, and still do, is free from all English claims and conquests. . . .

"It is true, when at Portsmouth, on Rhode Island, some of ours, in a General Assembly, motioned their planting on this side Pawcatuck. I, hearing that some of the Massachusetts reckoned this land theirs, by conquest, dissuaded from the motion, until the matter should be amicably debated and composed; for though I questioned not our right, etc., yet I feared it would be inexpedient and offensive, and procreative of these heats and fires. . . .

---

[72] The colonies employed him to break the league between the tribes against each other and the whites, to win support by a league of the Narragansetts and Mohegans, and to act as interpreter and intelligencer for the colonies and Indians. See Bradford: *History of Plimouth*, p. 364. Winthrop: *Journal*, Vols. I and II. All of which and much more than was requested, he did for those who previously had banished him, without any charge or reward.

"6. Some time after the Pequod war and our charter from the Parliament, the government of Massachusetts wrote to myself, then chief officer in this colony, of their receiving of a patent from the Parliament for these vacant lands, as an addition to the Massachusetts, etc., and therefore requesting me to exercise no more authority, etc., for they wrote, their charter was granted some weeks before ours . . . only it is certain, that, at Gorton's complaint against the Massachusetts, the Lord High Admiral, President, said openly, in a full meeting of the commissioners, that he knew no other charter for these parts than what Mr. Williams had obtained, and he was sure that charter, which the Massachusetts Englishmen pretended, had never passed to table.

"7. Upon our humble address, by our agent, Mr. Clarke, to his Majesty, and his gracious promise of renewing our former charter, Mr. Winthrop, upon some mistake, had entrenched upon our line, and not only so, but, as it is said, upon the lines of other charters also. Upon Clarke's complaint, your grant was called in again, and it had never been returned, but upon a report that the agents, Mr. Winthrop and Mr. Clark, were agreed, by mediation of friends, and it is true, they came to a solemn agreement, under hand and seal, which agreement was never violated on our part. . . .

"9. However you satisfy yourselves with the Pequod conquest, with the sealing of your charter some weeks before ours; with the complaints of particular men to your colony; yet upon due and serious examination of the matter, in the sight of God, you will find the business at bottom to be,

"First, a depraved appetite after the great vanities, dreams and shadows of this vanishing life, great portions of land, land in this wilderness, as if men were in great necessity and danger for want of great portions of land, as poor, hungry, thirsty seamen have, after a sick and stormy, a long and starving passage. This is one of the gods of New England, which the living and most high Eternal will destroy and famish.

"2. An unneighborly and unchristian intrusion upon us, as being the weaker, contrary to your laws, as well as ours, concerning purchasing of lands without the consent of the General Court. This I told Major Atherton, at his first going up to the Narragansett about this business. I refused all their proffers of land, and refused to interpret for them to the Sachems.

"3. From these violations and intrusions arise the complaint of many privateers, not dealing as they would be dealt with, according to the law of nature, the law of the prophets and Christ Jesus, complaining against others, in a design, which they themselves are delinquents and wrong doers. I could aggravate this many ways with Scripture, rhetoric and similitude, but I see need of anodynes, as physicians speak, and not of irritations. Only this I must crave leave to say, that it looks like a prodigy or monster, that countrymen among savages in a wilderness; that professors of God and one Mediator, of an eternal life, and that this is like a dream, should not be content with those vast and large tracts which all the other colonies have, like platters and tables full of dainties, but pull and snatch away their poor neighbors' bit or crust; and a crust it is, and a dry, hard one, too, because of the natives' continual troubles, trials, and vexations.

"10. Alas! Sir, in calm midnight thoughts, what are these leaves and flowers, and smoke and shadows, and dreams of earthly nothings, about which we poor fools and children, as David saith, disquiet ourselves in vain? Alas? what is all the scuffling of this world for, *but, come, will you smoke it?* What are all the contentions and wars of this world about, generally, but for greaer dishes and bowls of porridge, of which . . . Esau and Jacob were types? . . .

"11. How much sweeter is the counsel of the Son of God, to mind first the matters of his kingdom; to take no care for to-morrow; . . . to consider the ravens and the lilies; . . . to be content wtih food and raiment; to mind not our own, but every man the things of another; yea, and to suffer wrong, and part with what we judge is right, yea our lives. . . [for the sake of principle.] This is humanity, yea, this is Christianity. The rest is but formality and picture, courteous idolatry and Jewish and Popish blasphemy against the Christian religion, the Father of spirits and his Son, the Lord Jesus. Besides, Sir, the matter with us is not about these children's toys of lands, meadows, cattle, government, etc., But here, all over this colony . . . [for a refuge is] provided this country and this corner as a shelter for the poor and persecuted, according to their several persuasions. And thus that heavenly man, Mr. Haynes, Governor of Connecticut, though he pronounced the sentence of my long banishment against me, at Cambridge, then Newton, yet said to me . . . 'I think, Mr. Williams, I must now confess to you, that the most wise God hath provided and cut out this part of his world for a refuge and receptacle for all sorts of consciences. I am now under a cloud, and my brother Hooker, with the Bay, as you have been, we have removed from them thus far, and yet they are not satisfied.'

"Thus, Sir, the King's Majesty, though his father's and his own conscience favored Lord Bishops. . . hath vouchsafed his royal promised under his hand and broad seal, that no person in this colony shall be molested or questioned for the matters of his conscience to God, so he be loyal and keep the civil peace. Sir, we must part with lands and lives before we part with such a jewel. I judge you may yield some land and the government of it to us, and we for peace sake, the like to you. . . . But to part with this jewel, we may as soon do it as the Jews with the favor of Cyrus, Darius and Artaxerxes. Yourselves pretend liberty of conscience, but alas! it is but self, the great god self, only to yourselves. . . . Our grant . . . is crowned with the King's extraordinary favor to this colony, as being a banished one, in which his Majesty declared himself that he would experiment whether civil government could consist with such liberty of conscience. . . .

"It is said, that you intend not to invade our spiritual or civil liberties, but only, under the advantage of first sealing your charter, to right the privateers that petition to you. It is said also that if you had but Misquomacuck and Narragansett lands quietly yielded, you would stop at Coweset, etc., Oh, Sir, what do these thoughts preach, but that private cabins rule all, whatever become of the ship of common safety and religion, which is so much pretended in New England? Sir, I have heard further, and by some that say they know, that something deeper than all which hath been mentioned lies in the three colonies' breasts and consultations. I judge it not fit to commit such matter to the trust of paper, etc. . . .

". . . Partly, you think that the King is an incompetent judge, but you will force him to law also, to confirm your first born Esau. . . . I judge your surmise is a dangerous mistake, for patents, grants and charters, and such like royal favors, are not laws of England, and acts of Parliament, nor matters of propriety and *Meum* and *tuum* between the king and his subjects, which as the times have been, have been sometimes triable in inferior Courts; but such kinds of grants have been like high offices in England, of high honor. . . yet revocable and curtable upon pleasure, according to the King's better information. . . ."

"16. Sir, I lament that such designs should be carried on at such time, while we are stripped and whipped, and are still under, the whole country, the dreadful rods of God, in our wheat, hay, corn, cattle, shipping, trading, bodies and lives. . . . When the French and Romish Jesuits, the fire-brands of the world for their god belly sake, are kindling at our back, in this country, especially with the Mohawks and Mohegans, against us, of which I know and have daily information.

"17. If any please to say, is there no medicine for this malady? Must the nakedness of New England, like some notorious strumpet, be prostituted to the blaspheming eyes of all nations? . . . I answer, the Father of mercies and God of all consolations hath graciously discovered to me, as I believe, a remedy, which, if taken, will quiet the minds, yours and ours, will keep yours and ours in quiet possession and enjoyment of their lands. . . will preserve you both in the liberties and honors of your charters and governments, without the least impeachment of yielding one to another. . . . If you will please to ask me what my prescription is, I will not put you off to Christian moderation or Christian humility, or Christian prudence, or Christian love, or Christian self-denial, or Christian contention and patience. For I design a civil, humane and political medicine, which if the God of Heaven please to bless, you will find it effectual to all ends I have proposed. Only I must crave your pardon, both parties of you, if I judge it not fit to discover it at present. I know you are both of you hot; I fear myself, also. If both desire, in a loving and calm spirit, to enjoy your rights, I promise you, with God's help, to help you to them, in a fair, and sweet and easy way. My receipt will not please you all."[73]

The basic principles of interstate relations enunciated in the foregoing letter are: (1) since each state is independent and naturally equal to every other state with a legal and political right to the independent control of its internal affairs, it ought to respect the equal rights of other states; (2) international agreements arrived at through mediation by the joint and free consent of all parties are sacred, and must be held inviolable until

---

[73] Letter: *To Major Mason,* 1670, N C P., Vol. VI, pp. 333-351.

changed or abrogated by joint and free consent of the parties;
(3) since arbitration of differences and conflicting interests is
politically, socially, and economically of more advantage than
war, the differences and disputes between states should be "amicably debated and composed"; (4) either military superiority or
conquest cannot justify invasion or violation of the rights of
other states; (5) only a defensive war is justifiable; (6) the
principle of ultimate expediency, of utility in the long run, should
guide states at all times in their external activities and policies,
rather than that of economic selfishness; (7) and relations between states ought to be conducted in a civil, humane, and political way, in order to guarantee to all their just rights. When
international affairs are regulated on these principles, Williams
hoped the states could enjoy their rights "in a fair, and sweet
and easy way." But he was aware that such a policy will seldom
please all parties to a dispute.

Numerous difficulties arose between the colonies and Indian
nations, for the country of New England to which the first
settlers came, was not an uninhabited wilderness.[74] It was occu-
pied by an unknown race in a state of barbarism. Although
agriculture was practised, the Indians were still in the hunting
stage of economic development and needed a wide territory to
supply their food. Furthermore, their political organizations
were misunderstood by the whites. The settlers failed to recognize that the Indian institutions had nothing in common with their
own. Naturally, endless trouble arose and much blood was shed
because the white men tried to interpret the Indian society they
came in contact with in terms of their own social life. Among
the Indians, articles of personal property were owned by the
individual, but the title to all lands was in the tribe. Their religious, social and economic life was no better understood than the
political. Because of this complete ignorance of Indian life, the
Christian whites looked upon the uncouth savage with a "sense
of scornful superiority."[75] The colonies considered the natives
merely as something to be "traded with, fought with, occasionally
preached to, and then, as far as possible, exterminated."[76] As
someone has remarked, when the Puritans landed in the new
world, first they fell on their knees, and then on the aborigines.

---

[74] Adams: *Founding of New England*, pp. 14, 24 f, 39 f, 198 f, 239 ff.
[75] Bryce: *The Relation of the Advanced to Backward Races of Mankind*, p. 4.
[76] Adams: *Founding of New England*, p. 14.

The inter-tribal politics of the New England Indians was advantageous to the white settlers.[77] Linguistically, the Indians were of the Algonquin stock. Because they had a single language, Roger Williams could act as their interpreter to the colonies. The Pequods were the leading Indian military power in southern New England, and jealous of their prestige. The fierce and restless Connecticut Mohegans, wedged in between the Mohawks and the Pequods, were eager for any alliance that would free them from their dangerous neighbors. The Narragansetts, while a strong military power, were the chief industrial and commercial tribe. The Wampanoags, after being reduced by the smallpox, were made tributary to the Narragansetts but formed an alliance with Plymouth for protection against their conquerors. This political situation made it possible for Roger Williams to form a league between the Plymouth, Connecticut, and Bay colonies and the Narragansett and Mohegan tribes against the Pequods. But it was also the source of future Indian troubles, which finally ended with the extermination of the Narragansetts. Of the latter the chief sachems, the aged Canonicus and youthful Miantonomic, were men of exceptional skill in statescraft. Remarkable ability was also exhibited by the chief sachems respectively of the Pequods, Mohegans, and Wampanoags—Sassacus, Uncas, and Massacoit.

Between the New England colonies and these tribes existed a deep enmity, due largely to differences of race and civilization, but fostered and provoked by the greed and treachery of the Christian white man. The Indians had attained to some degree of social organization, unrecognized by the colonies. Clan members had the right to elect and depose the sachem and chiefs; they had "mutual right of inheritance in the property of deceased members, were obliged to defend one another, and participated in the council."[78] The government was essentially democratic, every man and woman in the clan having a voice. The sachem was merely a civil officer, and his office was usually hereditary through election. The chiefs were the military officials. Both sachems and chiefs attended the larger councils of the tribes. This political organization, Williams held, was sufficient to classify the Indian tribes as a state, independent and on an equality with any other state.

[77] Richman: *Rhode Island*, Vol. I, pp. 63 f.
[78] Adams: *Founding of New England*, p. 17.

The chief ground for misunderstanding between the colonists and Indians was a "difference of their notion as to property."[79] The Indians had not yet reached the stage of society "in which property is apportioned out to individuals and made descendable to their heirs." They "ordinarily held property in common . . . [and] could form no idea of any piece of land becoming so entirely the property of an individual as to make it a crime for another to trespass upon it."[80] They probably never meant the transfer of the land to the white man to be for more than a short period. That the Indian had this particular notion of property is borne out by the testimony of Roger Williams that the common Indians held their land at the will of the sachem and returned it upon demand.[81] Moreover, the white man considered the Indian an inferior being—a beast with a man's brain; while the latter felt that the white man was an intruder without an iota of right to the land, whose standards of honor and justice were dictated entirely by sordid self-interest.[82] These conflicting attitudes and interests Williams had consecrated himself to harmonize, with what success history clearly points out.

The relation between the colonies and Indian tribes, Williams regarded as that between equal and independent states.[83] By means of commissions, arbitration, leagues and treaties, the various state affairs were arranged and composed between the Indian and white man. Each colony selected its representatives for the purpose. The Indian tribes were represented by their sachems, who usually made the arrangements for them. These tribes were recognized as fully and legitimately organized states,[84] and so dealt with. The fact that they were inferior in civilization and constituted an ever-present menace, never caused Williams to waver in his desire that they must be dealt with honorably, humanely, and justly. That it was prudence alone which urged him to cultivate their good will, is denied by his whole conduct[85] in defense of their just and legal rights. To secure them justice,

---

[79] Potter: *Narragansett*, p. XI.
[80] *Ibid*, p. XII.
[81] *Key*, N C P., Vol. I, 50 and 89.
[82] Letters: N C P., Vol. VI, *To Major Mason*, pp. 333 ff; *To the General Court of Massachusetts*, pp. 269 ff; and numerous other letters to the General Court, etc., bring out this quite forcibly.
[83] N C P., Vol. VI. Most of his letters in this volume contain references to Indian affairs.
[84] *Key*, N C P., Vol. I, 89.
[85] Potter: *Narragansett*, p. XI.

he held a part of the collective responsibility of the New England colonies. Each tribe is to be treated as an absolute, independent state: "I know that it is said," argues Williams, "the Long Islanders are subject; but I have heard this greatly questioned, and, indeed, I question whether any Indians in this country, remaining barbarous and pagan, may with truth and honor be called the English subjects."[86]

Yet he had no confidence whatever in the Indian veracity: "I believe nothing of any of the barbarians on either side, but what I have eye sight for, or English Testimony."[87] This mistrust of his is not strange, since he failed to have any confidence in the motives of his fellow colonists. "Concerning Indian affairs," he wrote to Winthrop, Jr., "reports are various; lies are frequent. Private interests, both with Indians and English, are many; yet these things you may and must do. First, kiss truth, where you evidently, upon your soul, see it. 2. Advance justice, though upon a child's eyes. 3. Seek and make peace, if possible, with all men. 4. Secure your own life from revengeful, malicious arrow or hatchet. I have been in danger of them."[88] And, because of his unselfish and disinterested devotion to the common welfare of the New England society of states, the Indians had an unflinching confidence in Williams' integrity and honor.[89] His advice concerning Indian affairs usually prevailed, during critical periods, in the councils of the United Colonies. He insisted that the savage tribes be dealt with on the principle of equality, no matter what rights civilization possesses *ipso facto* over the unsettled and barbaric parts of the earth. Civilized states have "no right however nomadic or savage they [the Indians] might be, to divest the title to the soil from the aborigines."[90]

In the relations between the Indians and colonies, or between the colonies themselves, the application of the principle of arbitration and commissions for settling differences expressed itself in various forms. For the purpose of drawing up treaties, agreements, or leagues between the various New England governments,

---

[86] Letter: *To the General Court of Massachusetts*, 1654, N C P., Vol. VI, p. 275.
[87] Letter: *To Mrs. Winthrop, Jr.*, 1649, N C P., Vol. VI, p. 177, and 1638, p. 101.
[88] Letter: *To John Winthrop, Jr.*, 1647, N C P., Vol. VI, p. 147.
[89] Letter: *To John Winthrop*, 1637, N C P., Vol. VI, p. 86. At all important conferences with the white man in New England, the Sachems requested the presence of Williams. See, Straus: *Roger Williams*, Indians.
[90] Scott: *Development of Constitutional Liberty*, p. 116.

committees were usually employed.[91] When the inter-colonial trouble involved more than two states, and the settlement included adjustment of claims as well as agreements, the representatives of the units were formed into commissions.[92] On numerous occasions when the disputes involved reciprocal claims, boundaries, or grave misinterpretations of the agreements or leagues, Williams enthusiastically presented the expediency and utility of compromise.[93] By these sundry means it was hoped that the affairs of state could be arranged on a basis of the independence and equality of each, and with justice, honor, and peace between them.

The terms compromise and arbitration have resident in them, when applied to members of a society of states, the idea of the external limitation of sovereignty. In the use of treaties a similar effect is produced upon the state. A still more permanent limitation of the state's sovereignty occurs in the formation of leagues and agreements. But, as in the case of individual liberty, the freedom of the state is enlarged by certain mutual restraints fixed by leagues and agreements between free and equal members of a society of states. Williams felt this strongly and favored the formation of a league in New England for the protection of his own colony and his neighbors'.[94] Each state, he believed, can be assured of its freedom only by the mutual interest of the others, secured through agreements and leagues. With this in view, in 1644 and again in 1648, Providence Plantations asked leave to join the Confederacy.[95] But the request was refused on the ground that they had no stable government within the colony. And again in 1655, Williams expressed the belief that Rhode Island would be benefited by membership in the Union, provided she could enter and act by joint and free consent as an independent and equal colony.

Until altered by mutual free consent, the leagues and treaties entered into must be observed by all parties.[96] This is a decided limitation of the state's sovereign power externally. At various

---

[91] R I C R., Vol. II, pp. 49, 72, 91, etc.

[92] Letter: *To the General Court of Massachusetts*, N C P., Vol. VI, pp. 320, 386, 393, 388. R I C R., Vol. II, pp. 309-328; 352, 164.

[93] N C P., Vol. VI, pp. 293, 43 f, 56 ff, 386; Letter: *To the Commissioners of the United Colonies on Claims*, 1677, pp. 387-394, has a modern flavor. R I H S P., Vol. 8, pp. 160 ff.

[94] Letter: *To John Winthrop*, 1637, N C P., Vol. VI, p. 47.

[95] Fiske: *The Beginning of New England*, p. 157.

[96] N C P., Vol. VI, pp. 55, 87, 93, 107, 260, 342, 269.

times, Williams suggested and formed leagues between the Indians
and colonies. Then again he urged the sacredness of agreements
between states. If a league or treaty is broken, the state responsible for the breach should be penalized. But the penalty
must be carefully applied so that "it may be with the safety of
the common peace," for he hopes "for the best to save blood."
Furthermore, it is essential to peace and order that promises and
pledges between states be open and carried out by each party.
The chief purpose of this mutual support of states through agreements and leagues, he considered utilitarian—that of self-preservation.[97] To "preserve plantation and public interest of the
whole New England," was one of the chief aspirations of his
whole life. The bitter experiences endured in trying to harmonize
the state affairs between the colonies, indelibly impressed upon
him that "to do judgment and justice is more acceptable than
sacrifice . . .," for he saw "the business . . . needs a patient and
gentle hand to rectify misunderstandings of each other and mis-
prisions."[98]

But Williams' greatest innovation in advancing the peaceful
relations between states was the introduction of the principle of a
third party to arbitrate between two or more of them. This third
party must, however, be an impartial, neutral peacemaker.[99] The
arbitrator must, also, have the respect and confidence of all the
parties involved.[100] In his advocacy of this principle, Williams
was steadfast in emphasizing that by the use of the third party
the many differences in the New England group of states, especially so if combined with the use of commissions and arbitration,
could be peacefully adjusted.

All wars except those actually and purely for self-defense,
Williams emphatically condemned. Christianity, humanity, experience and expediency deny the use of arms. "I yet doubt, now
since the coming of the Lord Jesus and the period of the National
Church, whether any other use of war and arms be lawful, but
in the execution of justice upon malefactors at home: or preserv-

---

[97] *Ibid*, pp. 21, 107, 23 ff, 287 ff, 296.
[98] Letter: *To Winthrop*, (no date), N C P., Vol. VI, p. 130.
[99] N C P., Vol. VI, pp. 153 f, 338, 391 ff, 388. In fact, the principle is
frequently referred to in this volume. Page 153 suggests Winthrop, Jr.,
as respected by all parties concerned, as a neuter.
[100] Letter: *To Thomas Hinckley*, N C P., Vol. VI, p. 395. "Both
parties yielded and proposed to submit to your decision, in active and passive obedience."

ing the life and lives in defensive war." Religious wars between states he considered illegal and incongruous because the church and state are separate institutions. "I must be humbly bold to say, that 'tis impossible for any man or men to maintain their Christ by their sword and to worship a true Christ."[101] Yet he conceded that under certain conditions a state may justly and legally wage war, internally and externally.[102]

Of legal wars that a state may wage, the internal war is the right and, at times, the duty of the state as an attribute of its sovereignty. And under certain conditions, civil punishments and civil restraints have a divine sanction. "We readily grant magistrates owned by *God* with a *Civil Sword* (Rom. 13) to execute vengeance against Robbers, Murthers, Tyrants, etc."[103]   Both expediency and prudence justify the state in the use of "punishments and weapons of a *Civill* nature,"[104] but not in spiritual misdemeanors because "the slander is of no civill nature."[105] "With respect to *civil matters*, I say the *civil state* must judge and punish the *offender*, else the *civil state* cannot stand." The use of the civil sword within the state "to subdue *Rebels*" is justified only after reason and persuasion have failed "powerfully to subdue their judgments and wills."[106]   But he never advocated death as a punishment for "rebels" simply because they were rebels and had done no crime justifying death. The treatment of Coddington, Dyre, and Harris, clearly shows his attitude toward "Rebels."[107] Although he opposed the arbitrary use of force by the state in internal affairs, he always granted the state a legal right to employ the force necessary to maintain civil peace and order. But in maintaining this peace and order, the punishment or penalty must be meted out on the basis of both humanity and justice.

Williams severely condemned the traditional penalties inflicted on the prisoners of war or civil rebellion, by the victors. "Sir, concerning captives, pardon my wonted boldness," he writes to Winthrop, "the Scripture is full of mystery and the Old Testament of types. If they deserved death then what punishments?

---

101 Letters: *To John Endicott*, 1651, N C P., Vol. VI, p. 225; *To John Winthrop*, N C P., Vol. VI, p. 139.
102 Letter: *To John Winthrop*, N C P., Vol. VI, p. 139.
103 *Queries*, N C P., Vol. II, p. 226.
104 *Bloudy Tenent of Persecution*, N C P., Vol. III, pp. 108 f.
105 *Bloudy Tenent Yet More Bloody*, N C P., Vol. IV, p. 148.
106 *Bloudy Tenent of Persecution*, N C P., Vol. III, p. 302.
107 Letter: N C P., Vol. VI, p. 267. At this time Europe still applied the death penalty to such cases.

Whether perpetual slavery . . .? I beseech you will weigh it after due time of training up to labor, and restraint, they ought not to be set free." Natural law and Scripture furnished him with a sufficient basis for the humane treatment of captives, even the Indians. The only right to hold the captive as a slave is "his good and the common"[108]—to train him to become a responsible member of a free state. For a humane treatment of them, he refers to the law of nature, because they are the "miserable drones of Adam's degenerate seed, and our brethren by nature." In the name of humanity, he pleads against the purposely inflicted injuries and for the captive's care and comfort. In reference to summary actions indulged in by Connecticut, he writes, "I fear some innocent blood cried at Connecticut." When the hands of the conquered Indians were cut off and sent to Boston, he united with Winthrop in condemning the act: "those dead hands were no pleasing sight. . . I have always shown dislike to such dismembering of the dead." In pleading for the care of war slaves he urges that "my humble desire is that all that have those poor wretches might be exhorted to walk wisely and justly toward them, so as to make mercy eminent." For the sake of expediency the Indians must be dealt with "wisely as with wolves endowed with men's brains" or they will join the enemy or "turn wild Irish themselves." Nor was the ruthless extermination of the Pequods, and later the Narragansetts, countenanced by him: "I must rejoice that, as he sayeth, some of the chiefs at Connecticut, Mr Heynes and Mr Ludlow, are almost adverse from killing women and children. Mercy outshines all the works." Instead of killing or enslaving those who surrender themselves, Williams asks that they be given houses, goods, and fields.[109] This last request goes beyond all bounds for mercy and generosity on the part of victors for his century. The plea for the merciful and generous treatment of prisoners of war he bases on Scripture, law of nature, humanity, justice, and political expediency.

That war between members of independent states could be entirely abolished never seemed more than a Utopian dream to Williams. "How should we expect that the streams of blood should stop the dregs of mankind [in New England] when bloody

---

[108] Letter: *To John Winthrop*, 1637, N C P., Vol. VI, p. 54. Williams accepted a youth to "bring up."

[109] Letters: *To John Winthrop*, N C P., Vol. VI, pp. 35, 48, 60, 80, 39 34, 36, 378.

issues flow so fresh and fearfully amongst the finest and most refined sons of men and sons of God. We have not only heard of the four northern nations . . . last year tearing and devouring one another . . . but we also have a sound of the Presbyterian's rage."[110]   Yet he would plead with the colonies, and with the Indians[111] for "more human consideration of so much blood spilt" in revenge and war. Both parties should keep the subscribed league and arbitrate; "that, and the common bond of humanity move me to pray yourselves [Massachusetts Bay] and our friends of Connecticut to improve all interests and opportunities to quench these flames. My humble requests are to the God of Peace that no English blood be further spilt in America: It is one way to prevent it, by loving mediation and prudent neutrality. Sir . . . you have not a truer friend and servant to your worthy person and yours, nor to the peace and welfare of the whole country, than the most despised and most unworthy, ROGER WILLIAMS."[112] Humane consideration of causes and effects, mediation and prudent neutrality, although they may not prevent wars in all cases, would, if employed, undoubtedly produce astonishing progress toward actual periods of universal peace.

In a letter to the General Court of Massachusetts, in October, 1654, Williams plainly states his views on war, its causes and effects. Much of it applies directly to conditions then existing in New England:

"MUCH HONORED SIRS: I truly wish you peace, and pray your gentle acceptance of a word, I hope not unreasonable.

"We have in these parts a sound of your meditations of war against these natives, amongst whom we dwell. I consider that war is one of those three great sore plagues . . . [pestilence, famine and war]. I consider, also, that I refused, lately, many offers in my native country, out of a sincere desire to seek the good and peace of this. . . .

"That at the subscribing of that solemn league, which, by the mercy of the Lord, I had procured with the Narragansetts, your government was pleased to send unto me the copy of it, subscribed by all hands there, which yet I keep as a monument and a testimony of peace and faithfulness between you both.

"That since that time, it hath pleased the Lord so to order it, that I have been more or less interested and used in all your transactions of war and peace, between the English and the natives, and have not spared

110 *Ibid.*, 1660, p. 307.
111 Letters: *To the General Court of Massachusetts*, 1654, N C P., Vol. VI, pp. 269 ff; *To Winthrop*, 1637, N C P., Vol. VI, p. 62.
112 *Ibid*, 1645, p. 145.

purse, nor pains, nor hazards, very many times, that the whole land, English and natives, might sleep in peace securely. . . .

"At my last departure for England, I was importuned by the Narragansett Sachems, and especially by Ninigret, to present their petition to the high Sachems of England, that they might not be forced from their religion, and, for not changing their religion, be invaded by war. . . .

"I never was against the righteous use of the civil sword of men and nations, but yet since all men of conscience and prudence ply to windward, maintain their wars to be defensive, as did both King and Scotch, and English and Irish, in the late wars, I humbly pray your consideration, whether it be not only possible, but very easy, to live and die in peace with all the natives of this country.

"For, secondly, are not all the English of this land, generally, a persecuted people from their native soil? and hath not the God of peace and Father of mercies made these natives more friendly in this, than our native countrymen in our own land to us? Have they not entered leagues of love, and to this day continued peaceable commerce with us? Are not our families grown up in peace amongst them? Upon which I humbly ask, how it can suit with Christian ingenuity to take hold of some seeming occasions for their destruction,[113] which, though the heads be only aimed at, yet, all experience tells us, falls on the body and the innocent.

"Thirdly, I pray it may be remembered how greatly the name of God is concerned in this affair, for it cannot be hid how all England and other nations ring with the glorious conversion of the Indians of New England. You know how many books are dispersed throughout the nation of the subject, (in some of them the Narragansett chief Sachems are publicly branded, for refusing to pray and be converted); have all the pulpits in England been commanded to sound of this glorious work, (I speak not ironically, but only mention what all the printed books mention,) and that by the highest command and authority of Parliament, and churchwardens went from house to house, to gather supplies for this work.

"Honored Sirs: Whether I have been and am a friend to the natives' turning to civility and Christianity, and whether I have been instrumental and desire so to be, according to my light, I will not trouble you with; only I beseech you consider, how the name of the most holy and jealous God may be preserved between the clashings of these two, viz.: the glorious conversion of the Indians in New England, and the unnecessary wars and cruel destruction of the Indians of New England.

"Fourthly, I beseech you forget not, that although we are apt to play with this plague of war more than with the other two, famine and pestilence, yet I beseech you consider how the present events of all wars that ever have been in the world, have been wonderful fickle, and the future calamities and revolutions, wonderful in the latter end.

"Heretofore, not having liberty of taking ship in your jurisdiction, I was forced to repair unto the Dutch, where mine eyes did see that first breaking forth of that Indian war, which the Dutch begun, upon the slaughter of some Dutch by the Indians; and they questioned not to finish

---

[113] Note the force of "to take hold of some seeming occasions."

it in a few days, insomuch that the name of peace, which some offered to mediate, was foolish and odious to them. But before we weighed anchor, their boweries were in flames; Dutch and English were slain. Mine eyes saw the flames at their towns, and the flights and hurries of men, women and children, the present removal of all that could for Holland; and after vast expenses and mutual slaughters of Dutch, English,[114] and Indians, about four years, the Dutch were forced, to save their plantation from ruin, to make up a most unworthy and dishonorable peace with the Indians.

"How frequently is that the saying in England, that both Scotch and English had better have borne loans, ship money, etc., than run upon such rocks, that even success and victory have proved, and yet are like to prove. Yea, this late war with Holland, however begun with zeal against God's enemies, as some in Parliament said, yet what fruits brought it forth, but the breach of the Parliament, the enraging of the nation by taxes, the ruin of thousands who depended on manufactures and merchandise, the loss of many thousand seamen, and others, many of whom worlds are not worthy?

"But, lastly, if any be yet zealous of kindling this fire for God, etc., I beseech that gentleman, whoever he be, to lay himself in the opposite scale. . . ."

"Now, with your patience, a word to these nations at war (occasion of yours), the Narragansetts and Long Islanders, I know them both experimentally, and therefore pray you to remember.

"First, that the Narragansetts and Mohawks are the two great bodies of Indians in this country, and they are confederates, and long have been, and they both yet are friendly and peaceable to the English. I do humbly conceive, that if God call us to a just war with either of them he calls us to make sure of the one to a friend. . . .

"2. The Narragansetts, as they were the first, so they have been long confederates with you; they have been true, in all Pequot wars, to you. They occasioned the Mohegans to come in, too, and so occasioned the Pequot's downfall.

"3. I cannot yet learn, that it pleased the Lord, to permit the Narragansetts to stain their hands with any English blood, neither in open hostilities nor secret murders, as both Peequots and Long Islanders did, and Mohegans also, in the Pequot wars. It is true, they are barbarians, but their greatest offences against the English have been matters of money, or petty revenging of themselves on some Indians, upon extreme provocation, but God kept them clear of our blood.

"4. For the people, many hundred English have experimented them to be inclined to peace and love with the English nation.[115]

"The cause and root of all the present mischief, is the pride of two barbarians, Ascassassotic, the Long Island Sachem, and Ninigret, of the Narragansett. The former is proud and foolish; the latter is proud and fierce. . . .

---

[114] Mrs. Anne Hutchinson was killed in this war.
[115] Williams then refers to "their late famous long-lived Canonicus" and his friendship.

"Honored Sirs. . .

"But I beseech you, say your thoughts and the thoughts of your wives and little ones, and the thoughts of all English, and of God's people in England, and the thoughts of his Highness and Council tender of these parts, if, for the sake of a few inconsiderable pagans, and beasts, wallowing in idleness, stealing, lying, whoring, treacherous witchcrafts, blasphemies, and idolatries, all that the gracious hand of the Lord hath so wonderfully planted in the wilderness, should be destroyed."[116]

In this letter Williams has pointed out three things—the slightness of justice in any war, the futility of it as a means of settling international disputes, and the method of preventing it in New England. Among the chief causes of past and contemporary wars he placed capricious violations of leagues and agreements between independent states; religious persecution and disputes; invasion for selfish economic purposes, or greed; invasion for political reasons, or desire for power on the part of leaders; refusal to mediate or compromise conflicting interests; and pride and false ideas of national honor. As a humane man and a student of history, conversant to some extent with the economic origins of wars, he realized that war results in the ruin of manufacture, merchandise, and commerce with its resultant human suffering through famine and pestilence, and in the destruction of so much property that no success can outweigh the loss sustained by the victors. Add to this the loss of thousands of lives of seamen, soldiers, and non-combatants, and ' the more immediate suffering of the "wives and little ones" and the "body of the innocent," for all of which no economic gains, not even "worlds," can possibly compensate. Are the fruits of victory, he asked, worthy of this suffering and loss? These general observations he applied to the question of threatening colonial and Indian wars in New England. One of the surest preventatives suggested is the formation of alliances to equalize the balance of political and economic power. Even though he sanctioned a righteous war, he also pointed out that all men "maintain their wars to be defensive." His inevitable conclusion on the subject is that "present events of all wars that ever have been in the world are wonderful fickle," and the seed-beds for "future calamities and revolutions."

Self-defense by the nation attacked[117] is legal and necessary,

---

[116] Letter: *To the General Court of Massachusetts,* 1654, N C P., Vol. VI, pp. 269 ff.

[117] *Bloudy Tenent of Persecution,* N C P., Vol. III, p. 160.

and the right and attribute of its sovereignty. In times of peace it may, moreover, make "just cautions and *provisos*" against external attack. Self-defense as a principle has divine sanction; for the fourth sword "is a civil Sword, called the Sword of Civill justice . . . which being of a material nature, for the defense of Persons, Estates, Families, Liberties of a City, or Civil State. . . . For other Wolves against the Civil State, we professe it to be the Dutie of the Civill State to persecute and Suppresse them." Even public defense may be prepared for in time, to assure protection; "Against the feare of Evill *practices* the *Wisdome* of the *State* may securely provide, by just *cautions* and *provisos,* as of Subscribing to Civill Engagement," etc.[118] The right of self-defense is not affected by the fact that "all civil contentions and wars" in the past have been started" for greater dishes and bowls of porridge" and that each contending state claims its war to be defensive. Such complications merely cloud the issues and make the justification of a war more difficult.[119]

Williams' peculiar theory of war and peace was put to a severe test during King Philip's War, in 1675. When the Indians carried the war into Rhode Island and besieged Providence, Williams took an active part in the defense of the colony and accepted a commission as captain.[120] But the colony waged a defensive war only, and had no part in the extermination of the tribe or in the spoils of war. "I presume you are satisfied," he wrote to Winthrop, Jr., in defense of his policy, "in the necessity of these present hostilities, and that it is not possible at present to keep peace with these barbarous men of blood, who are justly to be expelled and subdued as wolves that assault the sheep."[121] In this war, provoked, as Williams believed, by the white men, the United Colonies took the offensive and finally exterminated the entire tribe of Indians for the sake of their lands. Although he denied sanctions to principles hostile to civil peace and the dictates of expediency, humanity, Scripture and reason,[122] Williams always advocated an intelligent state policy of public

---

[118] *Bloudy Tenent of Persecution*, N C P., Vol. III, p. 160. *Queries*, N C P., Vol. II, p. 274, *Bloody Tenent Yet More Bloody*, N C P., Vol. IV, pp. 313 f.

[119] Letter: *To Major Mason,* 1670, N C P., Vol. VI, p. 343.

[120] R I C R., Vol. II, p. 547. N C P., Vol. VI, p. 375, note. Williams at this time was about seventy-two years of age.

[121] Letter: *To John Winthrop, Jr.,* 1675, N C P., Vol. VI, p. 377.

[122] The Allegory of the Ship of State. N C P., Vol. VI, pp. 278 ff.

defense against internal and external attack. But he condemned offensive warfare. The only just war is that of self-defense, and that only.

In his effort to secure the integrity and independence of the Providence Plantations amidst the wars, jealousies, and conflicting desires and claims of the savage natives and the Christian white men, Roger Williams worked out and presented certain general principles that should underlie the interstate relations in the society of states in the new world. Incidentally, by analogy and illustration he held these principles of general and universal significance. (1) In international relations, each state remains the absolute and independent sovereign within itself with the right of resistance to foreign interference in its internal affairs, ecclesiastical or civil. (2) Legally and politically, it has an equal capacity for rights in the international society. (3) The form of the civil government of a state does not in any manner affect its sovereignty, nor its equal legal and political rights with other states. (4) No state can with equity claim authority over another by Right of Discovery or Conquest. (5) The limitation of the state's activities, externally, by means of arbitration, treaties, agreements, and leagues arranged between free and equal states enlarges the freedom of the state by the mutual restraints. (6) The use of commissions and arbitration for settling the disputes and conflicting interests of the various states, instead of war, can be justified on the basis of experience, reason, expediency, and humanity. (7) Leagues, treaties, and agreements arrived at through mediation by the joint free consent of all parties are sacred and inviolable until changed by free mutual consent. (8) The peaceful relations between states can often be secured by the principle of a third acceptable, neutral party to arbitrate or compose the conflicting claims and interests. (9) Military superiority and desire for conquest can never justify an invasion or violation of the rights of other states. (10) Two kinds of wars are justifiable: an internal war for the sake of peace and order and the protection of citizens; and a war of self-denfense against the attack of another state. (11) All prisoners of war should be treated with mercy and generosity because that alone is natural, equitable, humane and politically expedient. (12) The best safeguards against war are mediation, compromise, humane and utilitarian consideration of causes and effects, respects for the rights

of other states and prudent neutrality.   When Williams argued
for the freedom and equality of the new society that he founded,
on the basis of medieval corporation law, law of nature, and his
concept of the origin and nature of the state and its sovereignty,
he was from the legal standpoint of his century on solid ground.
But he needed a still broader foundation upon which to carry on.
And so to corporation and natural law and his concept of state,
he added the arguments from Scripture, humanity, equity, reason
and expediency, in upholding his thesis that the relation between
states should ever be civil, humane and political.

PART 4

INTERNATIONAL RELATIONS AND THE MODERN STATE

International affairs were of absorbing interest and concern to Roger Williams because of their bearing upon the welfare of the individual man in society. In this respect he is the Tom Paine of the seventeenth century. His interests were not limited to the selfish provincial affairs of Rhode Island. His concerns and his sympathies in life were universal. Neither race, station in life, nor nationality could circumscribe his public interests. He yearned to enlighten and free through reason, will, argument and love, the whole human race. The Indian, the Jew, the Turk, all mankind, though barbarian, "proud, and angry and covetous and filthy, hating and hateful," he considered, nevertheless, his "brethren by nature." In his contact "with shadows and fables" of life, he was able to "see the vain and empty puff of all terrene promotion . . . all dashed in a moment in the frowns of such in whose friendship and love lay [the] chief advancement." This gave him an astonishing clarity of insight in and definiteness of outlook upon the multifarious problems around him.[123] In public affairs, "I respect," he affirms, "not one party more than the other, but I desire to witness truth. And as I desire to witness against oppression, so also against the slighting of civil, yea, of barbarous order and government, as respecting every shadow of God's gracious appointment. . . .[124] My humble desires are to contribute my poor mite, as I ever have, and I hope ever shall, to preserve plantation and public interest of the whole New England and not the interest of this or that town, colony, opinion, etc."

All his life Williams was an apostle of peace. If a state because of greed and selfishness, civil or religious, fails to respect the rights of another, then self-defense to him becomes a virtue. Desire for property and lands, or wealth and power, either religious or civil, he recognized as the "fickle" underlying causes of past wars.[125] What could be more fickle than England's war

---

[123] Letters: *To John Winthrop*, N C P., Vol. VI, pp. 306 ff, 310 ff, 101, 35, 114. Numerous passages will show his interest in international affairs.

[124] Letter: *To the General Court of Massachusetts*, N C P., Vol. VI, p. 327.

[125] R I H S P., Vol. 8, p. 159. Letter: *To Winthrop*, N C P., Vol. VI, pp. 269 ff, 306, 310, 319, 272. He mentions state affairs of Spain, Portugal, Sweden, Norway, Denmark, Spanish America, England, Scotland, New England.

of 1652, when "your English Seas contend[ed] with a neighbor *Dutchman* for the motion of a piece of silk?"[126]   Is a piece of silk, he wonders, of more civil and humane importance than the destruction of immense wealth and thousands of lives and the subsequent poverty? He even notices that man is imbecile enough to want to drench several colonies with human blood for the sake of two hundred goats. "Sir," some of the soldiers said here that " 'tis true the Narragansetts had yet killed no English, but they had killed two hundred of Mr. Winthrop's goats . . . that Mr. Winthrop was robbed and undone. . . . I hope to hear . . . that notwithstanding any private loss, yet that noble spirit of your father still lives in you, and will still work." In his relentless efforts to prevent another war, he writes, "Capt. Patrick also informs me of a great itch upon the soldiers to fall foul upon our neighbors. Little sparks prove great fires. The God of Peace who is only wise be pleased to guide us."[127] While the other colonies were designing and waging war "for greater dishes and bowls of porridge," Williams discovered "it hath pleased God, mercifully to help me to do many things, with my great hazard and charge, when all the colonies, and the Massachusetts, in special, have meditated, prepared and been, sometimes many hundreds, among the march for war against the natives in this colony. Of this my promise and duty, and constant practice, mine own heart and conscience before God,"[128] has unflinchingly been devoted to "endeavors of preserving the public peace."

In interstate affairs, Williams recognized and employed various degrees of relationships. But none of these relations in any way affects the nature of the internal sovereignty of state. Instead, they guarantee a far greater liberty of internal activity than would otherwise be possible. Each relation, furthermore, assures a varying degree of security. And in proportion to the security obtained, reciprocal obligations are increased. The first kind of relationship between states, that of simple physical contact between states, is exceedingly dangerous. It resembles the condition

---

[126] *Bloody Tenent Yet More Bloody*, N C P., Vol. IV, p. 10.   Preface to Parliament.

[127] Letter: *To John Winthrop, Jr.*, N C P., Vol. VI, pp. 277, 35 f.

[128] Letter: *To Sir Robert Carr*, 1665, N C P., Vol. VI, pp. 321 f. Even if allowance is made for the fact that Williams is writing to a member of the royal Commissioners visiting the colonies in the interest of the home government, what he states here is borne out by Winthrop and the Records of the United Colonies, and Connecticut, Massachusetts and Plymouth.

of men without a form of government. No treaties or other obligations restrain the actions of the states in such relations. And, because there the only rule is that of the law of nature and of God, the condition of relations is more apt to resemble that of barbarism. The second, that of deliberate mutual agreements and treaties provides more security for both parties. But this form of relationship must come from a free joint consent between the parties[129] and be held morally binding until changed by the consent of all parties. By the third, that of the defensive alliances, a still greater degree of safety is assured. And lastly, the confederate or league of states form of relationship, is represented in the United Colonies of New England, organized in 1643. But the functions of the league may cover only points of common interest and safety. Its powers, at any time, cannot be more than the people of each state by joint consent are willing to give it from time to time. In the last two kinds of association he holds that each and every state is to be admitted, whatever the form of government, the representatives to be appointed for a central conference as occasion arises.[130] Whatever the form of relation may be that exists between free states, that relation is a sacred obligation to each party, and, instead of limiting the freedom of the state, if it is just and honorable, it enhances the state's liberty.

The principle of arbitration was, indeed, not a new instrument in international affairs. It was known to the Greeks and the Romans. It was used in the fifteenth century by Poland, with salutary effects. But it was never a popular principle with statesmen of powerful or victorious states. As an active principle in practical statesmanship, arbitration became again internationally recognized through the Jay Treaty with Great Britain in 1794. In the seventeenth century the one man who vigorously advocated the use of the principle to settle both internal and external problems of state was Roger Williams.[131]

Although independent and equal, every state in the new society has certain reciprocal obligations. Internal sovereignty "is compatible with numerous restrictions upon the state conduct in

---

[129] Letter: *To the General Court of Massachusetts,* 1655, N C P., Vol. VI, p. 295. See also pp. 401 ff.

[130] N C P., Vol. VI, p. 387. *To the Commissioners of the United Colonies.* See *Ante,* Chapters II and III.

[131] *Ibid,* pp. 149 ff, 393, 265. He repeatedly advocated this principle throughout this volume. R I C R., Vol. I, The Proposals of 1640.

matters in which the advantage of an orderly adjustment of claims by an adoption of a common rule of law have come to be recognized."[132] Williams fully appreciated that interdependence has a higher claim than independence in the relation between states. And he vehemently and definitely denounced all rights in international relations to arbitrary decisions.[133] States continue free agents in respect to other matters which remain outside the law of nations. No obligation can be imposed upon them, by whatever majority of the international community, against their individual will, and each state remains the guardian of its own interests and the arbiter of its own destiny.

For centuries the philosophers and publicists, anticipating in theory what Williams set out to establish in fact, had been dreaming of a state that represented the collective will of the people. They had visions of a state in which every citizen was a free and equal unit, subject only to the free and equal rights and privileges of his fellow citizens; in which rulers and leaders are chosen not because of accident of birth or the voice of a few privileged burghers and noblemen, but by the whole people because of their superior abilities and unselfish interests in the state; which would consider itself a member of the society of states, each of which was willing to work for the common and collective welfare; and which would be, as free and equal among other states, great and small, as the humblest and poorest citizen is free and the equal of the wisest or wealthiest—in civil, humane and political things. Luther, when he broke the temporal and economic stranglehold which the papacy then had upon the temporal powers of Europe, prepared the soil for the realization of this dream of the centuries.[134] But to Williams belongs the honor of attempting to make this dream a practical thing, a reality, and of providing the warp and woof of a new social fabric out of which could be fashioned the modern state.

---

[132] Fenwick: *International Law,* p. 45.
[133] N C P., Vol. III, pp. 327, 321, 366, 387; also Vols. IV and VI, Palfrey: *History of New England,* Vols. I, p. 390; II, pp. 110, 327, 326.
[134] See Waring: *The Political Theories of Martin Luther,* pp. 108 ff.

V

THE PURPOSE OF THE STATE

PART 1

THEORIES OF THE SEVENTEENTH CENTURY

The seventeenth century political thought on the purpose of the state may be broadly divided into the absolutist and republican viewpoints.[1] The two schools agreed that the state, of necessity, must carry out its functions of war, police and justice. But they were at variance in regard to the ideal ends of these functions. A wide difference of opinion was found, even among the republicans, on how far the state may interfere with individual rights. Nor could they agree on the real content of the word, "liberty," or the ultimate significance of the term, "public welfare." In fact, there was no concurrence among any of the theorists regarding the significance of these terms in practical politics. Yet, upon their meaning depended largely the view taken by each writer on the ideal object and purpose of the state.

Hobbes,[2] foremost among the absolutists, held the end of the commonwealth to be "particular security. . . . One person" is given the complete authority "to the end that he may use the strength and means of them all as he shall think expedient, for their peace and common welfare . . . to peace at home and mutual aid against the enemies abroad." Spinoza[3] was greatly influenced in his theory of state by Hobbes. James I and Filmer[4] in their defense of the Divine Right of Kings, substantially agreed with Hobbes and Bodin[5] in the arbitrary and irresponsible power, *legibus soluta,* as the essential character of every state.

In opposition to the absolutists, the republican theorists denied that the state's authority is either arbitrary or irresponsible. Harrington[6] followed in the footsteps of Aristotle and Machiavelli. To him the end of the state is the common welfare, both

---

[1] Gooch: *Political Thought from Bacon to Halifax; Democratic Ideas in the Seventeenth Century.* Dunning: *Political Theories: Luther to Montesquieu.*
[2] *Leviathan.*
[3] *Tractatus Politicus.*
[4] *True Law of Free Monarchies.* Filmer: *Patriarcha.*
[5] *De la République.*
[6] *The Commonwealth of Oceana.*

as to material conditions and psychological influences at work in the political institutions.   The Independents and the Army declared the state must regard man's "naturall rights derived from Adam and right reason."[7]   The natural rights embraced those of life, liberty, and property, freedom of conscience and expression, and equality in political privileges.[8]   In the various manifestoes of the Levellers this new motion is constantly brought forward— "common rights, liberty, and safety" and "safety and well-being of the people."[9]   To Milton, liberty is the "birthright" of men and nations and assures to the individual a wide sphere of action unrestrained by any government.   Man is born with the right and power of self-defense and preservation.   The state is to execute justice between men, which, except for the bond of nature and of covenant, man must have executed for himself and for one another.[10]   "And it is not without reason," Locke writes, "that he seeks out and is willing to join in society with others who are already united, or have a mind to unite for the mutual preservation of their lives, liberties and estates, which I shall call by the general term—property."   In the "well-ordered commonwealth, where the good of the whole is so considered as it ought[11]. . . the great and chief end, therefore, of men uniting into commonwealths . . . is the preservation of their property."[12]   Although the political writers and statesmen of the seventeenth century differed in their conception of the inclusive and exclusive purpose of the state, they, nevertheless, expressed the ultimate end in the same general terms of "security," "common peace," and "common welfare" of the commonwealth.

Like a true child of the seventeenth century, Roger Williams used the same terms as the other political writers and thinkers of his century whenever he referred to the end and object of the

---

[7] Edwards: *Gangrœna.*

[8] *The Agreement of the People,* 1647; *Heads of Proposals,* 1647. Gardiner: *Constitutional Documents,* pp. 316 ff

[9] Gardiner: *Civil War. Ante,* note 1.

[10] *Tenure of Kings and Magistrates,* 1649.   The freedom of action is not as wide in scope as that demanded by most of the modern individualists.

[11] Locke: *On Civil Government,* II, 123, 143.   Compare *A Model for Church and Civil Power* by Ministers of Massachusetts Bay Colony, about 1635: "For in a free State no magistrate hath power over the bodies, goods, lands, liberties of a free people, but by their free consents."   But by means of numerous qualifications, this is twisted into a theocratic purpose.   N C P., Vol. III, p. 234.

[12] *Ibid.* II, 124, 222, 229, 136, 146.

state.[13] But he used them with the connotation applied to them by the popular sovereignty advocates of the Middle Ages and the Reformation, with, however, certain striking modifications. To the Town of Providence he wrote that the "Ship of State" must use its authority for their "common peace and preservation." To Winthrop, he urged that the state must look to "the public peace and welfare. . . While we are here, Noble Sir, let us *viriliter hoc agere, rem agere humanam, divinam, Christianam,* which I believe is all of a true public genius." While all the other colonies of New England were on the warpath, he was tirelessly striving to bring about public peace through agreements and arbitration.[14] To him, public peace and welfare of the people were not merely theoretical terms of a speculative philosophy of state, but ideas real, practical, and necessary to the ultimate and highest end of human existence. In his letter to Major Mason, his advanced conception of the purpose of the state is clearly indicated; in it, he asserted that the peace and welfare of a community can exist only when each individual possesses "temporal and soul liberties." But this peace and welfare is not to be merely a local symptom. The state establishes its government machinery "for the peace and good of Mankind."[15] To Williams, then, the ultimate purpose of the state is to provide a means whereby not only the individual and the community will be preserved in common peace and well-being; but "Mankind," as a universal society, will be assured the use and advantages of life, liberty, and property in the interest of all.[16]

---

[13] Gooch: *Political Thought from Bacon to Halifax.*
[14] N C P., Vol. VI, pp. 278, 279, 319, 321 f, 117 ff.
[15] *Ibid,* pp. 333 ff, 401 f.
[16] R I H S P., Vol. 8, pp. 147 ff, Letter: *To the Town of Warwick,* 1666.

PART 2
WILLIAMS' EXPOSITION OF THE AIMS OF THE STATE

The unusual environment and economic life of New England, undoubtedly, had an inestimable influence upon the inquiring and sensitive mind of Williams.[17] In its intolerance and flagrant disregard for individual rights, the Bay colony represents the necessary link between his early theory and later practice. That no state long continues in *statu* was vividly demonstrated to him by the rapid political and social changes in Rhode Island, the other New England colonies and Europe. He recognized, as few in his age did, the influence of social changes, economic tendencies and political attitudes upon the means by which the ultimate aims of the state may be achieved. These factors, he realized, create the complexity or the simplicity of the problems the state must treat, and therefore dictate the form of government machinery to be employed. But, in spite of the influences at work or the means required to meet them, the highest aim of the state remains always "our temporal and soul liberties."[18]

In reply to the authors of *A Model of Church and Civil Power*,[19] Williams rejected their paradoxical statement that the object and end of church and state are the same, and substituted his own notion:

"Whereas they say, that the *Civill Power* may erect and establish what *forme* of *civill Government* may seeme in *wisedome* most meet, I acknowledge the *proposition* to be most true, both in itself, and also considered with the end of it, that a *civill Government* is an *Ordinance* of *God,* to conserve the *civill peace* of people, so farre as concernes their *Bodies* and *Goods*. . . .

"But from this *Grant* I infer, (as before hath been touched) that the *Soveraign, originall,* and *foundation* of *Civill power* lies in the *people*. . . . And if so, that a People may erect and establish what *forme* of *Government* seems to them most meete for their *civill condition*. . . .

"*Lawes* respecting *Religion* are two-fold: First, such as concerne the *acts* of *Worship* and the *Worship* itself. . . .

---

[17] Scott: *Development of Constitutional Liberty*, p. 112. N C P., Vols. I-VI, continually stress this idea.

[18] R I H S P., Vol. 8, p. 154. N C P., Vol. VI, pp. 262 ff, 334.

[19] *A Model of Church and Civil Power*, Williams believed to have been written by John Cotton; but it is now believed to have been written by Richard Mather of the Bay Colony before the end of 1635. See Bibliography. Partly quoted by Williams in the *Bloudy Tenent*, pp. 221 ff.

"Secondly, *Lawes* respecting *Religion* may be such as meerly concerne the *Civill State, Bodies* and *Goods* of such and such persons, professing these and these *Religions,* viz. that such and such persons, notorious for *Mutinies, Treasons, Rebellions, Massacres,* be disarmed: Againe, that no persons *Papists, Jewes, Turkes,* or Indians be disturbed at their worship. . .

"These and such as are of this nature, concerning only the *bodies* and *goods* of such and such *Religious persons,* I confesse are meerely Civill.[20]

"We have formerly viewed the very nature and essense of a *Civill Magistrate,* and find it the same in all parts of the *World,* where evere people live upon the face of the *Earth,* agreeing together in *Townes, Cities, Provinces, Kingdomes.* . . The Object of it, viz. the *common-weale* or *safety* of such a people in their bodies and goods. . .

"This *civill* Nature of the *Magistrate* we have proved to receive no *addition* of *power* from the *Magistrates* being a *Christian,* no more than it receives diminution from his not being a *Christian* even as the *Commonweale* is a true *Common-weale,* although it have not heard of *Christianitie.* . . .

" . . . The worke of the *Civill Magistrate* under the Gospel, Rom. 13., expressly mentioning (as the *Magistrates* object) the duties of the *second Table,* concerning the *bodies* and *goods* of the *subject.*

"The *reward* or *wages* which people owe for such a worke, to wit, (not the *contribution* of the *Church* for any *spiritual work,* but) *tribute, toll, customs* which are *wages* payable by all sorts of men, *Natives* and *Forreigners,* who enjoy the same benefit of the *publick peace* and *commerce* in the *Nation.*

"Since the *civill Magistrate,* whether *Kings* or *Parliament, States,* and *Governours,* can receive no more in *justice* then what the People give, and are therefore but the *eyes* and *hands,* and *instruments* of the people (simply considered without respect to this or that *Religion.*[21]. . .

"The Civill horne or power being . . . but of an humane and Civill nature and constitution, it must consequently be of a humane and Civill *operation,* for who knows not that operation followes *constitution?.* . .[22]

The authors, Williams claimed, having made an excellent confession of the:

"proper end of the *civill Government,* being the preservation of the *peace* and *welfare* of the *state,* they ought not to break downe these *bounds,* and so to censure immediately for such *sinnes* which hurt not their *peace.* And in the last place, they acknowledge the *Magistrate* hath

---

[20] *The Bloudy Tenent of Persecution,* N C P., Vol. III, pp. 249, 252. "This is cleare not only in Reason, but in the experience of all commonweales, where the people are not deprived of their materiall freedom by the power of tyrants."
[21] *Ibid,* pp. 354 f. "Civil Magistrates" here means the civil machinery.
[22] *Ibid,* p. 372.

no power to punish any, for any such offenses as break no *civil Law* of *God*, or *Law* of the *state*, published according to it: For the *peace* of the *state*, say they, being preserved by wholesome *Lawes*, when they are not hurt, the *Peace* is not hurt."[23]

The state establishes a civil government to carry out its purpose. This government and also the *"Emperours, Kings* and *Rulers* of the earth" must be "qualified with *political* and state abilities to make and execute such Civill Lawes which concerne the common *rights, peace* and *safety* (which is worke and business, load and burthen enough for the ablest shoulders in the *commonweale.*) The *Civill Magistrates* [have] the common care and charge of the *commonwealth*, the peace and safety of the *Towne: City, State* or *Kingdom*. . . . For what is a *Commonweale*, but a *commonweale* of *Families* agreeing to live together for common good."[24] In the Instructions to the Committee representing Providence in 1647, at the formation of the government, Williams writes that the purpose of the state may coincide with that of England "so far as the nature and constitution of this place will admit." Otherwise the committee is to strive for "whatever may tend unto the generall peace and union of the colony and our own particular liberties and privileges . . . always reserving our equal votes and equal privileges in general." In the Constitution of 1647, the Towns agree "to maintayne each other by the same authority, in his lawful right and liberty . . . to the end that we may give each to the other. . . as good and hopeful assurance as we are able, touching each man's peaceable and quiett enjoyment of his lawful right and libertie," of life, property and equal justice.[25] With the formation of the civil government, therefore, the members of the state no longer possess absolute individual liberty and rights, but only *lawful rights and liberties,* or civil liberties.

In reconciling the interests of the state and individual, Williams made another of his chief contributions to political theory and practice. In his effort to establish order and co-operation among his fellow-colonists, he continually stood for political and civil freedom over against an over-emphasis of individual freedom. The unrest in the colony was the natural result of the extreme individualistic tendencies among his followers. They took their

23 *Ibid*, pp. 384 f.
24 *Ibid*, pp. 366, 128 f, 242.
25 R I C R., Vol. I, pp. 42 ff, 156 ff.

stand for natural and absolute individual rights with no reciprocal
duties. Civil liberty, Williams explained, is "lawful right and
Libertie" fixed by an agreement, and carrying with it reciprocal
duties and obligations toward the other individuals and the community or state—"We enjoy liberties of soul and body," he wrote
to Winthrop, "but it is license we desire."[26] His fellow men for-
got that "there is a civil *faithfulness, obedience, honesty, chastity,
etc.* even among such as own not *God* nor *Christ*."[27] The political
freedom of the colonists of Rhode Island was established by the
constitutions which they formed from time to time. In these instruments the people were considered the original and permanent
source of authority, as expressed by their votes and the joint and
individual referendum and recall. Their individual freedom was
assured them by a Bill of Rights which recognized the private
rights of life, liberty of conscience and thought, property, equal
justice, and peace in harmony with the common welfare of the
whole. Arbitrary government was replaced by a somewhat uni-
form regulation of public affairs, and the government and officials were made responsible agents of the people.[28] In this manner civil liberty—as defined and elaborated by Martin Luther—
became for the first time a practical reality.

Nor did he consider state authority and civil liberty in essence antagonistic. The civil authority, instead of destroying,
in fact creates and maintains civil liberty by administering civil
justice. "*Scandalous offendours* against . . . the *life, chastity,
goods* or *good name* in the rest, is properly transgression against
the *civill State* and *Commonweale,* or the *Wordly State* of *Men*:
And therefore consequently if the *World* or *Civill State* ought to
be preserved by *Civill Government* or *Governours*: such scandalous offendours ought not to be tolerated, but suppress according to the wisdome and prudence of the said *Government* . . . In
the Civill state from the beginning of the World . . . Magistrates are to judge, and accordingly to punish such sinners as
transgress against the good and peace of the Civill state, *Families, Townes, Cities, Kingdomes* . . . and seasonably suppress, as

    [26] Letter: *To John Winthrop.* 1654, N C P., Vol. VI, p. 287. Wil-
liams quotes, as he closes, Queen Elizabeth: "*Profecto omnes sumus
licentia deteriores.*"
    [27] R I H S P., Vol. 8, p. 152.
    [28] R I C R., Vols. I and II. N C P., Vol. III, pp. 164, 298, 249.

may best conduce to the *publicke safetie*[29] . . . I never denied, that notwithstanding this liberty, the commander of this ship [of state] ought to command the ship's course, yea, and also command that justice, peace and sobriety be kept and practiced."[30] The civil justice which enlarges the civil liberty of man in the modern state deals with affairs of a *"material civil nature*, for the *defense* of *Persons, Estates, Families, Liberties* of a *Citie* or *Civill State."* And, since the government and the laws are the creation of the people, the purpose of the state can be changed at any time by the consent of the people as a whole.[31] If the majority actually rules, can the authority of the state be opposed to civil liberty? Some hold that it may be a tyranny; but, since the actual majority has probably never ruled in any state, probably not even in Williams' Rhode Island, the assumption is futile. In a summary manner Williams states that "it is *civil Justice* to preserve the *civil rights*: and the *Rights* of a *civil society* ought to be *preserved* by a *civil State."*[32]

In achieving its ultimate end, the state limits, in certain respects however, the freedom of action of the individual. That this should be so was taken for granted by Williams and most of his followers. Moreover, they considered civil restraint essential to the highest degree of civil liberty, for law and order enlarge the scope of freedom of individual action. "It is reasonable," argues Williams, "to expect and demand of such as live within the *state* a *civil maintenance* of their *civil officers* and to force it where it is denied." Furthermore, "it is gentlemen, in the power of the body to require the help of any of its members." In fact, *"active obedience* cannot be *given* but to a *competent judge."* and not "to him that hath no *Activitie* and *Abilitie* to command and rule."[33] In the compact and constitutions of the colony a similar position was taken: "We whose names are hereunder. . . do promise to subject ourselves in active and passive obedience to all such orders and agreements as shall be made for the public good of the body in an orderly way by the major

---

[29] *Bloudy Tenent of Persecution,* N C P., Vol. III, pp. 171, 108 f.
[30] Letter: *To the Town of Providence,* N C P., Vol. VI, p. 279.
[31] *Bloudy Tenent of Persecution,* N C P., Vol. III, pp. 160, 116, 249 ff, 398 ff; *Ante,* Chapter II, the definition of the state.
[32] *Bloody Tenent Yet More Bloody,* N C P., Vol. IV. p. 74; N C P., Vol. I, p. 51.
[33] *Bloudy Tenent of Persecution,* N C P., Vol. III, pp. 299; N C P., Vols. IV, p. 300, and VI, p. 150.

consent." These limits must, however, be equally applicable to all citizens in order to secure civil justice and peace.[34] For partiality will always in the end breed internal disorder. The principle which makes this limitation of individual liberty acceptable, is that it assumes freedom for each individual to do what he wills, provided he does not infringe upon the equal right to freedom of the other individuals.

His most concise statement of the principle of civil liberty is contained in a letter to the Town of Warwick, in 1666:

"Beloved Friends and Countrimen

"My due respects presented with heartie desires to your present and eternal prosperitie when this short Life is over: I was resolved to haue visited you my selfe this winter and to haue persuaded with Arguments of Trust and Loue the finishing of the payments relating to his Majesties Royall Graunt and Charter to us. . . .

"On 2 hinges my discourse shall turne: First the Fairness and Equity of the Matter: 2, the damage and Hazard if not performed.

"As to the first: The Fairnes of the Matter, please you to heare 2 or 3 witnesses: the first is common honestie and Common Justice in Common dealings between Man and Man: This giues to every man his Due, a penyworth for a peny. . . and will cry shame upon us that Mr. Clarke should be undone yea destroyed and ruined, as to this world, for his so great and so long pains. . . .

"These very Barbarians when they send forth a publike messenger, they furnish him out, they defray all payments, they gratifie him with Rewards, and if he proue lame and sick and not able to return, they visit him, and bring him home upon their shoulders, and that many Scores of Miles, with all care and Tenderness.

"At first Rhode Island, but afterward the whole Colony requested, employed, and sent to Mr. Clark a Commission and Credentials sealed, with which the King was satisfied, and owned him for our publike Agent. . . .

"At our Gen: Asembly when Mr. Clarkes accounts were fairly brought in of what he had recd and what he had borrowed, upon the Morgage of his house and Land, to goe through our Worke, the Assembly appointed a Committee of able and judicious Men to examine the accounts: upon whose Report and upon their owne further Examination and Consideration they saw cause to agree upon a Very moderate and Equall summe to be raised throughout the Colony, to be discharged unto him.

"Worthy friends it is Easy to find Cloaks and Coulours for Denyalls or Delays to any Business: we haue no mind to: I have visited most of my neighbors at Prouidence this winter: Some say they are sory and

---

[34] R I C R., Vol. I, 1636, p. 14. This is Williams' own draft; p. 323. N C P., Vol. VI, p. 262.

ashamed of it: Some say they like not some Words in the Charter:
some say they will pay if all doe: some are against all Gouernment and
Charters and Corporacions: some are not so bad and yet cry out against
Thieues and Robbers who take anything from them against their Wills:
some say they will see what became of their former payments before
they will part with any more: some say let those that sent Mr. Clarke into Engl: at first pay him: An some say other things, but none say ought,
in my judgment, which answers the Witnes of Common Honestie: For
the whole summ and scope of his Majesties Royall graunt and charter to
us is to bestow upon us 2 inestimable Jewells.

"The first is peace, commonly calld among all men the. Kings
peace (among) ourselues and among all the Kings subjects and Friends
in this Countrey and wheresoeuer: And further at our Agents most sea-
sonable peticion your King prohibites all his subjects to act any Hostilitie
toward our Natiues inhabiting among us without our Consent, which
hath hietherto bene otherwise practiced to our Continuall and great
grievance and disturbance.

"The 2 Jewell is Libertie: the first of our spirits which neither
Old nor N. Engl: knowes the like, nor no part of the World a greater.

2. Libertie of our persons: no Life no Limbe taken from us: No
Corporall punishment no Restraint, but by knowne Lawes and Agreements of our owne making.

"3. Libertie of our Estates, Howses catle, Lands, Goods, and not
a peny to be taken by any rate, without euery mans free debate by his
Deputies, chosen by himself and sent to the General Assembly.

"4. Libertie of Societie and Corporacion: of sending or being sent
to the Gen: Assembly: of choosing and being chosen to all offices, and
of making or repealing all Lawes and Constitutions among us.

"5. A Libertie, which other Charters haue not, to wit of attending to the Lawe of Engl: with a favourable mitigacion viz: not absolutely but respecting our Wilderness Estate and Condicion.

"I confess it were to be wished that these Dainties might haue fallen
from God and the King like showers and Deawes and Manna from
Heaven, gratis and free, like a joyful Harvest and vintage without any
paine of our Husbandry: But since the most Holy God the first Cause
hath ordained second Causes, and Meanes and Agents and Instruments;
it is no more honest for us to withdraw in this case then for Men to
come to an Ordinary and to call for the best wine and Liqours, the best
Meats Rost and bak't, the best Attendance etc and to be able to pay for
all and yet most unworthily steale away and not discharge the Reckoning.

"My 2nd Witnes is Common Gratitude, famous among all Mankind
yea amongst Bruit Beasts euen the Wildest and fiercest for Kindnes
received. . . .

"I will . . . present you with my 3rd Witnes of the Fairnes of this
matter which is Christianitie, which we all of us pretend to, though in
various and different persuasions. . . .

"Give me now leaue therefore to mencion my 2nd part or Hinge, which is the Hazard we run by not a free discharging. . . . 3. the Rate must be taken by distraint in the Kings name and Authoritie, and this we know will be more grievous and more chargeable: yet cannot be avoided, if we resolve not to turne Rebells, nor loose Vagrants to be catchd up by the other Colonies, Liues and Governments: or else to leaue our Catle, Children Wiues and Liues to be torne out of our bozomes by the strongest Arm, Catch who catch can: It is true that Honestie and Innocencie, Reason and Scripture are infinitely Excellent in ther Way, but are they Sufficient to charme, except God please to giue his spirit, Adders Serpents, Foxes, Wolues, etc. yea or to order tame Beasts without Bit or Bridle, as David speaks by which we all know what David meanes.

"If we wholy neglect this business what will become of our credit? . . . Again who knowes what stormes and Tempests yet abide us?. . . What a worme and sting of Bitternes will it be to us, to remember, like Jerusalem in the days of affliction, all our pleasant things? such peace, such security, such Liberties for Soule and Body as were neuer enjoyed by any English men, nor any in the World that I haue heard off?. . . Let us not sooth and sing our selues asleep with murthering Lullabies: Let us provide for charges and by timely humiliation preuent them: For my selfe, seeing what I see ouer all N. Engl. I can but say with David Psal. 119. My flesh trembleth for feare of thee and I am afraid of thy Judgments.

"I remain

"Longing after your present and eternal peace

R.W."[35]

Civil liberty, as Williams considered it, sets certain limits to state interference with individual rights.   Yet he also recognized that a certain increase of state authority and administrative action may actually increase opportunities for individual expression and action.[36]   To protect the individual in civil society, "the *civil state* may bring into *order,* make *orders,* preserve in *civil order* all her members."   In addition to the limits set by civil liberty, the civil state is limited in another direction.   It has no spiritual power "within the *sphear* of *civil jurisdiction* [for] the body or *Commonweal* is merely *civil,* the *Magistrate* or *Head* is a *civil head,* and each *member* is a *civil member.*"[37]   The state's power and weapons do not reach to the impiety and ungodliness of tongue and hand; it has no power "to punish. . . any such offenses as break no *civil Law of God,* or *Law* of the *State,* published according to it."[38]

---

[35] R I H S P., Vol. 8, pp. 147 ff.

[36] *Bloudy Tenent of Persecution,* N C P., Vol. III, p. 354.

[37] *Bloudy Tenent Yet More Bloody,* N C P., Vol. IV, pp. 80, 74, 199.

[38] *Bloudy Tenent of Persecution,* N C P., Vol. III, pp. 270, 384 f.

This twofold limit, of civil and spiritual liberty, fixed upon the state's endeavor to attain its chief object, the United Colonies of New England strenuously opposed and condemned. In his letter to Leverett, in 1675, Williams stated that the arbitrary governments of the Union imagined "Two dangerous, supposed, enemies: 1. dissenting and non-conforming worshippers, and 2. liberty of free, really free, disputes, debates, writings, printing, etc.; the Most High hath begun and given some tastes of these two dainties in some parts, and will more and more advance them when (as Luther and Erasmus to the Emperor Charles V, and the Duke of Saxony,) those two gods are famished, the Pope's Crown and the Monk's bellies."[39] These two supposed enemies, civil and spiritual liberty, the United Colonies felt must be either suppressed or banished if the theocratic state is to have internal peace. Williams and others had been banished from the Bay for proclaiming and defending these "enemies." Many others were suppressed, or threatened as John Cotton had been before the Cambridge Synod. Massachusetts, Connecticut and Plymouth unanimously, but with varying emphasis, insisted that the ends of the church and state are identical and that the individual is the servant of the state instead of its master. Roger Williams and most of his fellow colonists in Rhode Island, on the other hand, defended and incorporated the two limits on state action in their civil polity as the natural, humane and civil rights of the individual in society.

That the ends of church and state are identical was completely rejected by Roger Williams. The church is like "unto a *Corporation, Society,* or *Company*" in a city or state. "The *essence* or being of the Citie, and so the well-being and *peace* thereof is essentially distinct from those particular *Society.*" Because the Authors of the *Model* were unable to see "a true *difference* between the *Church* and the *World* and the *Spiritual* and *Civill State,*" they held the end of both to be "mans eternal felicitie." But Christ at his coming dissolved the National Church of Israel, and definitely stated that the church and state have different and distinct purposes. In the state, therefore, a subject or magistrate may be "good in respect of *civill* or *morall goodness,*"

---

[39] N C P., Vol. VI, p. 374.

though Godliness be entirely wanting.⁴⁰ But the Authors of the
Model held that the magistrate, as a magistrate has spiritual power to governe the *Church*. . . . That such *Lawes* properly concerning the church from the People; undeniably it followes, that a
people, as a *people,* naturally considered (of what *Nature* or *Nation* soever. . . have fundamentally and originally, as men, a power to governe the *Church*. . . . That such *Lawes* properly concerning *Religion, God,* the *Soules* of Men, should be *Civill Lawes* and
Constitutions; is as far from *Reason,* as that the *Commandments*
of *Paul,* which he gave the *Churches*. . . concerning *Christs worship*. . . were *Civill* and *Earthly constitutions;* Or that the *Can-
ons* and *Constitutions* of either *Œcumenicall* or *Nationall* Synods
concerning *Religion,* should be *Civill* and *State conclusions* and
agreements." Yet there are "many civill states in flourishing
peace and quiett," Williams argued "where the Lord Jesus is
not found." Nor can any one show a commission from the Son
of God to unite church and state; nor has the civil power a
divine commission giving it authority over the spiritual life. The
New Testament has nothing concerning such a delegation. Neither
is the "National State of Israel . . . a president or patterne" for
the state now to control the church of Christ. "So unsutable is
the commixing and intangling of the *Civill* with the *Spirituale*
charge and *Government* that. . . the Lord *Jesus* and his *Apostles*
kept themselves to one."⁴¹

"The *Magistrate* should encourage and countenance the
Church, yea and protect the persons of the *Church* from violence,
disturbance, etc. it being truly noble and glorious." On the other
hand, "Gods people must pray for and endeavour the peace of the
state they live in, although Pagan or Popish." The civil power
being of a human and civil nature, owes three things to the true
church of Christ:

"First, *approbation* and *countenance,* a reverent esteeme and honorable *Testimonie,* according to *Isa* 49. *Revel* 21, with a tender respect
of *Truth,* and the *professours* of it

"Secondly, Personall *submission* of his (officers) owne Soule to the
power of the *Lord Jesus* in that *Spiritual Government* and *Kingdome.* . . .

"Thirdly, *Protection* of such true *professours* of *Christ,* whether

---

⁴⁰ *Bloudy Tenent of Persecution,* N C P., Vol. III, pp. 73 f, 234 f, 239,
246 f. Uses the Latin phrase, *Bonus vir.*
⁴¹ *Ibid,* pp. 250, 253, 251, 277, 297, 315, 367.

apart, or met together, as also of their *estates* from violence and in-
jurie. . . .

"Now Secondly, if it be a false Religion (unto which the *Civill
Magistrate* dare not adjoyne, yet) he owes,

"First, *Permission* (for *approbation* he owes not to what is evill)
and this according to *Matthew* 13, 30, for publike peace and quiett sake.

"Secondly, he owes *protection* to the persons or goods of any Rom,
13."[42]

The end of the church is separate and distinct from that of
the state, because each differs in its source of immediate origin
and sphere of activity:

"That the civill state and the spirituall, the Church and Commonweale, they are like Hippocrates twinnes, they are borne together, grow
up together, laugh together, weepe together, sicken and die together,"
Williams scorns as "a witty, yet most dangerous *Fiction* of the *Father
of Lies,* who hardned in *Rebellion* against *God* perswades *Gods* people
to drink downe such deadly poison, though he knowes the truth of these
five particulars, which I shall remind you of."[43]

The church has its origin in, and is the creation of, God:

"unless Master *Cotton* can prove that all nations of the *world* have
spiritual power, Christs power, naturally, fundamentally, and *originally*
residing in them (as they are people and *inhabitants* of this world) to rule
. . . the *church.* . . .[44] What impudence and indiscretion is it in the most
common affairs of life, to conceive that *Emperours, Kings,* and *Rulers* of
the earth must not only be qualified with *political* and *state abilities* to
make and execute such *Civill Lawes* which may concern the common
rights, peace, and *safety* (which is worke and business, load and burthen
enough for the ablest shoulders in the *commonweal*) but also furnished
Spiritual and heavenly *abilities* to governe the *Spirituall* and *Christian
commonweale.* . . . If so, then the *finall cause* of both these Commonweales or States cannot be the same. But although the *End* of the *Civill
Magistrate* be excellent, to wit, well to administer the *Common-weale,* yet
the end of the *Spirituall Common-weale* of *Israel* and the officers thereof,
is as *different* and *transcendent* as the *Heaven* is from the *Earth.*"[45]

In the civil state is lodged the means for carrying out the
purpose or final cause of the individual in civil society. The end
is "common peace and liberty" of the passengers of the "Ship of
State."[46] As a visible organization of the state, the *"Civill Government* is an *Ordinance* of *God,* to conserve the *civill peace* of

---

[42] *Ibid,* pp. 280, 236, 372 f.
[43] *Ibid,* p. 333.
[44] *Bloody Tenent Yet More Bloody,* N C P., Vol. IV, p. 187.
[45] *Bloudy Tenent of Persecution,* N C P., Vol. III, pp. 366, 410.
[46] Letter: *To the Town of Providence,* N C P., Vol. VI, pp. 278 f.

the people, so farre as concernes their *Bodies* and *Goods*. . . . The proper end of this *civill Government*, being the preservation of the *peace* and *welfare* of the *State*." The "*Civill Magistrate*, whether, *Kings* or *Parliament*, *States* and *Governours*, can receive no more in *justice* then what the People give." It is the "eyes and hands and instruments" of the people, and acts merely as "Derivatives and Agents" immediately created and employed as hands and eyes "serving the good of the whole. . . ."[47]

The chief object of the state is, therefore, the "*commonweale* or *safety* of such a *people* in their *bodies* and *goods*."[48] And the ideal purpose of the civil officers and machinery is to "well administer the *Common-weale*."[49] How the means and end of the state are attained Williams illustrated by comparing a civil pilot with a pagan and Christian pilot of a ship: "he performes the same worke, (as likewise doth the Metaphoricall *Pilot* in the ship of the *Commonweale*) from a principle of *knowledge* and *experience*."[50] In the well-being of its individual members lies the chief purpose of the state's existence. Its object and administration is founded not on pure theory, but on knowledge and experience as a means and agent of the people. And its ultimate end is best accomplished by correction and regulation.

To the final cause of the state, the form of civil government is a non-essential. "Every *lawful Magistrate*, whether succeeding or elected is. . . the servant of the people" whose distinct sphere of activity in public affairs is "given him, in *commission* from the people."[51] This is true with regard to all "Gentile Princes, Rulers, and Magistrates, (whether *Monarchicall, Aristocraticall*, or *Democraticall*)."[52]For even the Scripture "leaves the *severall Nations* of the *World*, to their owne *severall Lawes* and *Agreements* (as is most probable) according to their severall *Natures, Dispositions* and *Constitutions*, and their *common peace* and *welfare*."[53] In the arguments of his Treatises,[54] he main-

---

[47] *Bloudy Tenent of Persecution*, N C P., Vol. III, pp. 40, 384, 355, 398.

[48] *Ibid*, p. 354.

[49] *Bloody Tenent Yet More Bloody*, N C P., Vol. IV, p. 410.

[50] *Bloudy Tenent of Persecution*, N C P., Vol. III, p. 399.

[51] *Bloody Tenent Yet More Bloody*, N C P., Vol. IV, p. 187; N C P., Vol. III, p. 41.

[52] *Bloudy Tenent of Persecution*, N C P., Vol. III, p. 343.

[53] *Bloudy Tenent Yet More Bloody* N C P., Vol. IV, p. 487.

[54] Especially Volumes III and IV, N C P.

tained the National Church of Israel is merely Typical since the beginning of the Christian era. Like numerous political thinkers of the twentieth century, (Laski, Duguit, Roscoe Pound, Arthur Bentley, Woodrow Wilson, and others) he recognized that the changing social conditions and tendencies demanded corresponding changes in the scope of the state's activities.[55] In order adequately to meet these ever-changing conditions, Williams postulated in the civil government a flexible agent and instrument of the state.

In the development of human society, the state fulfils its ultimate purpose. By regulation, correction, and adjustment of individual and community interests through law and justice, it assures individual liberty. In fact, the civil state is the mark of civilization. By giving every man equal consideration in civil life, the state fosters political, social, and individual liberty. Without some civil regulations men, through greed and selfishness, "would hunt and devoure each other."[56] Man, therefore, must be ever alert to defend the "fundamentall liberties of the country" against the anarchistic Harrises. "If any should preach or write that there ought to be no commanders or officers, because all are equal in Christ, Therefore no masters nor officers, no laws nor orders, no corrections nor punishments;—I say, I never denied, but in such cases whatever is pretended, the commander or commanders may judge, resist, compel and punish such transgressors, according to their deserts and merits."[57] For "if the *sword* and *balances* of *justice* (in a sort or measure) be not drawn and held forth, against *scandulous* offenders against the *Civil State*, that *civil state* must dissolve by little and little from *civility* to *barbarism*, which is a *wildernesse* of *life* and *manners*."[58] Without the civil state, the *"barbarism* and *confusion"* in which man "would hunt and devoure each other" would result in the loss of the two "inestimable Jewells" for which the state chiefly exists—"Peace & Libertie."

To evaluate the more complex individual and common public interests and to act as the public servant or service for regu-

---

[55] R I H S P., Vol. 8, p. 154. N C P., Vol. IV, p. 12. *Preface to Parliament.* Nor can your most prudent Heads and potent Hands possibly erect that Fabrick which the next Age (it may be the next Parliament) may not tumble down. . . ."
[56] *Bloudy Tenent of Persecution,* N C P., Vol. III, p. 398.
[57] N C P., Vol. VI, Letters: *To Winthrop,* 1637, p. 23; *To the Town of Providence,* 1654, p. 279.
[58] *Bloody Tenent Yet More Bloody,* N C P., Vol. IV, pp. 222 f.

lating and adjusting them, becomes an essential duty of the modern state. Here again Williams and his followers made a striking innovation in building up their new society. In this position Williams is in harmony with contemporary publicists and jurists who consider the state a public service agent or corporation serving a free citizenship in society.[59] Through his efforts to maintain peace and liberty, he discovered that each individual is the subject of numerous interests which must be peaceably adjusted with other individuals and the community. These interests must be evaluated by each individual from the viewpoint of public peace, safety and good.[60] "For all experience tells us," writes Williams, "that Public Peace and Love is better than abundance of corne and Cattell, and so forth." But public peace comes only when "all unite for true public good."[61] The Proposals of 1640 finally concluded: "Yet so farre as we can conceive in laying all things together we have gone the fairest and equallest way to produce peace. . . friends and neighbors being freely willing and have bound themselves to stand to our Arbitration of all differences amongst us to rest content in our determination. . . . After many considerations . . . we apprehend no way so suitable to our condition as government by way of arbitration. But if men agree themselves by Arbitration, no State we know disallows that, neither doe we; But if men refuse that which is but common humanity between man and man, then to compel."[62] Williams advocated arbitration, adjustment and compromise of differences between individuals, and the individual and community, throughout his career in the colony. The compact of 1636 suggests it; and his letter to Thomas Hinckley in 1678 emphasizes that "both parties yielded and proposed to submit to your decision, in active and passive obedience."[63]

Through arbitration and accomodation of differences in civil and social affairs, each party, under the supervision of the civil government, yields abstract individual rights for a higher good of "peace and publike Ends." Duties and responsibilities and serv-

---

[59] Laski: *A Grammar of Politics.* Duguit: *Law in the Modern State.* Oppenheimer: *The State.* Gettell: *History of Political Thought.*

[60] R I H S P., Vol. 8, pp. 157 ff, 160 f. R I C R., Vol. I, p. 39. N C P., Vols. VI, pp 48, 117, 321 ff, 395, and III, 355, 398.

[61] R I H S P., Vol. 8, p. 159. R I C R., Vol. I, p. 39.

[62] R I C R., Vol. I, pp. 27 ff. Written in 1640.

[63] N C P., Vol. VI, pp. 395 f.

ice will have to replace the exclusive character of the fictitious individual right. Force and authority will always be present, but merely as a latent factor. "I therefore humbly offer," Roger Williams writes to Sir Robert Carr, "intercession and mediation. . . in which time a peaceable and loving agreement may be wrought to mutual consent and satisfaction."[64]   To Providence he suggests, "if you will now profess not to have disfranchised humanity and love, but that. . . you will sacrifice to the common peace, and common safety, and common credit, that which may be said to cost you something. . . . Send unto your opposites such a line as this: Neighbors . . . both for pacification and accomodation of our sad differences . . . we are persuaded to remove our obstruction, viz. . . to meet with, and debate freely, and vote in all matters with us . . . If aught remains grievous, which we ourselves, by free debate and conference, cannot compose we offer to be judged and censored."[65]   But Williams did more than advocate compromise; he often practised it. Questions of property and personal right were in "no way ponderous with myself," he says, "but higher Grounds for peace and publike Ends." When the original settlers and new-comers quarreled about Providence and Pawtuxit lands, he came forward with the only reasonable solution, "for peace sake I persuaded both sides to Arbitration."[66]

His letter to the Town of Providence, in 1648, explains his method of applying the unique political principle of compromise and adjustment:

"WORTHY FRIENDS, that ourselves and all men are apt and prone to differ, it is no new thing. In all former ages, in all parts of the world, in these parts, and in our dear native country and mournful state of England, that either part or party is most right in his own eyes, his cause right, his carriage right, his arguments right, his answers right, is as woefully and constantly true as the former. And experience tells us, that when the God of peace have taken peace from the earth, one spark of action, word or carriage is too powerful to kindle such a fire as burns up towns, cities, armies, navies, nations, and kingdoms. And since, dear friends, it is an honor for men to cease from strife; since the life of love is sweet, and union is as strong and sweet and since you have been lately pleased to call me to some public service and my soul hath been long musing how I might bring water to quench, and not oil or fluid to the flame. I am now humbly bold to beseech you, by all

[64] *Ibid.* pp. 321 ff.
[65] *Ibid.* Letter: *To the Town of Providence*, p. 265 f.
[66] R I H S P., Vol. 8, pp. 157 ff, 160.

those comforts of earth and heaven which a placable and peaceable spirit will bring you, and by all those dreadful alarms and warnings, either amongst ourselves, in deaths and sicknesses, or abroad in the raging calamities of the sword, death and pestilence; I say, I humbly and earnestly beseech you to be willing to be pacifiable, willing to be reconcilable, willing to be sociable, and to listen to the (I hope not unreasonable) motion following: To try out matters by disputes and writings, is sometimes endless; to try out arguments by arms and swords, is cruel and merciless; to trouble the state and Lords of England, is most unreasonable, most chargeable; to trouble our neighbors of the other colonies, seems neither safe nor honorable. Methinks, dear friends, the colony now looks with the torn face of two parties, and that the greater number of Portsmouth, with other loving friends adhering to them, appear as one grieved party; the other three towns, or greater part of them, appear to be another: Let each party choose and nominate three . . . let authority be given to them to examine every public difference, grievance and obstruction of justice, peace and common safety: let them, by one final sentence of all or a greater part of them, end all, and set the whole into an unanimous posture and order, and let them set a censure upon any that shall oppose their sentence. One log without your gentle help, I cannot stir; it is this: How shall the minds of the towns be known? How shall the persons chosen be called: Time and place appointed in any expedition: For myself I can thankfully embrace the help of Mr. Coddington or Mr. Clarke, joined or apart, but how many are there who will attend, (as our distempers are) to neither: It is, gentlemen in the power of the body to require the help of any of her members, and both King and Parliament plead, that in extraordinary cases they have been forced to extraordinary ways of common safety."[67]

Such shrewd and politic pleas were usually able to secure an adjustment of differences between individuals and between communities.

Impartial service to the people who compose it, Williams considered the untiring duty of the state. The civil machinery of the state is, indeed, nothing more than a corporate organization[68] for public service and need, in which every citizen is a member with interests to protect and advance. This idea is resident in such terms as: common peace, common safety, common welfare, common credit, public good, preservation of peace and order, common peace and subsistence, common peace and liberty, derivative and agent, eyes and hands and instrument, and minister

---

[67] Letter: *To the Town of Providence*, N C P., Vol. VI, pp. 149 ff. Compare, Duguit: *Law in the Modern State;* Laski: *A Grammar of Politics.*
[68] *Bloudy Tenent of Persecution,* N C P., Vol. III, pp. 72 ff. Compare also Vols. IV and VI.

and servant. In his letter to Providence, in 1651, he emphasizes the public service in settlement of controversies, care of orphans, widows, the poor and the insane; in a letter, in 1667, he encourages the building of roads and bridges.[69]   At other times, he requests the regulation of trade, commerce, industry, the liquor traffic with the Indians and the citizens, and the protection of cattle from wild beasts.   This is indeed a diverse regulative service for the civil state to achieve.

As a public service to carry out the purpose of the state, the government, according to Williams, must be as flexible and variable as the circumstances and the nature of the times demand. The sensitiveness of the civil machinery to public need is assured through annual elections of all officers and the ability of the people to repeal any portion of the laws or the constitution itself that no longer serves the good of the whole.   Such a system of government guarantees efficient service and quick relief. It seldom, if ever, in the case of Rhode Island, resulted in rash or tyrannical legislation.   Williams recognized and encouraged change in the scope of the state action necessary to meet the new conditions as they arise: "Hence in many former changes of estates. . . the childrens work hath been to tumble down their fathers buildings.   Nor can your most prudent Heads," he informs Parliament, "and potent Hands possibly erect that Fabrick which the next Age (it may be the next Parliament) may not tumble down.[70]. . . Yet, I cannot but expect changes," he writes to Winthrop, "yet dare I not despise a liberty. . . if for mine own or others peace."   With such a variable "Fabrick" of government, the acts of the state can be shaped "with effectual endeavour for true public good."[71]

The highest end and purpose of the state as set forth by Roger Williams grows out of his concept of its origin, nature and necessity, and the nature and essence of its sovereignty. Since the state is natural, humane and civil; and its supreme power is lodged perpetually and inalienably in the body of people, its proper object in operation cannot be otherwise than civil and humane.   In the state he located the means for carrying out

---

[69] N C P., Vol. VI, pp. 206 ff, 324 f.
[70] Ibid, Vol. IV, p. 12, in Preface to Parliament.
[71] Ibid, Vol. VI, Letters: To Winthrop, 1636, p. 5; To John Winthrop, p. 315.   To the Town of Warwick, 1666, R I H S P., Vol. 8, p. 154.

the final cause of the individual in the new society that he founded. In order to steer the colony of Rhode Island toward the goal which he set for it to achieve, Williams continually stressed the salient principles by which it could attain its ultimate purpose. (1) The purpose of the state is the common well-being and safety of a people in their bodies and goods. (2) The end of the church is spiritual, and separate and distinct from that of the state which must, however, permit the church and protect it in civil things. (3) The state creates a civil government, indirectly as an ordinance of God, whose proper end is well to administer the commonwealth so as to preserve the peace and welfare of the state. (4) In the creation of the civil state, certain natural individual rights are given over by man and replaced by lawful civil rights and liberties which limit to some extent the freedom of individual action. (5) While civil liberty restrains individual action in society, it also sets limits to state interference with certain fundamental individual rights contained in the term "temporal and soul liberties." (6) In this new society, state authority, instead of being antagonistic, enlarges the freedom of action of the individual members and fosters political, social and individual liberty. (7) The means by which the state achieves its purpose is shaped by the knowledge and experience gained through its administrative organs. The means to the end, therefore, become variable and experimental. (8) Since the end of the state in operation is civil and humane, the chief functions are no longer war, police and justice; but the chief functions become justice, correction, regulation and arbitration in the effort to evaluate and adjust the more complex individual and public interests and differences. In the new social structure erected by Williams, public welfare and service are made the real, practical and necessary civil functions to assure the highest end of human existence in civil society.

PART 3

A SOCIAL EXPERIMENT IN CIVIL LIBERTY

The state is universal in its object and significance—the "preservation of Mankind, in civill order and peace."[73] After the founding of his colony, Roger Williams held steadfastly to the civil and humane purpose underlying the new social experiment. Although his social principles were never formulated into a system of political theory as in the case of men like Hooker, Grotius and Hobbes, yet they were clear-cut and definite to him. The state is entirely distinct from and independent of religion, for he held that "the roots and foundations of all common societie in the world"[74] are humane, natural and civil. All states, therefore, have equal rights in international relations, and their purposes must ultimately harmonize because of their common source and nature. But of equal importance is the harmony of the individual men within each state. Like that of the members of the society of states, the members of a state have ultimately and should actually possess equal civil rights and duties. The principles of civil liberty, for which he unflaggingly struggled, are frequently set forth in his letters to his friends and the colony. Political and individual liberty are both contained in his concept of civil liberty through law and order; civil liberty is to be substituted for license; religious liberty is guaranteed to each individual by the very origin, nature and object of the state as distinct from the church; economic liberty is an essential element of true civil liberty—"liberty and equality in land and government." Inseparably connected with civil liberty is the right of "really free" disputes, debates, writing, printing, and the like, and the search after truth; and for the complete fulfilment of it, the state must act from the principles of humanity and love, and common peace, safety and credit. Without the public supervision of internal improvement, trade, commerce, work of mercy and general welfare, full civil liberty is not attainable. But to guarantee the full exercise and privileges of this liberty to the individual, the state must be unhampered in its external relations. And so, to achieve the ideal purpose of any state in New Eng-

---

[73] *Bloudy Tenent of Persecution,* N C P., Vol. III, p. 398.
[74] *Ibid,* p. 415.

142

land, a society of states is necessary for mutual support and trade, and the advancement of mankind in peace and order.[75] When the state guarantees to all the privilege of arbitration, regulation, and adjustment of individual and common interests and differences, both in internal and interstate affairs, it fulfils its purpose to the individual, the society, and the society of states.

But the heartless school of experience discovered to Roger Williams that the ultimate purpose of the state is seldom, if ever, attained in actual practice. He was never incurably optimistic about the continuing success of his social experiment; nor did he forget that those who should be most magnanimous seldom act except "for the filling of their *paunches*." Not infrequently does he turn aside for the purpose of making some pertinent reference to the motives and factors that influence the actions of political and religious leaders. "It is one thing," he states in reference to the difference between the "ought to be" and the actual, "what persons are in *fact* and *practice;* another what they ought to be by *right* and *office*[76]. . . wise men used to enquire, what Motives, what Occasions, what Snares, what temptations were there which moved, which drew, which allured, etc. . . . Surely, Sir," Williams wrote to John Endicott, "the baits, the temptations, the snares laid to catch you were not few, nor common. . . . Sir, it is no small offer, the choice and applause and rule over so many towns, so many holy, so many wise, in such a holy way as you believe you are in: To say nothing of strong drinks and wines, the fat and sweet of this and other lands."[77] On numerous occasions Williams accused John Cotton of having bartered liberal principles of church and state for the flesh-pots of New England: "The *Martyrs* and *Witnes* of *Jesus* in all *Ages,* and the *cry* of the *Soules* under the *Altar*, may bring againe to his *Remembrance,* if *New Englands peace, profit, pleasure,* and *Honour,* have lulled him into *Forgetfulnesse* of the *principles* of the Lord *Jesus Christ.*"[78] But it is seldom that Williams becomes personal in his condemnation. More often his references to the motives that influence men in authority are of general ap‧ plication—"and yet to what other end have and doe, ordinarily,

[75] N C P., Vol. VI. pp. 262 f, 296, 374, 206, 333, 395; Vol. III, pp. 354 ff. R I C R., Vols. I and II. R I H S P., Vol. 8, pp. 147 ff.
[76] *Bloudy Tenent of Persecution,* N C P., Vol. III, p. 238.
[77] Letter: *To John Endicott,* N C P., Vol. VI, pp. 222 f.
[78] *Bloudy Tenent Yet More Bloody,* N C P., Vol. IV, p. 409.

Kings of the *Earth* use their *power* and *authority* over the *Bodies* and *Goods* of their Subjects, but for the filling of their *paunches* like *Wolves* or *Lions,* never pacified unless the peoples *bodies, goods,* and *Souls* be sacrificed to their *God-belly* and their owne *Gods* of *profit, honour, pleasure, etc.*"[79]   Prosperity and desire for pleasures and honor actuating men endowed with civil power are a continual menace to the actual attainment of the true purpose of the state, for "he that is in a pleasant *Bed* and *Dreame,* though he talke idly and insensibly, yet is loath to be awakened."[80]   History and his own experiences in old England and the New England colonies vividly impressed upon him that *"Liberty of searching out Truth* [is] *hardly got,* and *as hardly kept."*[81]

Roger Williams deliberately rejected any special form of civil government or civil action for the carrying out of the general principles upon which he built his civil state.   For new conditions and tendencies, he devised new means and appropriate action.   Hence, his apparent inconsistencies and the charge by his contemporaries that he was "an impracticable person, presumptuous, turbulent, and even seditious"—a man with a "windmill" in his head.   In each particular controversy he had, however, a definite purpose: "For I design," he wrote to Mason, "a civil, a humane and political medicine, which, if the God of Heaven please to bless, you will find it effectual to all the ends I have proposed. . . ."[82]   He could, indeed, be of no particular self-interested political group in the building of the new state, for his interests and sympathies in affairs of state were only humane and civil.

For the principles of civil rights and liberties, Williams dared and suffered ignominy, vilification, loss of friends, home, and the comforts of civilization.   For them he dared all that men usually hold most dear and priceless—even life itself.   With them he founded a state, unsurpassed before or since in the measure of economic, political, and individual liberty secured to all its citizens.   With these as a basis, he erected a civil government to act in the best interests of the people and community.   Because the application of these principles depended on peaceful inter-

[79] *Ibid,* p. 402. Tyler: *History of American Literature,* p. 143.
[80] *Ibid,* p. 403.
[81] *Ibid,* p. 30.
[82] Letter: *To Major Mason,* N C P., Vol. IV, p. 350.

state relations, he saved the other colonies, in return for the ignominy and vilification heaped upon him, from annihilation by an
impending Indian confederacy. Under these principles in actual
practice, Rhode Island enjoyed, he claimed, "such Peace, such
Security, such Liberties of Soule and Body as were never enjoyed by any English men, nor any in the World I have heard
of."[83]

In his theory of state and the practice of it, Williams belonged to no particular group of political thinkers. In his political thought, as in his religious, he remained until the end of life
a Searcher and Seeker after ultimate Truth. For this reason,
he was misunderstood by the leaders of the other New England
colonies. Their middle class minds and outlook made the leaders
of the other colonies simply incapable of grasping significant
world-moving "truths." As a true Seeker, he was "never quiet
settled on all questions in the Universe; at almost every moment
on the watch for some new idea about that time expected to heave
into sight; never able by the ordinary means of intellectual stag-
nation to win for himself in his life-time the bastard glory of
doctrinal consistency; professing many things by turn"[84] so
that no one was ever able at any time to know what his position
on any question was going to be. In this he was fortunate. For,
because of it, he was able to act as arbiter in the many local
problems of government and social adjustment. Although cur-
ried for favor and backing by each, party, he adroitly kept in the
background until he had decided what would conduce to the highest common interests and satisfaction. With his decision made,
he would at times, to their utter astonishment, vigorously and
vehemently support his most bitter former opponent. But, whatever he decided as the most expedient thing to do, he always
entered the controversy zealously and stubbornly determined to
succeed. His services were eagerly sought by the other colonies
in their disputes with the Indians; while his pleas for moderation
and mercy to the vanquished foe were as eagerly ignored. Even
his seeking and examining attitude aroused much animosity
toward his radical ideas and conclusions, his unyielding and uncompromising zeal for justice and truth, as he saw it, made him
one of the most influential men of his age. But Williams could
identify himself with no particular political group, because civil
liberty demands continual experiment and readjustment in social
life. Mankind, the good of humanity, was his only passion.

[83] R I H S P., Vol. VIII, p. 153.
[84] Tyler: *History of American Literature*, p. 141.

VI

ACTIVITIES OF THE STATE

PART 1
VIEWS OF THE SEVENTEENTH CENTURY

English political theory of the seventeenth century agreed in separating the chief functions of the state.[1] But with regard to the scope of these functions, the political thinkers divided into two main camps. The one group held that the chief functions of the state are those of law and order. It sanctioned no ideas of communism or social equality, and definitely repudiated the republican doctrine of the century. Among the leaders of this group were Hobbes, Locke, Filmer, James I, and Halifax,[2] of which Hobbes and Locke may be considered as representative. According to Hobbes' *Leviathan*, the sovereignty is established to furnish protection to its citizens. The obligation of the citizens ceases when the sovereign fails to fulfil this function. A paternalistic government is rejected. And the state is merely a necessary evil, supreme in spiritual and temporal affairs. According to Locke,[3] to preserve life, liberty and property is the chief function of the state. But it can only act within a specified and limited sphere. Its powers, instead of being invested in one individual, rest permanently in the community as a whole. In the contract, the state receives the power to execute the natural law between man and man, but has no power over men's other natural rights. Its chief purpose is the preservation of social and civil order. The executive and judiciary, in his theory, are dependent on the lawmaking body. In the utilitarian happiness of its citizens by maintaining law and order, according to this group, lies the chief function of the state.

Under republicanism may be included most of the opposing liberal group of political writers and thinkers of the seventeenth century.[4] In addition to preserving law and order within itself and regulating its affairs with other nations, the state, they postu-

---

[1] Gettell: *History of Political Thought*, pp. 194-229. Dunning: *Political Theories: Luther to Montesquieu.*

[2] Gooch: *Political Thought from Bacon to Halifax.*

[3] *On Civil Government.*

[4] Dunning: *Political Theories: Luther to Montesquieu.*

lated, is also responsible for the general welfare of its members. The extent and effect of these functions, enunciated by them, ranged from the communism of the Army to the extreme individualism of Milton. A republican like Harrington[5] considered the chief function of the state to be that of balancing the economic forces within itself for the general welfare. To do this, a system of universal and compulsory education should be carried on by the state. But above all else, it must maintain civil stability by economic means. In the *Tenure of Kings and Magistrates,* Milton opposed government restriction and supervision and became one of the earliest prophets of nineteenth century individualism. By delegating and limiting the powers of state, he made the executive an agent of the people, and by the same means restricted the state's action to police and protection and the execution of justice between man and man. In the Puritan Commonwealth, the political ideas were largely shaped by the influence of Roger Williams;[6] his *Bloudy Tenent* represents the more extreme and rationalistic tendencies of the Levellers.[7] It is essentially the mouthpiece of the Independents against the Presbyterians; and the full implication of Williams' theory is revealed by the political revolution of the Army in 1647-48. Cromwell and Ireton were, however, more conservative, believing that manhood suffrage[8] would endanger property. The radical followers of Roger Williams' theory demanded their natural rights of civil and social equality, the freedom of conscience and expression. These rights were to be assured to the citizens through limiting the essential functions of the state and widening its non-essential functions, by law.[9] The republican group demanded a re-evaluation of the functions of the state in order to guarantee man's natural right to political and civil freedom.

And it was not without good reason that the most radical men both in church and state in England looked to Roger Williams for inspiration, and even guidance. His rationalism and experimental attitude were the harbingers of a new age in political

---

[5] *The Commonwealth of Oceana.*

[6] Dunning: *Political Theories: Luther to Montesquieu,* p. 234. Gettell: History of Political Thought, p. 211.

[7] Gooch: *Democratic Ideas,* pp. 141, 200.

[8] Dunning: *Political Theories: Luther to Montesquieu.*

[9] Wilson: *The State,* pp. 42 ff. Wilson divided the functions of the state into the Constituent, those necessary for state existence, and the Ministrant, those not necessary for state existence but for general welfare.

thought and practice. His ideas were also the heralds of a new religious and political attitude within the church. Indeed, Williams was a strong "voice crying in the wilderness" proclaiming a new age in the structure and internal relationships of civil society.

Although Williams presented few political ideas that were entirely new in the field of political speculation, he gave the oft-repeated ideas a new and practical setting. The radical thinkers of the Middle Ages postulated in theory a state and society much like that erected by Williams; Aristotle and the ancients practised much of it, but from the viewpoint of benefit to the state, instead of the individual.[10] Martin Luther[11] re-emphasized the ideas in a reformation background; but the political, economic and social forces that had at the first aided him, now, in turn, defeated him and fostered a despotic nationalism. Evidently a new setting was needed for the new political practices. The American wilderness and the intelligent, self-reliant fellow-colonists provided Williams with the necessary preparation and setting for this new state with "such unheard of Liberties." Rhode Island, through Williams' far-seeing statesmanship, came to be the first federal state based on the "Rule of Law," in which the chief functions were no longer police and military but the general welfare of and public service to the people. It was the first state to provide, for a time at least, a complete "free-citizenship" with religious, political and economic freedom and equality. To Roger Williams belongs the credit of having first established and set forth more fully than any other man before the republicans of the eighteenth century, the political principles of "the Rights of Man and the Individual."[12]

---

[10] Gierke: *Political Theories of the Middle Ages*, pp. 62 ff, 109 ff, discusses the medieval conceptions of state functions that have since been accepted in liberal state policies.

[11] Waring: *Political Theories of Martin Luther*. The chapters on the functions and limits of the state.

[12] Jellinek: *Declaration of the Rights of Man and of Citizens*. Jellinek considers Roger Williams as the forerunner of eighteenth century republicanism.

WILLIAMS' ATTITUDE TOWARDS STATE ACTIVITIES

In order to set forth clearly Williams' position on the powers and activities of the state, it is requisite that a study be made of his theory together with the practices of Rhode Island colony up to the end of his life. These activities, according to Williams, are of three kinds and all of them essential.[13] The state must defend itself against external aggression by agreements and arms; it must prevent internal encroachment upon the individual, and assure him religious, political and economic freedom and equality; and it must exercise directing and restraining powers for public ends. The functions both within and without the state were in his scheme of things essentially humane and civil. Force is to be used only as a last resort; for the state can, he held, force obedience in civil things.[14] But this force is merely a means to an end, namely, to conserve the *"Bodies* and *Goods"* of the people and the "peace and good of mankind" at large. The agent of the people is the civil government created through a commission which specifies and limits its scope of action.[15] To meet the demand of the times, the commission, and therefore the action of the agent, is subject to continual modification by the sovereign people. Nothing in the state is rigid—neither state, constitution, laws, nor civil government. Yet all are protected in their civil operations because "in civil things nothing is lawful but what is according to law and order."[16]

The system of federalism of the colony inaugurated by the Constitution of 1647 was indeed epoch making.[17] It divided the powers of the state into central and local activities or governments, on the basis of general or merely local concern. For administering the general functions of the state, the framers of the constitution created the legislative, executive and judicial de-

---

[13] Wilson: *The State*, pp. 42 ff. He divided the functions into the constituent or essential and ministrant or non-essential. Many of the contemporary political writers follow this division pedantically.

[14] *Bloody Tenent Yet More Bloody*, N C P., Vol. IV, pp. 313, 80. "The *civil state* may bring into *order*, make *orders*, preserve in *civil order* all its members." p. 313.

[15] *Bloudy Tenent of Persecution*, N C P., Vol. III, pp. 249, 397, 116; *Letters*, N C P., Vol. VI., p. 401 f.

[16] *Cottons Letter Examined*, N C P., Vol. I, p. 48.

[17] R I C R., Vol. I, p. 147.

partments of the central government. This central government was made the agent of the people to carry out the will of the major part of them. A code of regulations fixed the individual rights, and restricted and limited the activities of the central government. The executive functions were placed in a "President" for the central government, and four "Assistants," one for each Town and selected by it. In the first part of its sitting, the General Court was to act as the legislative body of the government. After the legislative work was finished, the General Court converted itself into a judicial court to try cases of general concern. The Court of Justice was a court of trial only, of the circuit type with trial by jury. For foreign commerce, the maritime code was the generally accepted "Code of Cleron." Both the government and officials were agents of the state directly responsible to the sovereign people, and subject to them. By means of a veto in the hands of the people in the form of a referendum and recall[18] for all actions of the government and officers, civil liberty was guaranteed to the members of the state. Because of a simple system of check and balance in the form of the referendum affecting all laws, the constitution and the governmental machinery, the state became a pliant and serviceable public corporation. The Assembly, or Representative General Court, was the chief regulating organ of the people. All the other departments or agencies of the government were subject to its orders.[19] With frequent elections and the referendum, reform became simple, quick, and effective; and by means of these two checks the founders of the civil government cleverly avoided the main cause for rebellion. The danger of tyranny was largely eliminated by not having an armed force in the hands of the central government to apply military pressure for private or class interests. The central government of the federal state of Rhode Island was a regulating and correcting and harmonizing agency to handle those internal and external affairs of the state that affected the general welfare and public interests.

Particularism was especially prominent in this federal system. Each town had full powers in definite home, or local, concerns.

---

[18] *Ibid,* Vol. I, pp. 151 (1647), 147 ff, 229 (1650). N C P., Vol. III, pp. 378, 398.

[19] *Ibid,* pp. 228 f (1650), 236 (1651).

To the local units—for each town had lost its sovereignty[20] upon the formation of the Constitution of 1647—were delegated the affairs that did not affect the common well-being of the whole. The administrative nature of these units in relation to the central state is cearly stated in the Charter of Civil Incorporation to the Town of Providence, in 1649: "Whereas the said towns of Providence, Portsmouth, Newport and Warwick are far remote from each other, whereas by so often and free intercourse of help, in deciding the differences and trying of causes and the like, cannot easilie and at all times be had and procured of that kind is requisite; therefore, upon the petition and humble request of the freemen . . . we the said Assembly, having duly weighed and seriously considered the premises, and being willing and ready to provide for ease and libertie of the people, have thought fit, and by the authoritie aforesaid, and by those present, do give, grant and confirm . . . a free and absolute charter of civill incorporation and government . . . together with full authoritie to governe and rule themselves, and such others as shall hereafter inhabit within any part of the said Plantation, by such a form of civill government, as by voluntarie consent of all, or the greater part of them, shall be found most suitable unto their estate and condition; and to that end, to make and ordaine such civill orders and constitutions, to inflict such punishments upon aggressors, and for execution thereof, and . . . so to place and displace officers of justice, as they or the greater part of them shall, by one consent, agree unto. Provided, nevertheless, that said lawes, constitutions and punishments, for the civill government of the said Plantation, be comformable to the lawes of England, so far as the nature and constitution of the place will admit, yet, always reserving to the aforesaid Generall Assemblie power and authoritie so to dispose the generall governmente of that plantation as it stands in reference to the rest of the plantations, as they shall conceive, from time to time, most conducing to the generall good of the said plantations."[21] In addition each town had its own trained militia, which it controlled and supported with only the restriction that it was by permission from the central government.[22]

---

[20] *Ante,* Chapter III, pt. II. These pioneers were at least quite intelligent and clear-sighted. In fact, they did not maintain the principle of "State's Rights," or the sovereignty of the administrative units, when such rights did not actually exist.

[21] R I C R., Vol. I, pp. 214 ff.

[22] *Ibid,* (1647), p. 153 f. The central government had no military organization of its own.

That the individual sovereign bodies which went to make up the federal state of Rhode Island lost their sovereignty by the formation of the Union of Towns was often reiterated by the General Assembly. The position of the assembly, which was that of the major portion of the citizens, was upheld by Roger Williams in theory and practice. One act by the assembly will make their position on the question of the sovereignty of the state through the central government clear: "It is ordered, that noe law or order appoynted and ordayned by ye generall or publicke authoritie of this Colonie, shall be any ways obstructed or neglected under the pretence of any authoritie of any of ye towne charters; but that ye general authoritie shall have it done and placed according to law in all the wayes."[23]

In the legislative assembly created by the constitution were placed the powers of interpreting the laws and the provisions of the constitution.[24] The first instance of the application of the principle of interpretation will suffice: "And it is further ordered, that, whereas in the engagement of ye Officers of State, there is a clause at the latter end thereof, vidg't, 'according to ye best of your understanding'." To avoid further confusion, the assembly "interprets their meaning to be that they are not, or shall not vary from the Letter of their Commission by any equivocall expositions." The assembly also was given the right to depose the "President" for misconduct or departure from the colony and to appoint a successor. "That if said President elect shall be found Guilty or being cleared of the said charges, refuse the place, [another] shall be invested in his place. . . . That if at any time hereafter, he that is made President shall happen to depart the Colony or Province into another Colony, or into Old England, or if ye said President shall dye; then the Generall Assistant of that Towne where the President was chosen . . . until the said President's returne, or a new be chosen at ye next General Court of Election ensuing."[25]

The General Court of Trial, on the other hand, unlike the Supreme Court of the United States, must apply itself only to the trial of specified civil and criminal offenses. It can undertake

---

[23] *Ibid*, (1656), p. 333. Roger Williams was president of the colony at this time.
[24] Compare with that of the United States, in which the Supreme Court decides all questions of constitutionality. Note also the English system.
[25] R I C R., Vol. I, (1648), pp. 210 f.

only "the Public Administration of Justice according to the Lawes agreed upon and established throwout the Whole Colonie."[26]   It is merely an agency of the whole colony to apply the constitution and laws to particular cases.   The local courts of justice are under the special supervision of the local or town governments and are distinct courts, from which appeals may, however, be made to the General Court of the colony.

Upon the functions of the General Court of Trial were placed definite limits.   The court may not even invade a certain restricted field of justice within the scope of the local unit, unless by request of that unit.   "It is further agreed, that these Colonie Courts of Tryall, shall appertaine the Tryall of such Crimes as may hazard Life, Limbe, Disfranchisement or Banishment; and such Trespasses, Debts, and differences (as by the Common Council eyther of Towne or Townes shall be judged too weightie for a more private determining).   Also, such matters of difference as fall out between Towne and Towne, or between parties dwelling in two Townes more remote, or in case of an arrest of a man belonging to a neighbor Colonie, or in cases of great importance; also, attaints of Inquests, and Tryalls of Perjurie, and finally all matters as are not referred, by any charter or order, unto any Towne apart, or to the Island, or two Townes joyntlie."[27]   Outside the action of the Court there remains a wide field of individual and community interests that may conflict, which are to be adjusted without the courts by arbitration and compromise.

The executive is a responsible officer of the state.[28]   To John Endicott, Williams wrote: "I stand accountable to our Generall Court and His Highness if I suffer such crimes unquestioned before my face."[29]   The civil magistrate, he frequently emphasized "is bound to preserve the *civill* peace and quiet of the place and people under him, he is bound to suffer no man to break the *Civill Peace*, by laying hands of violence upon any.[30]

In the Constitution of 1647, the executive, with other civil officials, is held directly responsible for carrying out the work delegated to him "nor though he be lawfully called and con-

---

[26] *Ibid,* (1647), pp. 191 f.
[27] *Ibid,* p. 191.   While "finally all matters" may seem a broad statement, it is, however, limited by numerous clauses and conditions not quoted here.
[28] N C P., Vol. III, Chapters 92-132.
[29] R I H S P., Vol. 8, p. 146 (1656).
[30] *Bloudy Tenent of Persecution,* N C P., Vol. III, p. 132.

firmed, presume to doe more or less than those that had power to call him, or did authorize him to do."[31]

In order to continue its existence with some degree of permanency, the state must secure civil order and provide for the enforcement of its laws. But civil laws Williams held to be beneficial in purpose and effect, and agreeable to all law-abiding members of the state. "Law is made or brought to light, not for the righteous, who is a Law unto himself, but for the lawless and disobedient in General but more particular for" such offenders as threaten to attack man "in his person, name and estate." I never was "against the righteous use of the civill sword of men or nations,"[32] Williams wrote to the General Court of Massachusetts Bay, in 1654. And in harmony with this admission, to protect his colony, he advocated the building of fortifications for self-defense.[33] His hearty approval was repeatedly given to a war "against offenders of public safety and the good and peace of the *Civill State*."[34] The civil sword of justice is to be used against "robbers, murderers, mutinies, tyrants, adulterers, oppression, sedition, lyers, etc." For no well-ordered state, he reiterated, will suffer or "connive at" such offenders.[35]

But the civil state gives over to the civil government the "common charge of the *Commonwealth* (the peace and safety of the *Towne, State* or *Kingdom*)." It has abilities to make such civil laws which may concern the "common *rights, peace* and *safety;*" for the life, liberty and property—"*bodies* and *goods*"— of the people are in its keeping.[36] In case of riot or rebellion, it shall "send the Ringleaders or Chiefs to prison, there to remain unto the Court," and when found guilty they are to be "fined as the law hath determined." The death penalty is provided for only six crimes: high treason, murder, manslaughter, witchcraft, burglary (above 14 years), and "burning of houses."[37] Violations

---

[31] R I C R., Vol. I, p. 157. See also *Ante,* Chapters III, pt. II, and V, pt. II.

[32] *Ibid,* pp. 158 f (1647), 293 (1654).

[33] R I H S P., Vol. VIII, p. 161. In King Philip's War, Williams took a personal part in repulsing the Indian attacks.

[34] *Bloudy Tenent of Persecution,* N C P., Vol. III, pp. 108 f.

[35] *Queries,* N C P., Vol. II, p. 26; N C P., Vol. III, pp. 124, 110, and Vol. IV, p. 108.

[36] *Bloudy Tenent of Persecution,* N C P., Vol. III, pp. 128 f, 366, 127, 124. N C P., Vol. IV, p. 161, and Vol. VI, pp. 255, 250.

[37] R I C R., Vol. I, p. 193. Only two death penalties were passed by the Court during Williams' life time, both during Court sessions at Newport in 1671: a Mr. Flounder for murder, and one man for burglary.

of civil peace, though out of conscience, must be punished "according to the *wisdome* of each state, each state is to provide for it selfe even against the *delusions* of hardned *consciences,* in any *attempt* which meerly concerns the civill state or *Commonweale* . . . . And therefore consequently if the World or Civil State ought to be preserved by *Civill Governments* or *Governors*: such scandalous offenders ought not to be tolerated, but supprest according to the wisdome and prudence of the said *Government.*"[38]

Upon the civil government also falls the task of making provisions for keeping the malefactors, offenders and scandalous persons in society in confinement as a safeguard to the general public. For this purpose prisons are to be provided. The General Assembly ordered, in 1648, that each town build and maintain a prison for self-defense, and that for the present the temporary prison at Newport be used by the whole colony. No record is available concerning the treatment of prisoners; but Williams records his disapproval, in a letter to the Bay Coloney, of the customary practice of treating all prisoners with cruelty and inhumanity. Stocks were used to some extent by the colony; and also fines were fixed, for penalties. It was not until 1658 that a prison was finally built at Newport, erected at the expense of and to be used by the whole colony.[39] What the colony did with its prisoners between 1636 and 1658, no records show with the exception of the order made in 1648; but the principle laid down by Williams is accepted, that "against the fear of Evill *practices* the *Wisdome* of the *State* may securely provide; by just *cautions* and *provisos,* as of *Subscribing Civill Engagement;* of *yielding* up their *Arms* . . . according to the *Wisdome* of the *State.* And without such like sufficient *cautions* given, it is not *Civill Justice* to permit justly suspected *persons,* dangerous to the *civill peace,* to abide out of places of *Securitie* and safe *Restraint.*"[40]

In regulating the civil finances, the government is rightly given supreme command. All values and usages of coin and moneys are under the regulating power of the civil state. "Usury," Williams argued, should be permitted, "for the preventing of a

[38] *Bloody Tenent Yet More Bloody,* N C P., Vol. IV, p. 91. *Bloudy Tenent of Persecution,* N C P., Vol. III, pp. 171, 111. N C P., Vol. VI, pp. 278 f.
[39] R I C R., Vol. I, pp. 310 (1653), 391 (1658); see also the Constitution of 1647.
[40] *Bloody Tenent Yet More Bloody,* N C P., Vol. IV, pp. 313 f.

greater evill, in the *civill Body*, as *stealing, robbing, murthering, perishing* of the poore, and the hindrance and step of *commerce* and dealing in the *Commonwealth.*" The finances necessary for the activities of the state machinery are to be obtained through taxation: "It is reasonable," continues Williams, "to expect and demand of such as live within the state a *civill maintenance* of their *civill officers,* and to force it where it is denied." But the state can lay only civil taxes and duties: "The *rewards* and *wages* which people owe for worke, to wit (not *contribution* of the *church,* for any *spirituall* work) but *tribute, toll, Custome,* which are *wages* payable by all sorts of men, *Natives* and *Forreigners,* who enjoy the same benefit of *publick peace* and *commerce* in the *Nation.*"[41] In addition to internal taxes, tax on imports was laid by the government, payable by citizens and foreigners, alike, within the jurisdiction of the colony. The Treasurer of the colony was made the ultimate custodian of all taxes and duties laid by the central government. The "fines, forfeitures, and amercements" were collected by the administrative units if within their corporation, otherwise by the central government. But in all cases, the treasurer "shall give account of in the Generall Assembly."[42]

Whenever it affected the general welfare and public interests, the trading carried on within the colony and with the outside world was regulated by the central government. Dutch and French traders were forbidden to barter with the Indians within Rhode Island territory. The "Lawes of Cleron" were made the basis for trade and justice with foreign vessels and their men. Land purchases from the Indians, as well as all other land transactions, were under civil supervision. All trading in liquors within the colony and with the Indians was strictly regulated by laws. No liquor was to be sold on Sunday, for the sake of public peace. Even the killing of goats and swine within the colony was supervised by the civil authorities.[43] To avoid extortion,

---

[41] *Bloudy Tenent of Persecution,* N C P., Vol. III, p. 169; the consensus of opinion of the seventeenth century was opposed to usury or the charging of interest. John Calvin and the Genevan merchants vigorously defended usury. Pp. 299, 355. N C P., Vol. VI, pp. 401 f. This letter on rates is also important with reference to the right of taxation because of representation.

[42] R I C R., Vol. I, p. 197.

[43] *Ibid,* pp. 152, 279, 151, 418, 435, 147 ff, 430, 307 f, 413, 331, 323; Vol. II, p. 500.

price-fixing was repeatedly resorted to by the Assembly. The prices were set on all necessities of life when conditions required regulation; wheat, pork, beans, peas, corn, venison, goods, peage, labor, all were subject to price regulation by the government. Especially, the price of spiritous liquors was very minutely provided for. No mercantile or commercial transaction that in any way affected the common interests of the whole or the public welfare, was allowed to escape the regulating and correcting hand of the civil government.[44]

The state, through its civil government, is bound to take cognizance of numerous civil matters that affect the religious, economic and civil well-being of the individual members of the new civil society. It must free all races within its civil control from the fetters of slavery. Since Williams held that each individual in organized society possesses *"natural & Civill Rights and Liberties,"*[45] it was only natural that he should condemn every type of slavery. In his opposition to slavery the major portion of the fellow-colonists seconded him. That the Indians captured in the wars, he wrote to Winthrop, be made perpetual slaves was unjust: "but I beseech you well to weigh it after a due time of training up to labor, and restraint they ought not to be set free."[46] In March 1675/6, Rhode Island decreed that "no Indian in this colony be a slave but only to pay their debts, or for their bringing up, or courtesy they have received, or to performe covenant, as if they had been countreymen not in war."[47] The only labor service that man or civil state may rightly exact, as set forth by both Williams in his writings and his fellow colonists with him in civil law, from any human being in civil life is a sort of apprenticeship according to contract or temporary employment for bringing up or payment of something owed.

In the mid-seventeenth century no state or nation took a more enlightened attitude against the institution of slavery than that of the Providence plantations. An act by Warwick and Providence, in 1652, put negroes, Indians, and whites on the same civil

---

[44] *Ibid,* pp. 481, 496, 217. N C P., Vol. III, p. 108. For an idea of the regulating action of this government see R I C R., Vols. I and II.
[45] *Bloody Tenent Yet More Bloody,* N C P., Vol. IV, p. 365.
[46] Letter: *To Winthrop* (1637) N C P., Vol. VI, pp. 54 f. Richman: *Rhode Island,* p. 40. Hall: *Roger Williams,* p. 128.
[47] Updike: *History of Narragansett Church,* p. 171. R I H S P., Vol. II, pp. 113 ff.

basis: "Whereas, there is a common course practised amongst English men to buy negers, to that end they may have for service or slaves forever; for the preventing of such practices amongst us, let it be ordered, that no blacke mankind or white being forced by covenant bond, or otherwise, to serve any man or his assighnes longer than ten years or untill they come to bee twentie four yeares of age, if they be taken in under fourteen, from the time of their coming within the liberties of this Colonie. And at the end of the terme of ten yeares to sett them free, as the manner is with English servants."[48] The history of slavery in Rhode Island from 1636 to 1676 is the history of the decay of this institution. Anti-slavery sentiment and agitation in America may be traced back to the time of Roger Williams, the founder of the colony. "The humane effect of Roger Williams and John Eliot to abate the seventy years of judgment against the captives, and mitigate the horrors of slavery"[49] in New England are worthy to be ranked among the noblest efforts in the history of man for complete individual liberty.

In the economic freedom and welfare of its members, the civil government is indeed to be vitally concerned. Williams ranks among the foremost men of his time in the advocacy of economic as well as religious and civil freedom of man. In 1638, in the second memorandum, he offered, some historians think under compulsion from his fellow settlers, equality in all things in these words: "I Roger Williams. . . do freely and fully pass grant and make over equal rights and power of enjoying and disposing the same ground and lands." This economic equality had been preceded by grants of civil and political equality and spiritual freedom.[50] The land was equally divided among the families; and specified portions were alloted to each new-comer upon the payment of a definite stipend. In a letter to Governor Hinckley, in 1679, Williams explains how political equality grew out of the very nature of the conditions of colonial life: "These 25 acre men encreasing the purchasers calld upon them to do service as well as themselves to Towne and Countrey they did so, and thereby came the priviledge of equall ordering of all Towne Af-

---

[48] R I C R., Vol. I, p. 243.
[49] R I H S P., Vol. 2, pp. 113 ff.
[50] R I C R., Vol. I, (1638) pp. 19 f, (1636) 14. N C P., Vol. VI, p. 5; see Vols. I-VI.

faires and equally paid (to a peny) to the later Purchase."[51]
His zeal for full and unrestricted equality in the colony was in
1650, he said, held against him as a weakness: "I have been
charged with folly for that freedom and libertie which I have
always stood for; I say libertie and equalitie, both in land and
government."[52]

The powers of the civil government in religious matters, Williams considered in no respect unlike that in any other society or
corporation within its jurisdiction. The church is merely a voluntary combination or corporation like that of the merchants or
traders or physicians. Interference by the government in church
affairs is permissible only when *"Evill* against the *Civill State"* is
done which is "punishable by that *civil sword* of his, as an *in-
civilitie disorder,* or breach of the *civill order, peace,* and *civility,*
unto which all the Inhabitants of a *City, Towne,* or *Kingdom*
oblige themselves." No civil pressure can be brought for the payment of church duties, for that is of a spiritual nature.[53] If
at any time a citizen interferes with the worship of another, he
is to be disenfranchised "for restraining the liberty of conscience."[54] Although laws concerning religion may be either religious or civil, the state can make only such laws as concern the
civil aspects of the religious associations—"Concerning only the
bodies and *goods.*[55] . . . When the Church offend against the Civill
peace of the State, by wronging the bodies and goods of any, the
Magistrate bears not the sword in vain. Ro. 13."[56] It is only
with the second Table of the laws of Moses that the civil state is
concerned. But, on the other hand, the *"Magistrate* should encourage and countenance the *Church,* yea and protect the persons
of the *Church* from violence, disturbances, etc." He sums up
his position on the function of the state in matters of the church
by declaring that the civil power in the church is "only a humane
and Civill *operation."* If the civil officials approve of the church,
they ought to give approbation, submission, and protection; if they

[51] R I H S P., Vol. 8, p. 158.

[52] R I C R., Vol. I, p. 351.

[53] *Bloudy Tenent of Persecution,* N C P., Vol. III, pp. 73 f, 163, 194 ff.
N C P, Vol. IV, p. 74.

[54] R I C R., Vol. I, p. 14. Case of Verein. Winthrop: *Journal,* Vol.
I, 1636-7.

[55] *Bloudy Tenent of Persecution,* N C P., Vol. III, p. 252.

[56] *Bloody Tenent Yet More Bloody,* N C P., Vol. IV, pp. 80, 145.

consider the church false or pagan, they ought to give it permission and protection.[57]

Marriage is essentially a civil institution, and has its basis in the nature of things.[58] In this respect Williams and his colony were in agreement with Martin Luther. The church has no authority in the institution of marriage. The Constitution of 1647 states: "It is agreed, and ordered by this present Assembly, for the preventing of many evills and mischiefs that may follow thereon, that no contract or agreement between a Man and Wife, shall be owned henceforth threwout the Whole Colonie as a lawfull marriage" or their children as legitimate "but such as are, in the first place, with the parents, then orderly published. . . and lastly confirmed before the head officer of the Towne." Divorce to be legal must be "sued for, by the party grieved" and only for "Adulterie; and that to be proved by the party grieved, eyther by Man against Woman, or the Woman against the Man." But divorce is not granted for self-accusation; the party must "sue to the Generall Assembly for divorce; then it being so granted each party shall be [as] free from each other as they were before they came together."[59]

That the state should care for the poor and give charity to the incapable was made an essential function of the government. This function was considered vital enough to be included in the fundamental law of the land. "It is agreed and ordered. . . that each Towne shall provide carefully for the relief of the poore, to maintayne the impotent, and to employ the able, and shall appoint an overseer for the same purpose."[60] In a letter to the town of Providence, Williams presents "in writing five requests. The first four concern either living and dead amongst us; the fifth, concerns myself."[61] The first four requests concern the care of and aid to orphans, widows, and the management of the estate of an incompetent widow.[62] The Colony passed an act in 1650[63] that any one "not worth five pounds" is to be aided "un-

[57] *Bloudy Tenent of Persecution,* N C P., Vol. III, pp. 280, 372 f.
[58] *Bloody Tenent Yet More Bloody,* N C P., Vol. IV, pp. 282 f. *The Hireling Ministry,* p. 179.
[59] R I C R., Vol. I, pp. 187, 231.
[60] *Ibid,* 148. The Constitution of 1647.
[61] Letter: *To the Town of Providence,* N C P., Vol. VI, pp. 206 ff.
[62] While in London, in 1643-44 and in 1652, Williams devoted much time to works of mercy in and around London. N C P., Vol. IV, p. 103.
[63] R I C R., Vol. I, p. 227.

der the title of form *a pauperis.*" The civil state is in duty bound
to provide for its citizens—the widows, dependent children, poor,
impotent and incapable—whenever they are in need, and helpless
to provide for themselves.

At no time in his writings did Williams make a definite
statement for or against the use of public funds for education.
Unfortunately, Rhode Island did not provide actual facilities for
education until some time after 1670.[64] Williams, however, openly condemned the universities of his day as nurseries for the
clergy—"All that I bear witness against, is the counterfeiting and
sacrilegious arrogating of the titles and rights of Gods, Saints
and Churches." According to the Testament of Christ Jesus "they
will be found none of Christs, and that in many respects."[65]
Tongues are "attainable out of Oxford and Cambridge," exclaimed
Williams, and besides, the universities are a place for the *"laze
and Monkish"* life.[66]

On the other hand, he disclaimed any prejudice against learning and education: "I heartily acknowledge that among all the
outward Gifts of God, humane learning and the knowledge of
Languages and good Arts, are excellent and excell other outward gifts, as far as light excells darkness. And therefore that
schools of humane learning, ought to be maintained, in a due way
and cherished." Again he says—"Far be it from me to derogate
from that honorable civility of training up of Youth in Language
and humane learning.[67] . . . I honour *Schooles* for *Tongues* and
Arts; . . . we count the Universities the Fountaines, the Sem-
inaries or seed-plots of all Pietie: but have not those Fountaines
ever sent what streames the Times have liked. And ever changed
their taste and colour to the Princes eye and Palate?"[68]

The fact that Williams encouraged the instruction of the
youth in New England and never opposed the town school of

---

[64] In 1663, the Assembly set aside 100 acres of upland and 6 acres of
meadow for the maintenance of education in Providence. The first record
of a public schoolmaster is that of William Turpin, June 11, 1684. *Annals
of Providence,* by William Staples, pp. 492 ff. The education of the youth
in the early days of the colony was carried on by private tutors, and by
instruction in the home in the elements of reading, writing and ciphering.

[65] *The Hireling Ministry None of Christs,* p. 171. N C P., Vol. III,
pp. 308 ff, footnotes.

[66] *Bloudly Tenent of Persecution,* N C P., Vol. III, p. 307.

[67] *The Hireling Ministry None of Christs,* pp. 171-175. N C P., Vol.
III, pp. 304 ff, footnotes.

[68] *Bloudy Tenent of Persecution,* N C P., Vol. III, pp. 305 f.

primary education in the Bay colony, seems to show him as not unfavorable to public education, as practised in the other New England colonies. Masson comes to this conclusion about the attitude of Williams on education: he would have been for no expenditure of public money on religious education of the young, and for the exclusion of all theological teaching out of existing schools and universities. But he honored schools, he says, "for *Tongues* and *Arts*." I have found no trace in him, concludes Masson, that the use of state funds for secular schools and universities is illegitimate.[69]

In the constitution of 1647, the tradition of primogeniture was definitely rejected by the colony. Under the title of "Probate of Wills," it expressly stipulated that in the case of no will the property of the deceased person was to be equally divided among his heirs or relatives. "Forasmuch, as all men are free to dispose of their owne as they please; be it enacted "that, in order to avoid confusion and distraction among the rightful heirs, they "draw up their Wills in writing, how their Houses, Lands, Goods and Chattells shall be disposed of after their deaths." And in case a man dies intestate, the head officer of the Town "shall Appoint one of his [the deceased] nearest kinsman to take with him two other honest neighbors, and make and bring in a true Inventorie of his goods, which being brought in, they shall then make an equal and just distribution of his Estate among those whom it does belong, this draught whereof being instead of the dead man's will."[70]

Since church and state are separate and distinct, the state is made responsible for the moral welfare of its people. Upon the moral purity of the members, Williams rested largely the internal order and peace of society. The Second Table of the Law concerns "our *walking* with man [Commandments forbidding, stealing, killing of fellowmen, adultery, perjury and covetousness] . . . and if there be any other Commandment, to be briefly comprehended in this saying, namely, *Thou shalt love thy neighbor as thyself*." Hobbes and Locke held that the state is a-moral. Williams held that it is non-religious but moral. "It is true the second *Table* containes the *Law* of *Nature*, the *Law Morall* and

---

[69] Masson: *Life of Milton*, Vol. III, p. 118. See also N C P., Vol. III.
[70] R I C R., Vol. I, pp. 188 ff.

Civill."[71] To offend any of these laws "is properly transgression against the Civill State and Commonweale, or the Worldly state of Men:" and if the civil state "ought to be preserved by *Civill Government,*" it must not tolerate the offender. Farther on he argues that the city of Pergamus ought to have suppressed "*Balaams* and *Iesabels* doctrine. . . of *corporall fornication*" practices, not from a religious but from a moral and social standpoint,[72] for it was primarily a moral problem of civil society.

In the new society erected by Williams, the civil government was vitally concerned with purely moral issues. The colonial government forbade certain acts that were of a moral nature in the fundamental laws of 1647. Among the acts prohibited were murder, misbehaviour, robbery, wanton destruction of property, "batteries and assaults," adultery, fornication, rape, whoremongering, fraudulent dealing, forgery, "liars," perjury, breach of covenant, slander, drunkenness, "loafing at alehouses," swearing and cursing.[73] The Assembly went so far as to require each Town to fix one day out of seven for recreation and rest for its servants and inhabitants. A rather close survey of the activities of the civil government in the moral life, always supported by Williams, will doubtless cause a student of early New England colonial life to wonder whether the colony really practised the lawless and unrestrained individualism, and even license, so emphatically reiterated against it by its enemies.

The common welfare and public safety functions of the state emphasized by Williams in his writings and by the government of Rhode Island were unusually comprehensive for his age. The common welfare functions of society include, in general, the economic, industrial, and moral interests of the people.[74] They are activities which,[75] if left in private hands, would not be performed at all or performed to the disadvantage of the people as a whole. Individual opinion of state functions ranges from that of unrestrained individualism to socialism and communism. In fact, no exact limit can be placed to governmental action, for all general

[71] *Bloudy Tenent of Persecution,* N C P., Vol. III, pp. 152, 171 ff, 355, 358, 173.
[72] *Ibid,* pp. 171 ff.
[73] R I C R., Vol. I, pp. 156 ff. Continual references to these internal problems occur throughout Volumes I and II.
[74] Willoughby: *The Nature of the State,* p. 338.
[75] Duguit: *Law in the Modern State.* "Public services are those activities that the government is bound to perform."

welfare activity rests entirely on a utilitarian basis. In its final analysis, the idea of common welfare includes "every activity that may in any way promote the general welfare."[76]

Williams used the term common and general welfare or its equivalent repeatedly in his letters and treatises: common weale, common good, public good, generall well-being, public well-being, common peace and welfare.[77] That he used the term in its ultimate meaning has, I hope, already been clearly pointed out. The state, and therefore the civil government, he held is charged with the "*Bodies* and *Goods* of the *Subject.*" His civil rights[78] must be defended—that is, his rights to political, religious and economic liberty and equality, for the sake of humanity and love of common peace, safety, and credit, either by force, persuasion or by the principle of arbitration and compromise.[79] Moreover, the civil government must "well administer the Commonweale," give the proper cognizance to the well-being of servants, children, wives, and husbands, and hear and help them against oppression and violence, in the interest of the individuals, families and communities.[80] As an agent and servant of the sovereign people, the government ought to look after their every interest and need.

In emphasizing the principles of common welfare and natural and civil rights and liberties of the individual as conditioning the functions of the state, Williams marks the definite beginning of a new society and the modern state. It is the first significant departure from the medieval state, in its grafting of the happy and virtuous life, the realization of the public weal and civic morality,[81] upon the medieval conception of the state functions of "maintenance of peace and order." To these conceptions Williams added the principle of the protection of the natural and civil rights and liberties of the individual—spiritual, economic, and political. Like many of the modern thinkers,[82] he maintained that common welfare consisted of public services that the government is bound to perform. But this public service is always varying,

---

[76] Willoughby: *The Nature of the State*, p. 338.
[77] N C P., Vols. VI, p. 5; III, Chapters 92-132; and IV, p. 487.
[78] *Ibid, Queries*, Vols. II, p. 14; and IV, p. 271.
[79] Letter: *To the Town of Providence*, N C P., Vol. VI, pp. 262 ff. R I H S P., Vol. VIII, pp. 147 ff.
[80] *Bloudy Tenent of Persecution*, N C P., Vol. III, pp. 389, 355, 164.
[81] Gierke: *Political Theories of the Middle Ages*, pp. 90 ff, 189, discusses medieval political theory and modern state practices.
[82] Duguit: *Law in the Modern State*. Laski: *A Grammar of Politics*.

and must be fitted to the interests of the community "as the nature and condition of the place will admit." In the founding of Rhode Island on this basic principle as its most vital function, Williams has the honor of having established the first modern state with "such unheard of Liberties" of religious, political and economic freedom and equality.

The functions of civil government in this federated state were indeed diverse. To the civil government were transferred all the activities arising out of the sovereignty of the state expressed in a constitution. All the separate units within this federal state became mere administrative organs with delegated and variant powers. The assembly received the legislative and unifying powers, and was made the interpreter of the constitution and laws. To the "President" were delegated powers comparable to those of a corporation executive. To the Court of Trial was given the power to administer justice within a limited field of judicature, but with no power within itself to establish precedents in law. The English common law was subordinated to the new needs of natural and civil rights. And to the central government was delegated enough force and authority to carry out its constitutional obligations. Provisions were made to safeguard the general public against attacks, either domestic or foreign. The government regulated the value and usage of coins and moneys, laid and collected civil taxes and duties, and in general controlled all finances. Even domestic and foreign mercantile and commercial affairs were minutely regulated, not with the view of protecting the middleman and manufacturer, but in the interests of common welfare. The civil aspect of church life was put under the control of civil authorities; marriage was made a civil institution only; primogeniture was replaced by the equal rights of heirs and the legality of wills and testaments; and education was provided for by the assembly through land grants. All moral affairs were of vital concern to the civil authorities and amenable to regulation. Slavery was prohibited. In the government was also placed the duty to provide for the poor and incapable citizens and to procure work for the able. In such a social structure, the civil government was not so much a display of force for theoretical civil peace and order, as a machinery of administration primarily concerned with regulating and correcting the civil and economic interests within the state in such a manner as to promote the general welfare of the individual members.

Among the many things that suggest themselves about Williams' contributions to the structural principles of the new society in Rhode Island, only three especially interesting aspects can here be noted. The first is his emphasis on the beneficent object of civil laws over against the assertion of those who hold them a necessary evil—beneficent because they have been made by the sovereign people themselves or their representatives. The second is that the taxes laid by the representative government of the sovereign people are justifiable and ought to be enforced: "There is no man that hath a vote in town or colony, but he *hath a hand in making the rates by himself or his deputies.*"[83] Words that call to mind the electrifying Revolutionary phrase: taxation without representation is tyranny. The last aspect is the close harmony existing between Williams' theory of state and the functions of the colonial government as seen in its constitution, laws, and actual practices. This fact clearly indicates his influence with his fellow-colonists in things social and civil. It suggests that Roger Williams was a great teacher and social and civil pioneer of these later centuries, who, like the founders of religions and philosophies in the past ages, passed on to posterity his contribution to the development of political thought and practice. He could train a group of followers to demonstrate and carry on his principles of liberty, equality and general welfare in such a "lively experiment" as to change public opinion and evolve a new structure for civil society.

---

[83] Letter: *To the Town Clerk of Providence*, 1680, N C P., Vol. VI, pp. 401 ff.

PART 3

FEDERALISM AND COMMON WELFARE

To the men in power in the Bay colony, the doctrines of Roger Williams sounded like the voice of anarchy. His theory of state was diametrically opposed to the structural principles of the Bay. He placed the sinner on equality with the saint in civil affairs, and for this he was banished.[84] To secure to each individual his *"naturall & Civill Rights and Liberties"* was made the chief object and function of the civil state.[85] This could be achieved only if the state remained the will of the people and was not perverted by private and class interests to assume a life and personality of its own apart from the people who created it. The state had no rights apart from the people; it had merely duties to perform. These duties it accomplished, by force if necessary, but only after it had failed "powerfully to subdue their judgments and wills, to lay down their *weapons*, and yield willing subjection; then come orderly into the city and so to Citie privileges."[86]

In his concept of state, Williams accepted the principle that not the will but the reason of the law is the basis for its justification and for granting obedience to it.[87] He repudiated government by privilege, the union of church and state, the accepted marks of the historical Christian church as the true marks of the church of Christ, the arbitrary use of force within and without the state, preservation of peace and order as its only essential functions and a rigid fundamental law and form of government. Instead of upholding the existing order of things in church and state, he became a Seeker in religion and social life; erected a flexible government with a flexible constitution; made the people the final voice in all state affairs through the use of compulsory referendum, joint and individual initiative of laws and the recall of all laws and the constitution; declared for religious, political, social, and economic liberty and equality; and substituted for arbitrary force, the principle of common welfare and arbitration and adjustment

---

[84] Cobb: *Rise of Religious Liberty*, pp. 433 ff.
[85] *Bloody Tenent Yet More Bloody*, N C P., Vol. IV, p. 365.
[86] *Bloudy Tenent of Persecution*, N C P., Vol. III, pp. 108, 302.
[87] *Ibid*, p. 257.

of public and private interests. The state by this new concept was changed from a military despotism to a social and public service corporation; man was converted from a mere servant of the state to a free citizen and individual in civil affairs; and the church was made a mere civil corporation within the state. Is it any wonder that Massachusetts Bay invoked the decree of banishment against Roger Williams? And yet what a grand gesture of poetic justice that an outcast from society should have contributed so much toward the founding of the new civil state.

In order to achieve the object of the new social organism, the functions which inhere in the sovereignty of the state are expressed in a government in and through its various departments and agencies. But the extent and effect of governmental activities vary with the social and economic conditions of the particular state. The criterion of just what powers shall be assumed at any particular time is solely one of expediency. This utilitarian basis for state action opens a problem to be solved mainly by practical politics. This solution Williams hoped to present in the joint and individual initiative of laws and civil reforms and the recall, through direct elections. In their functions governments differ, he held, according to their origin, histories, and the circumstances which have guided them; and consequently each particular government must continually adjust its activities to the particular need of the times. His concept of state powers emphasized the modern idea of state, that it no longer absorbs the individual but only serves him. And although the civil agencies in operation interfere with individual freedom of action for the general well-being, yet Williams contended that only by some form of organization and by a certain measure of obedience to civil laws could the citizen secure real civil liberty. The several departments of the government he made subservient to the legislature under the direction of the fundamental laws, instead of allowing them to remain direct agents of king or executive. By making the legislature, representing the will of the people, the regulating authority in the government, and by separating the chief functions of the state, Williams was able to secure immediate civil attention to the present needs of the whole social group.

The separation of the chief functions of the state has been

recognized since the days of Aristotle.[88]   According to him, the
three functions or powers are deliberative, magisterial and judicial.[89]   Although variously distributed under different governments,
these powers are generally accepted as separate and distinct.
Bodin is considered the first to point out that the prince ought
not to administer justice in person.   Liberty, he asserted, is possible only when the judicial function is separated from the executive and legislature[90]   Montesquieu[91] was the first modern pub-
licist to suggest a subjective as well as an objective separation
of these functions.   For the sake of civil freedom and security,
he held that the different public functions should be exercised by
different persons.   To maintain a unity of power in the state, the
several powers must not, however, be absolutely separated; for
these powers are not equal, they are merely distinct.   A regulating and controlling power is necessary to determine the laws
and the relations between the parts of the whole.   That particular
function distinct from all the others which fixes the permanent
relation of the whole and belongs to the whole body politic, is
the legislative.

The framers of the constitution of the United States recognized the principle of the federal state that each of the chief
powers or agencies of the state must remain within its own particular sphere of activity.   In a letter to John Taylor, John
Adams presented the view, then held, of this system of checks and
balances of state activities: "First, the states are balanced against
the general government.   Second, the house of representatives is
balanced against the senate and the senate against the house.
Third, the executive is in some degree balanced against the legislature, the executive, and the state governments.   Fifth, the senate
is balanced against the president in all appointments to office and
in all treaties.   Sixth, the people hold in their hands the balance
against their own representatives by periodical elections.   Seventh,
the legislatures of the several states are balanced against the senate by sexennial elections.   Eighth, the electors are balanced
against the people in choice of president and vice-president."[92]

---

[88] Bluntschli: *The Theory of State*, p. 515.
[89] Aristotle: *Politics*, IV, 14-16.
[90] Bodin: *De la République*, Part I.   This separation was, however,
suggested in the Middle Ages.
[91] *Spirit of the Laws*, XI, 6.
[92] Adams: *Works*, Vol. VI, p. 476, Letter to John Taylor.

In contrast to the complex machinery of counterbalances in the United States government, that of Rhode Island had a more simple system of checks and balances which gave it greater flexibility: the towns against the central government; the executive against the legislature; the people against the government through the initiative, referendum and recall; the people against the legislature through annual elections; the constitution against the government, and in some degree against the people; and the legislature against the several towns.

Federalism occupies a large place in the public mind today. In contrast to the various forms of union among states, a federal state is that type of political life in which the separate units, retaining their governments and control over certain internal interests, have by voluntary union lost their sovereignty and exist as component parts of a single sovereignty.[93] The formation of a federal state, like the formation of every state, is a revolutionary act. The former separate sovereign commonwealths disappear, and, in turn, become from a legal point of view mere administrative districts. Sovereignty, thenceforth, resides in the federal state, while both local and central governments become its agents, neither being able to determine its competence or destroy the other.

In a federation the distribution of powers between the central government and various local governments becomes a problem of prime importance. The general division of powers is made by a constitution which is usually considered rigid.[94] Modern federal states agree in giving the central government control over certain functions essential to state existence and common welfare; and affairs of local concern alone, demanding different treatment because of sectional differences, are properly left to the control of the component units. In the federal system there is always a marked tendency toward increasing authority on the part of the central government. This tendency is especially marked in the United States. Against the numerous advantages of the federal plan, its serious defects in actual operation are so grave that some authorities refuse to recognize it as more than a mere makeshift. Others hold that "present political expediency, as well as past necessity, has found value in federalism, and many

---

[93] Gettell: *Political Science,* p. 181.
[94] Gilchrist: *Principles of Political Science,* p. 351.

writers predict a further unification of states, at present independent, on a federal basis."[95]

In the breakup of the medieval concept of society through the influence of the Renaissance and the Reformation, a new attitude toward the relation between the state and individual was gradually taking form in the European schools of philosophy. Liberty and natural rights of the individual in society were brought forward in the conflict with the feudal ideal of an absolute state. In the early sixteenth century when Luther championed the Reformation in church and state, feudalism was rapidly passing away. Throughout the Middle Ages the functions of government were those of proprietorship. The state belonged to the baron or king; he was actually the state. The conscience of the prince was the standard of justice; the state had become a private estate; and the power of the prince was the only conclusive test of prerogative. Luther in his appeal to the German princes marks a step in the transition from absolutism to the modern idea of state. He recognized the different spheres of the three great functions of state. "He appealed for the enactment of certain legislation; he urged the execution of the laws; he declared that matters of legal right and of constitutional law should be left to the jurists and courts."[96] These departments are, Luther asserted, by their nature obliged to fulfil the general aims and objects of the state. To the several agencies represented by the temporal authorities belong the matters of money, property, life and honor, judgment according to the law of the land, education of the youth, care for the poor, and protection against monopolies, gambling and public immorality. But it remained for Roger Williams to establish in practical politics the principle of public well-being as the highest function of the state.

In Williams' theory of state, the functions which the state ought to undertake were diverse and numerous. It must defend itself against foreign aggressions by establishing an adequate national defense, and especially through agreements, arbitration and adjudication. Ample provisions must be made to protect itself against internal attacks. But the state must also prevent internal encroachment upon the individual and assure him of his natural and civil rights and liberties. To facilitate the carrying out of these

[95] Gettell: *Political Science*, p. 189.
[96] Waring: *Political Theories of Martin Luther*, pp. 190-231.

activities, force either active or latent is to be used as a means to an end. None of the means is in essence fixed, but must change to meet the changing conditions of social life so that the government machinery can fully exercise the directing and restraining powers for public ends.

In the development of the machinery of federalism, the state of Rhode Island made a distinct contribution to political theory. The hegemony of Greece and other Greek attempts at federation lacked the essentials of self-government. But the central government of Rhode Island was made an agent of the people. By means of a constitution, Williams fixed individual rights, and restricted and limited the activities of the central government and local administrative units. The powers of the state were divided into central and local activities and governmental units. The central government became the regulating, correcting and harmonizing agent for handling all civil affairs. To the local units were given limited powers to carry on affairs that were only of local concern, but always in harmony with the central government. In organizing the central government, he recognized the necessity of separating the powers into judicial, executive, and legislative functions. The judicial functions were placed in a General Court of the circuit type to try general cases, and in local courts of justice for affairs of concern to the local units. In a "President" and his assistants were located the highest executive functions, which were limited by a commission through the constitution; the executive was merely the head of a corporate political organization. The legislature was the chief regulating and correcting instrument of the government because it represented the will of the people expressed through the ballot, and to it was given the sole power to interpret its own laws and also the fundamental law.

As the corporate machinery created to serve the members of society, the government had placed upon it various checks and duties. A veto of all actions of the civil machinery was placed in the people in the form of referendum and recall. In order to guarantee civil liberty, a simple system of checks and balances and the joint and individual initiative and referendum were made a part of the fundamental law. In this manner the government became a pliant and sensitive instrument chiefly concerned with the public welfare and economic interests. Internal problems that in any way affected the common interests became a matter for regulation or correction by the central government, such as control of finances, moneys, taxes, duties, mercantile and commercial affairs, slavery and apprenticeship in trades, civil activities of church bodies, marriage, inheritance, care of poor, incapable and orphans, instruction of youth, and the moral welfare of society. But the extent of civil interference was definitely fixed by a bill of rights which guaranteed to each individual such an amount of civil rights and liberties that the contemporary leaders in the Bay and Plymouth colonies talked much of anarchy in the Rhode Island Plantations.

Williams believed the government in actual operation is justified not only in maintaining its own existence and the life, liberty and property of its citizens, but also in undertaking such other functions as, under existing conditions, may also promote the general welfare. Among the most important duties of the state, he recognized its obligation to maintain a wide sphere of individual liberty protected from governmental and private interference. In this concept of the modern state, the action of the government may vary from the policy of extreme interference of socialism to the extreme non-interference of individualism, but the policy is never wholly sympathetic to either of these two partisan activities. The common welfare, or public well-being, view of Williams rests on an individualistic basis which he so modified by utilitarian and opportunistic motives that in the application of each function the criterion for the action muct rest upon the utilitarian and humanitarian basis of the best interests of the individual and society.

VII
LIMITS OF STATE POWER

PART 1
ATTITUDE OF THE SEVENTEENTH CENTURY

In seventeenth century England, the contest between absolutism and popular rights for the control of the state powers and activities, began to assume a paramount place in political theory and practice. The conflict caused both schools of political thought to arrange their ideas into a more formal system. Of seventeenth century absolutist views on the limits to be placed on state functions, Hobbes, in the *Leviathan,* may be taken as the most representative exponent. He declared that the sovereign can do no injustice to the subject because the sovereign has unlimited power and unfettered discretion as to ways and means of attaining his end. The state also has unrestricted power over property and private rights. Since the people give up their natural rights and power in the contract that forms the state, they may have no rights whatever, and rebellion is unjust. The king, on the other hand, is the third party to the contract, and therefore retains all his natural rights and powers. Consequently, the king is absolute in all things relating to his subjects, who have no freedom of speech, thought, action, or religious belief.

The individualism of the republicans and more liberal publicists resulted in widely diverging views on the limits of state action. The Social Contract, Locke[1] held, places definite limits on the action of a state, which has no "right to destroy, enslave, and designedly to impoverish the subjects." At no time may it rule arbitrarily; for the state is limited to securing the "life, liberty, and property" of its citizens. It must stay within limits fixed by law, must not take property or transfer it, must secure equality for rich and poor before the law, and must not tax the people without their consent. The state, according to Milton,[2] is merely the agent of the people, with the sphere of action limited by a constitution. In his theory of state limits, he was an individualist. Liberty to him meant a wide sphere of action unrestrained by gov-

---

[1] *On Civill Government.* Especially, Sections 134-142.
[2] *Tenure of Kings and Magistrates.*

ernment. Laws are merely to be for punishment of crimes; absence of laws best promotes virtue in life. The natural laws grant to every man the right of rebellion, freedom of speech and press, and religious toleration. In 1649, the Commonwealth Army[3] demanded a constitution with a list of rights "fundamental to our common right, liberty and safety." The bill of rights was to protect the individual against encroachments by the government. The Army, furthermore, asked for a guarantee that rebellion, if these fundamental rights were violated, could not be considered as treason. The apex of the individualism postulated by Milton and the Army was not reached until the end of the eighteenth and early part of the nineteenth centuries.

The doctrine of state limits held by Roger Williams was unique for his day, and the most advanced of the seventeenth century. Although he was an individualist, the individualism peculiar to Williams was to find its fullest expression through limits on both the state and individual through law.[4] He postulated that complete individual liberty is attainable only through law. Absence of law in the present stage of civilization can result in nothing but a return to barbarism, and social and political disorder. The state, as expressed in a government, is community consciousness of solidarity and common interests. It is distinct from and superior to the church in all civil things. The church, as one of the civil corporations, has authority only in the doctrines, morals and administration of its own organization—it is superior in spiritual things alone. All temporal affairs are exclusively of civil and secular concern. The member of a church is subject in secular matters not to the church but the state. Even the church as a corporation is subject to civil law in civil things; and religious disturbances of the civil peace are to be suppressed by civil force. The civil government is a servant and agent of the people that ought to act in their best interests. It is to control the relations between the people in external things only. It must, in addition, maintain civil peace and order within itself; when necessary, it must even defend the church in civil matters. Civil law exists only for offenders and evil-doers, and to the law-abiding it is beneficent. Coercion is a prerogative of

---

[3] *The Agreement of the Army,* 1649.
[4] N C P., Vols. I-VI, especially the *Letters* in volume VI, pp. 178 ff, 400 ff. R I H S P., Vol. VIII, pp. 147 ff.

the civil government only. Neither state nor church can bind the individual conscience. In all things the activities of the state must be shaped to serve the common peace, safety, and welfare. To do this the state must respect individual right of religious opinion and worship, and grant liberty of conscience, debate, speech, writing, etc., as a natural, human, and civil right of every individual, subject only to the similar rights of others. It must respect the inalienable right possessed by each man to think as he pleases in matters of religion, politics, and social life. It must, furthermore, recognize the right of association and arbitration with others for indifferent civil ends. In man's reaching and searching after truth, the state has no right to interfere. And, although every man ought to oppose tyranny and oppression, it is, nevertheless, his duty to obey the lawful civil government and perform that part of the civil duties incumbent upon every citizen. In such a state or society, even though the common welfare is paramount, all the powers and interests of the state are formed to guarantee to each member the fullest opportunity for individual development and liberty.

WILLIAMS ON THE LIMITS OF THE STATES

The limits of state action cannot be even approximated in general terms, unless some limits on individual right of action within civil society are recognized. In no uncertain terms, Williams undertakes to limit the state in its absolute and arbitrary functions and to elevate the individual to a place of paramount interest in civil affairs. To reorganize society in harmony with the new concept of state, Williams found it essential to qualify and limit active sovereignty in its relation to religion, individual social relations, individual natural rights and civil liberties, bodies and goods, and individual development and common welfare. Only upon a full appreciation of the effect of these limits on civil power is it possible to see the full implication of the new social structure erected by Williams with the aid of his fellow colonists.

To Roger Williams must be accorded the honor of having set forth and applied for the first time as a fundamental principle of state the great gift of America to civilization and the world— pure religious liberty. It has among the principles of state "no equal for moral insight, and for recognition both of the dignity of the human soul and the spiritual majesty of the church of God."[5] Its chief import is the complete separation of church and state. The idea received acceptance and' came into practice only after much interference through the ages by the civil powers, and after centuries of struggle and bloodshed. Liberty of conscience as a principle of civil life has received so many partial interpretations during the last four centuries that some explanations and definitions are needed to clear away the confusing débris heaped upon and around it through agelong controversy.

The Puritan colonies of New England held to a "fundamental error," the necessity of a union between church and state for civil and international peace. "To this they clung as to an ark of safety."[6] In Plymouth, Massachusetts, and Connecticut "the Congregational Church was established by law, with more or less of proscription of other forms of worship. This establish-

---

[5] Cobb: *Rise of Religious Liberty*, p. 2.
[6] Story: *Massachusetts and Her Early History*, p. 34; Cobb: *Rise of Religious Liberty*, p. 158.

ment was not by charter or by imposition of external authority, but by act of the colonial legislature at the beginning of the colonies, in conformity with the will of the great majority of the people. . . . Theocratic Massachusetts and New Haven reverenced the order as the chosen instrument of God, with which a man could interfere only to his peril, and on conformity to which all civil rights depended. Plymouth and Connecticut loved it as a seemly thing and as conducive to religion and social prosperity, but at the same time recognized the claims of charity toward men of other minds."[7] With the exception of Rhode Island, all the colonies of New England, and foremost among them Massachusetts, were theocratic states, copies of the Old Testament theocracy of Israel.[8]

In order to understand the principle of religious liberty, it is necessary to make clear such terms as freedom of conscience, persecution, toleration, and religious liberty, by definitions. Freedom of conscience is not synonymous with religious liberty. In reality the conscience is always free, and the mind is free, from direct civil or religious interference. The civil power can only reach to silencing the expression of the conscience,[9] but cannot force the mind to a change of attitude. It can compel conformity of outward expression but cannot change the inner man, or convert unbelief to faith.[10] "Thoughts are free," is an old German Law, Lieber points out, "conscience lies beyond the reach of government."[11] This fact was understood and recognized by Williams: "I acknowledge that to molest any person, *Jew* or *Gentile,* for either professing *doctrine,* or practicing *worship* meerly *religious* or spiritual, it is to persecute him, and such a person (whatever his *doctrine* or *practice* be true or false) suffereth persecution of *conscience* . . . this *distinction* is not full and complete: For beside this that a man may be persecuted because he holdeth or practiseth what he believes in *conscience* to be a *Truth* . . . a man may also be persecuted, because he dares not be *constrained* to yield obedience to such doctrines and *worships* as are by men

---

[7] Cobb: *Rise of Religious Liberty,* p. 133. The churches of Massachusetts Bay dropped congregationalism in 1639, and became a synodical organization in fact.

[8] *Bloudy Tenent of Persecution,* N C P., Vol. III, pp. 416 ff.

[9] *Letters,* N C P., Vol. VI, dealing with the case of William Harris. R I C R., Vol. I. pp. 361 ff.

[10] *Bloudy Tenent of Persecution,* N C P., Vol. III, p. 4.

[11] *On Civil Liberty,* Vol. I, p. 118, Note.

invented and appointed.[12]. . . But I speak of conscience, a persuasion fixed in the mind and heart of a man, which enforceth him to judge . . . and to do so and so."[13]   Freedom of conscience, according to Williams, includes freedom from state compulsion to yield obedience to any specified religious creed and formula, and freedom from state interference with the practice and profession of a "Truth" or any religious doctrine and worship, as the natural and civil right of every man, so long as no purely civil aspect is in opposition to civil laws.

Roger Williams uses persecution in a limited sense in his letters and treatises. Despotism or tyranny and persecution are not the same thing, although both may be employed against the conscience. Tyranny is the civil attempt at oppression of or interference with the conscience. Persecution is interference with religious doctrines and practices held for conscience's sake. To persecute is "to molest any person *Jew* or *Gentile,* for either professing *doctrine,* or practicing *worship* meerly *religious* or spiritual."[14]   It is "soul yokes, soul oppressions, plundering, etc.;" it is "uniformity of Religion to be enacted and inforced in any civil State;" it is "suppressing, preventing and extinguishing such doctrines or practices [of religion] by weapons of wrath and blood, whips, stocks, imprisonment, banishment, death, etc."   Not only is religious persecution a civil injustice, but it is also possible that by it the government may "persecute Jesus in some of them."[15]   Persecution is an error because religious liberty is "not hurtfull to any commonwealth, and it depriveth not Kings of any Power given them of God."[16]   To persecute for religion's sake is "opposite the very nature of a Christian Church. . . . Opposite the very tender Bowels of Humanity. . . . Opposite to the very essential and Fundamentalls of the Nature of Civill Magistracie, a Civil *Common weal* or *combination* of Men which can only respect *civill* things. . . . Opposite to Civill Peace, and the lives of millions. . . . Opposite to the Souls of all Men. . . . Opposite to the best of God's servant who in all Popish and

---

[12] *Bloudy Tenent of Persecution,* N C P., Vol. III, p. 63.
[13] Letter: *To Endicott,* N C P., Vol. VI, p. 219.   "This consicence is found in all Mankind more or less, in Jews, Turks, Papists, Protestants, Pagans, etc."
[14] *Bloudy Tenent of Persecution,* N C P., Vol. III, p. 63.
[15] Letter: *To Endicott,* N C P., Vol. VI, p. 225.
[16] *Tracts: Persecution for Religion Judged and Condemned,* 1615, pp. 85 ff.

Protestant States have been commonly esteemed and persecuted
. . . . Opposite the Light of Scripture. . . . All this in all Ages
experience testifies, which never saw any long lived Fruit of
Peace or Righteousness to grow upon that fatal Tree."[17]

In the principle of toleration is resident a definite denial of
the principle which underlies Williams' idea of religious liberty.[18]
Religious liberty asserts that in matters of religion all men are
equal before God and the civil law. Toleration assumes that all
men are not equal in matters of religion—one form of religion
has a better right. To tolerate is merely to endure something under force of necessity or for expediency. Toleration is a "gift
from a superior to one who is supposed to occupy a lower station
in the scale of rights."[19] Religious toleration has found advocates throughout recorded history.

Roger Williams, however, made a distinction between toleration and religious liberty, and between the equity of toleration and
its necessity. In his treatises he passes in review the important
acts and practices of toleration in Europe since the introduction of
Christianity. Concerning more recent acts of toleration, he declared "Your honors know what blood bickerings and bloodshed
have been in later times in *Germany,* in *France,* in *England,* in
Polonia, in *Hungaria, Bohemia, Transilvania,* etc. about the Freedome of mens Consciences and worship? . . . Some have said
that *worldly policie* perswaded, as well as *State-necessity compelled*
the States of *Holland* to prudent permission of different *Consciences.* And that the said *State-policie* perswaded some *Dutch*
to wish that *England* might not tolerate, least a permission of
Conscience in England." But Williams deals with a great principle and goes to the root of the question: "I most humbly and
earnestly beseech your *Honors* to mind the *Difference* between
State *Necessity* of *Freedome* to different *Consciences,* and the
Equity and *Piety* of such a *Freedome. State Policie* and *Necessity* of *Affairs* drew from great *Constantine"* the Edict of Milan
granting freedom of conscience; but Maximilian II comes "nearer
to the *Life* of the *Businesse"* in these words: *"There is no sin
ordinarily greater against God,* said he, *then to use violence*

---

[17] *Queries,* N C P., Vol. II, p. 35.
[18] *Bloudy Tenent of Persecution,* N C P., Vol. III, p. 4.
[19] Cobb: *Rise of Religious Liberty,* p. 8.

against the Consciences of Men."[20] "Toleration," wrote Tom Paine "is not the opposite of intolerance, but the counterfeit of it. Both are despotisms. The one assumes to itself the right of withholding liberty of conscience, and the other of granting it. The one is the pope armed with fire and faggot, the other the pope selling or granting indulgences."[21]

Religious liberty, or the equality of all men in matters of religion, does not even include toleration.[22] "Soul liberty" is of God; and conscience is by nature free[23] and beyond the control of men or states. The idea of religious liberty must be sought in two things: its origin in the will of God, and its relation to civil law.[24] The first point will be assumed without discussion. The chief interest lies in seeing what authority civil law and society has to interfere with this inalienable God-given right. Williams argues for "soul liberty" from the vantage points of utility, expediency, and necessity, as well as the equity and piety of it.[25] Not only does he conclude that God enjoins it, but also discovers it politically and socially expedient. The roots and essence of this right he grounds in the natural and divine principles of life itself.

Liberty from external interference with conscience "turns upon two Hinges." Civil government may not restrain any one from "the *worshipping* of a *God* or *Gods,* which the *Consciences* of Men in their respective worships, all the world over believes to be *true.* Secondly, [a civil government cannot compel] the practicing or countenancing of that whereof their consciences are not perswaded."[26] With one exception all governments of his day assumed the right to determine the religious belief and life of their people. Rhode Island stood alone as the champion of the religious liberty proclaimed by its founder. Even more significant than this, was the fact that no mention of religious matters was

---

[20] *Bloody Tenent Yet More Bloody,* N C P., Vol. IV, pp. 11; 8, p. 6, the Edict of Milan was published in 312 A.D.; 7, Maximilian II became Emperor in 1564.

[21] Tom Paine: *The Rights of Man,* p. 31, (Ed. of 1883).

[22] *Bloudy Tenent of Persecution,* N C P., Vol. III, p. 4.

[23] Scott: *Development of Constitutional Liberty,* p. 112.

[24] Cobb: *Rise of Religious Liberty,* p. 9.

[25] *Bloudy Tenent of Persecution,* N C P., Vol. III, Chapters 97, 101, 103; N C P., Vol. IV, Chapter 59. Williams' utilitarianism in both religious and political ideas is a forecast of later rationalism.

[26] *Bloody Tenent Yet More Bloody,* N C P., Vol. IV, p. 7.

made by the Charter of 1644.[27]   This omission was the only "confirmation of the rights of conscience which Williams could consistently admit, and was therefore the more acceptable, for to receive religious liberty as a concession from any power would be virtual recognition" that any power could of right take away or deny religious liberty.[28]

Probably no better or clearer statement of the general principle of religious liberty has been made than that by Roger Williams in 1643: "All *Civill States* with their *Officers* or *Justice* in their respective *constitutions* and *administrations* are proved *essentially Civill*, and therefore not *Judges, Governours* or *Defendours* of the *Spirituall* or *Christian state* or *Worship*. . . . It is the will and command of God, that (since the coming of his Sonne the Lord Jesus) a *permission* of the most *Paganish, Jewish, Turkish,* or *Antichristian consciences* and *worships,* bee granted to all *men* in all *Nations* and *Countries*: and they are onely to bee *fought* against with that *Sword* which is only (in *soule matters*) *able* to *conquer,* to wit, the *Sword* of *Gods Spirit,* the *Word* of *God* . . . . *God* requireth not an *uniformity* of *Religion* to be *inacted* and *inforced* in any *civill state;* Which inforced *uniformity* (sooner or later) is the greatest occasion of *civill Warre, ravishing* of *consciences, persecuting* of *Christ Jesus* in his servants, and of the *hypocrisie* and *destruction* of *millions* of *souls* . . . . An inforced *uniformity* of *Religion* throughout a *Nation* or *civill state,* confounds the *Civill* and *Religious,* denies the principles of Christianity and civility, and *Jesus Christ* is come in the Flesh . . . . True *civility* and *Christianity* may both flourish in a *state* or *Kingdom,* notwithstanding the *permission* of divers and contrary *consciences,* either of *Jews* or *Gentiles*."[29]   Roger Williams transformed the idea of freedom of conscience in religious matters into a living force "and to him is due the honor of being the first who recognized it as a constitutional principle, and who atcually created a polity that had it for a foundation stone."[30]

A practical test of Williams' theory of freedom for "all kinds of consciences" was made in the founding and political development of Rhode Island.   No church organization was formed in

[27] R I C R., Vol. I, pp. 12-207.
[28] Straus: *Roger Williams,* pp. 122 ff.
[29] *Bloudy Tenent of Persecution,* N C P., Vol. III, pp. 1 f.
[30] Scott: *Development of Constitutional Liberty,* p. 107.

the colony until 1638. Among his fellow colonists were radicals of every shade of opinion. When Verein interfered with the liberty of worship of his wife, he was disfranchised and fined. The coming of the Quakers to Providence was, perhaps, the severest test put to this principle. Before their coming, all people of whatever creed or no creed were made welcome. But when the Quakers were welcomed, the United Colonies of New England, including Massachusetts, Plymouth, Connecticut and New Haven, sent a note that "Quakers, ranters and such notorious heretics" be removed from the colony and prohibited to enter in the future.[31] To this the General Assembly replied that "concerning these quakers, so-called . . . we have no law among us whereby to punish any for only declaring by Word and so forth . . . . And we, moreover, finde, that in those places where they . . . are most of all suffered to declare themselves freely . . . there they least desire to come . . . surely we find that they delight to be persecuted by Civill powers."[32] They added, "freedom of conscience . . . was the principle ground of our Charter . . . which freedom we still prize as the greatest hapiness that men can possess in this world." But in civil matters the Quakers must subject themselves "as other members of Civill societies."[33]

Still another test was made of the principle of religious liberty. In his *Bloudy Tenent* Roger Williams maintains all men have equal rights to protection while resident within a state without regard to race or religion. "Many *seducing teachers,* either of the *Paganish, Jewish, Turkish,* or *Antichristian* Religion, may be clear and free from *scandalous offences* in their life, as also from *disobedience* to the Civil Lawes of a State." The state is a creation of the *"people,* as a *people,* naturally considered (of what *Nature* or *Nation* soever in *Europe, Asia, Africa* or *America."*[34] This principle when applied to practice in Rhode Island would require the recognition of Jews, Indians, etc., to the full protection of the civil state in all civil things. When the Jews came to Rhode Island, the Assembly again upheld the principle of the modern state laid down by Roger Williams twelve years before, by con-

---

[31] R I C R., Vol. I, pp. 374 ff.

[32] This is a shrewd bit of advice in statesmanship.

[33] R I C R., Vol. I. pp. 375 ff.

[34] *Bloudy Tenent of Persecution,* N C P., Vol. III, pp. 171 ff, 250. See also Richman: *Rhode Island: A Study in Separatism,* pp. 126 f.

cluding: "we declare that they [the Jews] may expect as good protection here as any stranger, not being of our nation, residing among us ought to have." The first Jews arrived in 1655. This people whose race for centuries had had no safe resting place, "entered the harbour of Newport to find equal protection, and in a few years to build a house of God for a Jewish congregation."[35]

Williams declared that the spheres of action of church and state are separate and distinct, both on the basis of religion and on that of the "radical difference of nature and aim between the two."[36] He argued that his opponents in New England were striving for their own religious freedom and went no further: "Yourselves pretend," he wrote, "a liberty of conscience; but alas! it is but self, the great god Self, only to yourselves."[37] His principle, on the other hand, was broad and universal—an essential of true religion and true humanity. He declared for a "liberty of all kinds of consciences." And since religious and civil affairs were separated, the excommunicated heretic could still be a good citizen, and if a law-abiding citizen, must receive civil protection. Moreover the demand for the union of church and state Williams considered economic on the part of the clergy, and political and economic on the part of the state,[38] motives entirely selfish and dangerous to public welfare.[39]

Because of the separate nature and aim of each institution, Williams rejected the state-church. No matter how a state-church might be administered, the purpose of each would be perverted, and confusion and disorder would eventually result. "For as it would be confusion for the *church* to censure such [civil] *matters,* and so such persons as belong to the *church:* So is it *confusion* for the *state* to punish *spirituall offenders,* for they are not within the *sphear* of a *civil jurisdiction.* The *body* or Com-

---

[35] Smith: *The Thirteen Colonies,* Vol. II, p. 333, quotes Daly: *The Settlement of the Jews in North America.* (Ed. by Max Kohler).

[36] Cobb: *Rise of Religious Liberty,* pp. 426 f.

[37] Letter: *To Major Mason,* N C P., Vol. VI, p. 346.

[38] N C P., Vols. III, pp. 386-395; II, *Queries,* p. 23; and IV, p. 4.

[39] When Williams first fixed on the principles of religious liberty is difficult to discover, but he himself states that it was before his escape from England. To Mrs. Sadlier, daughter of the great jurist, Sir Edward Coke, he writes, "My conscience was persuaded against the national church and ceremonies, and bishops, beyond the conscience of your dear Father." N C P., Vol. VI, p. 239. And therefore he did not feel it prudent to call on his Mentor, Sir Edward, before leaving for America.

monweal is meerly *civil,* the *Magistrate* or *head* is a *civil head,* and each *member* is a *civil member:* and so far forth as any of this *civil body* are spiritual, or act spiritually, they and their actions fall under a *spiritual cognizance* and *judicature.* . . . The *civil state* and *Magistrate* are meerly and *essentially civil;* and therefore can not reach (without transgressing the bounds of *civility*) to judge matters *spiritual,* which are of another *sphere* and nature than *civility* is: Now it is most just and proper, that if any member in a *civil body* be opprest, that *body* should relieve it: As also it is just and proper, that the spiritual *state* or *body* should relieve the soul of any in that spiritual combination oppressed."[40] The sphere and nature of the two differ so greatly that each needs a peculiar treatment of its own, for any disease within or upon its organization. Furthermore, the magistrate has a right to act in the church not as a civil officer but only as a personal member of the church body.

Through interference of the civil power, Williams pointed out that both conscience and church are made to suffer in their particular purpose, and usually diverted from their distinct activities. "The *straining* of mens consciences by *civil power,* is so far from making men faithful to *God* or man, that it is the ready way to render man false to both: my ground is this: *civil* and *corporal punishment* do usually cause men to play the *hypocrite,* and dissemble in their *Religion,* to turn and return with the tide, as all *experience* in the *nations* of the *world* doth testify now, This *binding* and *rebinding* of *conscience,* contrary or without its own *perswasion,* so weakens and defiles it, that it (as all other *faculties*) loseth its strength, and the very nature of a common honest *conscience.* . . . This *Tenent* of the *Magistrates* keeping the *church* from *Apostizing,* by practicing *civil force* upon the *consciences* of men, is so far from preserving *Religion* pure, that it is a mighty *Bulwark* or *Barricade* to keep out all true *Religion,* yea, and all *godly Magistrates* for ever coming into the *World.* . . ."[41] A *Tenent,* all besprinkled with *bloudie murthers, stobs, poysonings, pistollings, powder-plots, etc.* against many famous *Kings, Princes,* and *States.* . . . A *Tenent* that *stunts* the *growth* and *flourishing* of the most likely and hopefullest *Common-weales* and *Countries,* while *Consciences,* the *best,* and the *best* deserving

---

[40] *Bloody Tenent Yet More Bloody,* N C P., Vol. IV, pp. 199, 203.
[41] *Ibid,* pp. 209 f.

Subjects are forct to flie (by enforced or voluntary *Banishment*) from their native *Countries*. . . . A *Tenent* whose grosse partialities denies the *Principles* of *common Justice*. . . . A *Tenent* that is but *Machevilisme*, and makes a *Religion*, but a *cloake* and *stalking horse* to *policie* and *private Ends* of *Jeroboams Crowne*, and the *Priests Benefice, etc*. . . . A *Tenent* that *corrupts* and *spoiles* the very *Civill Honestie* and *Naturall Conscience* of a *Nation*. . . . Yea, the *bloudiness* and *inhumanitie* of it is such" that the persecutors "have been forced to arme themselves with the faire *shewes* and glorious *pretences*, of the *Glory* of *God*, and the *zeale* for that *Glory*, the *Love* of his *Truth*, the *Gospel* of *Christ Jesus*, *love* and *pitie* to mens soules, the *peace* of the *Church*, *uniformitie*, *Order*, the *peace* of the *Common-weale*, the *Wisedome of the State*, the *Kings, Queenes*, and *Parliaments* proceedings, the *odiousness* of *Sects, Heresies, Blasphemies, Novelties, Seducers* and their *Infections*: the *obstinacie* of *Hereticks*, after all *Meanes, Disputations, Examinations, Synods*, yea after *Conviction* in the poore *Hereticks* owne *Conscience*: Add to these the flattring sound of those glosing *Titles*, the *Godly Magistrate*, the *Christian Magistrate*, the *Nurcing Fathers* and *Mothers* of the *Church, Christian Kings* and *Queenes*."[42]

"Roger Williams," says Newman, "advocated the most complete separation of Church and State at a time when there was no historical example of such separation . . . and when to the mass of Christian men everywhere such a separation was almost inconceivable. . . . While we accord all honor to Roger Williams for advocating liberty of conscience in all its length and breadth at a time when he was almost alone among men of his class and condition in grasping this fundamental Gospel principle, we must beware of looking with contempt on men like Cotton and Mather and Hooker and Winthrop," because the contemporary theologians and political thinkers of Europe agreed in regarding this doctrine of liberty of conscience as utterly impracticable, and as sure to result in civil and religious anarchy.[43]

"It is impossible to imagine," writes Cobb, "a distinction more radical and broader than that between things of this spiritual nature and the functions of civil government."[44]   But in surveying

---

[42] *Ibid*, pp. 493 ff.
[43] Newman: *Roger Williams*, pp. 60, 78. N C P., Vol. I, pp. 40 ff.
[44] Cobb: *Rise of Religious Liberty*, pp. 527 f.

the religious attitude of Roger Williams, it is well to notice that he was "not a Liberal in religion, but a religious liberal," concludes Straus. "He was not lax in faith; on the contrary, he was even more tenacious of his creed than Cotton or Hooker; he was unnecessarily scrupulous about many minor points of doctrine and policy. His piety was never impugned or censured by his enemies. Yet he was tender of consciences of others and granted them the same freedom as he himself claimed."[45] Fiske came nearer to a correct estimate of Williams' religious attitude, when he called him the forerunner of that Protestantism "which, in the natural course of development, is coming to realize the noble ideal of Roger Williams, but from the very thought of which such men as Winthrop and Cotton and Endicott would have shrunk with Dismay."[46]

The American idea of religious liberty laid down by Roger Williams is a complete separation of state and church in their peculiar activities. The church has no power in the direction of civil affairs, except indirectly by the influence of its teachings upon the public opinion through its members; nor can it look to the state for any support from civil government other than that granted to all corporations, in which case all state action is not religious but merely civil. The state, on the other hand, has no power in, or over, the church or the individual in matters of religious doctrine or practice, unless that doctrine or practice endangers society by disturbing the civil peace; it can not appropriate money for any type or quality of religious activity; it must maintain a balance of common justice among the various church bodies; equality before the law and equality of protection in civil affairs must be meted out to all people of the state; it can make no distinction between its citizens because of religion in any thing that concerns the natural, humane and civil life of each individual. "Thus the severance of the state from church—of the civil power from all concernment for religion—is made thorough to the minutest detail."[47]

Not only ought the civil state not to interfere with liberty of religion and individual conscience, but it must respect and guard a circumscribed field of individual duties, obligations, natural

[45] Straus: *Roger Williams,* p. 71.
[46] Fiske: *The Beginnings of New England,* p. 151.
[47] Cobb: *Rise of Religious Liberty,* pp. 15 f.

rights and civil liberties. In the new social structure planned by Williams, the limits of state interference are literally fixed in "non-rigid" fundamental laws. But it is only upon a recognition of these individual duties and obligations in the new civil society that the limits of state functions laid down by Williams can be fully understood. Consequently, it is necessary to make a brief review of Williams' individualism before approaching his presentation of the individual civil liberties guarded from state interference.

No obligation of the individual in society is higher than that of each individual's responsibility for the rights, liberties, and welfare of the other members. Here is the crux of Williams' peculiar individualism, by emphasis upon which he achieved a singular harmony and social order while allowing for the most extreme individual opinions and consciences in the new civil society. No other leading statesman of the century made this concept a part of the constitutional law. It is in this aspect that he differs widely from the individualism of the eighteenth and nineteenth centuries. The doctrine of *laissez-faire,* or arbitrary individualism, of the last century and a half had no place in the political structure conceived by Roger Williams. But the philosophic individualism which sprang into prominence during the latter part of the last century and the first two decades of the present, and was upheld by many liberal and radical political thinkers of this period, agrees with Williams in opposing state interference in indifferent and non-essential civil affairs.

When an individual enters a society of men, the least that can be expected of him is that he respect the same rights in others that he himself claims. Consequently the social problem becomes not so much that of individual rights as of individual duties, obligations and interests in common with his fellow members. Certain individual duties and obligations are incumbent upon each member of society in order that each and every individual in it can be guaranteed his individual natural, humane, civil rights and liberties. The impartial attitude of this noble form of individualism is given by Roger Williams when he says, "I desire not that liberty to myself, which I would not freely and impartially weigh out to all the consciences of the world beside: and therefore I do humbly conceive, that it is . . . the express and absolute Duty of the Civil powers to proclaim an absolute freedom

. . . in all the world,"⁴⁸ and to limit the action of the civil government in indifferent civil things.

In the formation of a civil society, a system of limitations was held by Williams a necessary civil caution on the part of both the individual man and the state. When he enters society, the individual by his free consent relinquishes certain of his natural rights and replaces them by civil rights and liberties, mutually guaranteed and respected. Certain of his natural rights, however, remain his more permanent possession. The only solution for the full realization of the individuality of each member of society is that of limiting individual rights and liberties by means of non-rigid civil laws. The degree of liberty must necessarily be conditioned by the age, place, and nature of the people of the particular society. How the guarantees are to be fixed, and what they ought to be, is the problem of each particular people in each age. In such a society, or state, it is not difficult to realize the paramount importance not of individual rights but of individual duties and obligations. The duties which limit the individual in his relation to the state and fellow-citizens are chiefly those of obedience to civil laws, service to society in "person or purse," and arbitration of conflicting interests.

"The *civil State* respecteth conformity and obedience to *civil laws*."⁴⁹ But this conformity and obedience, although it is among the foremost duties of the individual to the state, can only be given to a competent and lawful government.⁵⁰ Obedience may be either active or passive. One form of passive obedience Williams calls subjection to pretenders or usurpers or cases pertaining to their cognizance or another tribunal without resistance to the unlawful rule. Such "undue proceeding is not tolerable in all well-ordered *states*."⁵¹ It is with active and passive obedience to lawful authority that Williams shows his chief concern as the only healthy civil condition of individual life. Obedience should, Williams argued, be given to lawful government: first because Christ commanded obedience to civil powers, and Paul and the Apostles did likewise, in civil things.⁵² Secondly, active and passive obedience should be given when it represents the major voice

⁴⁸ *The Hireling Ministry*, p. 176.
⁴⁹ *Bloody Tenent Yet More Bloody*, N C P., Vol. IV, p. 219.
⁵⁰ *Ibid*, p. 300.
⁵¹ *Ibid*, p. 267.
⁵² *Bloudy Tenent of Persecution*, N C P., Vol. III, pp. 4, 364 ff.

of the society; for he claims "There is a civil faithfulness, obedience, honestie, chastity, etc," requisite of all members of society without regard to creed, race, or form of organization.[53]   But active obedience cannot be given to "him that hath no *Activitie* nor *Abilitie*" nor lawful competence to command and rule and judge.[54]   This allows for rebellion against the civil government when incompetent or unlawful.   Williams' principle of obedience as a limit upon individual action in society was carried into practice by his fellow colonists and made part of constitutional law in 1640 and 1647.   The simplest statement of this principle is found in the agreement of 1636: "We . . . do promise to subject ourselves in active and passive obedience to all such orders as shall be made for public good of the body in an orderly way by the Major Consent."[55]

In a letter to the town of Warwick, in 1666, Williams gave a lengthy and comprehensive analysis of the reasons for civil obedience to civil laws.[56]   He argued for obedience first from the standpoint of equity and fairness, the ethical and philosophical basis, "Common Honestie and Common Justice in common dealings between Man and Man;" secondly, that of internal and external "Hazards" to the state resulting from disobedience, a utilitarian and rational basis for obedience.   Williams' principle of active and passive obedience based upon the individual right and duty to judge the competence and lawfulness of the civil government and laws is a not inconsiderable motivating force in his individualism.

Individual freedom of action in the new society is also limited by man's duty to serve the state "in person," and "to perform their services."   A refusal to serve the lawful part and perform the rightful tasks as a member of the social group is to be punished "according to their deserts and merits."[57]   Such service can be required "towards the common charges or defence" at any time.   This civil duty was laid down as a constitutional principle in the Rhode Island Plantations: "And then in case a man be

---

[53] *Bloody Tenent Yet More Bloody,* N C P., Vol. IV, pp. 267, 313. N C P., Vol. III, pp. 108 f, 366.

[54] *Ibid,* pp. 300 f, 267 ff.

[55] R I C R., Vol. I, p. 14.   See N C P., Vol. VI, pp. 4 f, where the idea as originally presented by Williams is given in the germ.

[56] R I H S P., Vol. VIII, pp. 147 ff.

[57] *Letters,* N C P., Vol. VI, pp. 178 ff, 401 ff, 265 ff; N C P., Vols. III and IV.   R I H S P., Vol. VIII, pp. 147 ff.

called unto Office by lawful Assemble, and refuse to beare office, or be called by an officer to assist in the execution of his office, and refuse to assist him, he shall forfeit as much again as his wages would have amounted unto, or be otherwise fined by the judgment of his Peers, and to pay his fine or forfeiture, unless the Colony, or that lawful Assembly release him. But in case of eminent danger, no man shall refuse."[58]

The individual, furthermore, owes to the civil state *"rewards and wages"* in the form of *"tribute, toll, custome,* which are *wages* payable by all sorts of *Men, Natives* and *Forreigners,* who enjoy the same benefit of *Publicke peace* and *commerce* in the *Nation."*[59] Each member of society is bound to serve in "purse" and "to pay their freight,"[60] for "no government," Williams wrote in 1680, "is maintained without tribute, custom, rates, taxes, etc." which should be paid "not only for fear, but for conscience sake." When lawful rates and taxes are resisted, the state may justly and reasonably demand the "Civill maintenance of their Civill officers and to force it where it is denied . . . it is folly to resist (one or more) [and] it is the duty of every man to maintain, and encourage, and strengthen the hand of authority" to collect the payment.[61] "But no man should be bound to maintain a worship against his own consent. . . . Christs labourers [are] worthy of their hire but from them that hire them."[62] The civil government as the agent and servant deserves its rewards and wages, the equal payment of which becomes a part of the civil duties of every inhabitant of the particular state.

As a means to the highest end of common welfare and liberty, every member ought to limit his freedom of action and espouse "government by way of arbitration" of differences and conflicting interests. "If men agree themselves by Arbitration, no State was know of disallows that, neither doe we. But if men refuse that which is but common humanity between man and man then to compel such unreasonable persons to a reasonable way" by arbitration and compromise through community or state direction. The arbitrators are to be paid for their trouble, and "the arbitrators to follow no other employment till the cause be ended

[58] R I C R., Vol. I, pp. 157 f.
[59] *Bloudy Tenent of Persecution,* N C P., Vol. III, pp. 299, 355.
[60] N C P., Vol. VI, pp. 178 ff.
[61] Letter: *To the Town of Providence,* N C P., Vol. VI, p. 402.
[62] *Bloudy Tenent of Persecution,* N C P., Vol. III, pp. 304, 299, 355.

without consent of the whole that have to do with the cause. Instance. In the first Arbitration the offender may offer reasonable terms of peace, and the [injured person] may exact upon him and refuse and trouble men beyond reasonable satisfaction, so for the last arbitrators to judge where the fault was . . . ."[63] The arbitrators are not to be persons out of touch with the actual conditions that gave rise to the differences and conflicts—a vital point in arbitration for the modern world to recognize. Nor are the arbitrators to make arbitration a profession; they are merely performing one of the many duties incumbent upon a citizen in a modern state.

The fostering of arbitration Williams considered a duty not only between man and man, but nation and nation. For the sake of common peace, safety, credit and liberty, sacrifice of some personal interests must be made by each individual "for pacification and accommodation of our sad differences;" he further suggested that Providence tell the other towns, "we are persuaded to remove our obstructions."[64] He repeatedly asked individuals, towns, and other colonies, to "agree to submit their differences to the wisdom of such solemn commissions chosen out of the Whole Country; the hearts of the claimers to acquiesce and rest in your determination. . . . I know there are objections, but also know that love to God, love to the Country and posterity, will conquer greater matters." In two undated letters to Providence, he requests "that our ancient use of arbitracion be brought in esteem again."[65] Compromise of interests and conflicting opinions is a fundamental duty of each individual member of society or society of states.

Only when the individual refuses to perform his duty or resists lawful requests for his service to the civil state, may the civil government use force to compel and punish him for neglect of his rightful duty. But the civil authority must first endeavor to secure "obedience through will" and reason, and especially through debates and disputes whereby public opinion is aroused, before force is to be applied.[66] Williams is tenacious in his in-

---

[63] R I C R., Vol. I, pp. 29 f.

[64] N C P., Vol. VI, Letter: *To the Town of Providence*, pp. 265 f.

[65] *Ibid, To Commissioners of the United Colonies*, p. 393. R I H S P., Vol. VIII, pp. 160 f.

[66] *Bloudy Tenent of Persecution*, N C P., Vol. III, pp. 257, 302.

sistence that the reason, will and purpose should be made the basis for obedience to a competent and lawful authority. But when some of the colonists claimed that since the government has no right to interfere with matters of conscience they could do with impunity whatever conscience dictated, and others went so far as to deny all state and governmental power and authority,[67] Williams replied in unmistakable terms in his "Parable of the Ship of State:" "If any of the seamen refuse to perform their services, or passengers to pay their freight; if any refuse to help in person or purse, toward the common charges or defence; if any refuse to obey the common laws or orders of the ship, concerning their common peace or preservation" or liberty, then the commander "may judge, resist, compel, punish such transgressions according to their deserts and merits."[68]

The individualism of Williams was to be achieved by establishing reciprocal duties, obligations and rights and liberty through the competent influences of reason, will and laws which guarantee to each individual member of society his natural and civil rights and liberties. This can be accomplished only by setting with the free consent of its members limits upon individual freedom of action within the social organism. The consensus of political thinkers today is against civil state interference in indifferent and non-essential matters. But when matters that formerly were considered non-essential matters of state action affect the well-being and equal civil freedom of the other members, then the state must remedy the evil. Milton's individualism was arbitrary individual freedom of action, and consequently largely destructive in its ultimate effect upon society. Williams' individualism is not arbitrary: the individual is free only as a member of a social group; he has rights in society only as a member of civil society; his freedom and his rights are dependent upon the similar freedom and rights of the other members. The individual is bound to be as watchful and anxious for the peace, life, liberty, and property of each of his fellow-members as for his own. His actual civil rights and liberties are dependent upon a similar condition for every other individual. This may be called a fanciful ideal, but to Williams it was the only means to the highest end and purpose of each individual in civil society.

---

[67] Staples: *Annals*, p. 45.
[68] Letter: *To the Town of Providence*, N C P., Vol. VI, pp. 178 f.

Against the cry that his individualism is the mere fiction of a dreamer may be placed the lesson that his fellow-colonists so well learned from him: "We . . . do engage ourselves to the uttmost of our Estates and Strength, to maintain the authority and to enjoy the liberty granted us by our Charter . . . and to mainteyne each other by the same authority, in his lawful right and liberties. . . . And now to the end that we may give, each to other . . . as hopeful assurance as we are able, touching each man's peaceable and quiett enjoyment of his lawfull right and Liberty."[69] No man has the social or civil right or liberty to do anything at any time that will interfere with "each man's peaceable and quiett enjoyment of his lawfull right and Liberty." This is true individualism, and Williams was a true seer when he saw it as the only possible form of civil duties consistent with individual welfare and common well-being in the new society.[70]

In addition to numerous individual civil duties, a citizen acquires certain individual civil rights and liberties in every *de jure* state. The Constitution of Rhode Island, in 1647, well illustrates how the powers of the civil government are limited to a specific field of action. The constitution places a twofold limit upon state activities. The first is a limit by means of a Bill of Rights: "That no person, in this Colonie shall be taken or imprisoned, or be disseized of his Lands and Liberties, or be Exiled, or any otherwise molested or destroyed, but by the Lawfull judgment of his Peers, or by some known Law, and according to the Letter of it, Ratified and confirmed by the major part of the Generall Assembly lawfully met and orderly managed." Secondly, limit to state action is set by an inclusive and exclusive statement of its right of action and the individual field of rights and liberties: "These are the Lawes that concern all men, and these are the Penalties for the transgression thereof, which by common consent are Ratified and Established throwout this whole Colonie; and otherwise than thus what is herein forbidden, all men may walk as their consciences perswade them, every one in the name of his God."[71]

---

[69] R I C R., Vol. I, pp. 156 ff.

[70] Fields: *History of Rhode Island*, pp. 434 f. A victim of an unjust and untruthful indictment found not guilty in Court might recover any costs to which he had been subjected, with damages, and complainant who had sworn falsely might be sentenced in stocks or fined twenty shillings.

[71] R I C R., Vol. I, pp. 157, 190.

Individual civil rights and liberties definitely limit the state in the powers and activities it can confer upon the civil government. Both the local and central governments are to be based on law and order, each with a limited field of action and power with respect to the individual.[72] This peculiar type of government by law as the "Means and Agents and instruments" Williams considered necessary to make civil liberty possible. "The 2 Jewell" argued Williams with the Warwick colonists, "is Libertie: the first of our spirits which neither old nor New England knowes the like, nor no part of the World a greater. 2. Libertie of our persons: no Life, no Limbe taken from us, no Corporall punishment, no Restraint, but by known Lawes and Agreements of our owne making. 3. Libertie of our estates, Howses, Catle, Landes, Goods, and not a peny to be taken by any rate from us, without every mans free debate by his Deputies, chosen by himselfe and sent to the General Assembly. 4. Libertie of Society or Corporacion: of sending or being sent to the General Assembly, of choosing or being chosen to all offices, and of making or repealing all Lawes and Constitutions among us. 5. A liberty of making laws "respecting our Wilderness Estate and Condicion."[73] The colony founded by Williams incorporated the concept of Liberty contained in his numerous letters and his treatises, and established a local self-governing unit in addition to a popular central authority. By making this concept of individual liberty a constitutional principle, Williams emphasized one of the most vital structural principles of the new social order.

With the first jewels "of Libertie," that of "our spirits," Williams demanded that the state should not interfere. When interpreted through his letters and treatises, this liberty is wide and comprehensive. It includes liberty of "all kinds of consciences," religious liberty and liberty of thought. In it is resident also the "liberty of free, really, free disputes, debates, writing and printing, etc." Especially emphatic is he in his stress on freedom of speech and the press. But this freedom is to be limited when it transgresses the civil peace and common welfare.[74]

Freedom of communion is one of the most precious and

---

[72] *Master Cottons Letter*, N C P., Vol. I, p. 48.
[73] R I H S P., Vol. VIII, p. 140.
[74] N C P., Vol. VI, pp. 374, 235, 246; Vol. III, p. 171.

necessary rights of the individual, and one of the indispensable elements of all civil liberty. A group of individuals may, even, organize and practise ordinances requisite for their particular society against the consent of the state, provided they are clear and free "from *scandalous offences*," as also from "disobedience to *civill* lawes of the state."   But in permitting this liberty of communion all "grosse partiality" must be eliminated; for all civil liberties and civil restraints ought to be administered on the basis of impartiality.[75]

That the civil state ought not to interfere with the freedom of assemblage, when not disturbing the civil peace and order, Williams often reiterated.   Likewise the colonists upheld this position on many occasions, including the episodes of the Quakers and Jews, and the gatherings of the Harris and Gorton followers.   In his reply to the authors of the *Model* he continues, "If they intend that the *civill Magistrate* should permit liberty to the free and voluntary Spiritual meetings of their Subjects, I shall subscribe unto them; but if they intend that *Magistrates* should give liberty only unto themselves, and not to the rest of their subjects . . . then I say (as before), it is to cause him to give Libertie with a *partiall* hand, and *unequall Ballance*."[76]

Right of rebellion and of forcing a change in civil institutions, either peacefully or if necessary by force, Williams assumes as a "natural and civil" right of the individual within the civil state. This does not deny the right of civil government to force its members to civil obedience.   In regard to rebellion he writes without further comment: "Some Papists and some Protestants agree in deposing of Magistrates. : . . If *Magistrates ought* (that is, ought only) to be chosen out of the Church, I demand if they ought not also to be *dethroned* and *deposed*, when they cease to be of the *Church*, either by voluntary departure from it, or by *excommunication* out of it."[77]   In the light of the previous quotation no extended interpretation need be applied to the following passage: "the *Soveraign, original*, and *foundation* of *civil power* lies in the *people* . . . and if so . . . It is evident that such *Governments* as are by them erected and established, have no more

---

[75] *Bloudy Tenent of Persecution*, N C P., Vol. III, pp. 389, 394, 171 f, 395. N C P., Vol VI, pp. 262 f, 278 f.
[76] *Ibid*, 389, 394 ff, 401 f.
[77] *Ibid*, pp. 415, 375, 377.

power, nor for no longer time, then the *civill power* or people consenting and agreeing shall betrust them with.[78] . . . The *civill Magistrates,* whether *Kings,* or *Parliaments, States, Governours* . . . must be considered (as formerly) invested with no more *power,* then the *people* betrust them with." And when they go beyond their commission then rebellion is justifiable. Civil reform, and even rebellion, is justified against tyranny and arbitrary civil government.[79]

Nor ought the state to obstruct the individual right of petition and suggestion with regard to policies of the civil state. Williams repeatedly practised it, not only in Rhode Island, but with the other New England colonies and the Parliament itself.[80] Furthermore, each citizen has a right to equal taxation for the support of the government, to the equal and equitable administration of justice and laws, and to equal political liberty. In order to assure to each member of the state equal *"naturall & Civill Rights & Liberties"* of thought, action, life, and property, a state must uphold "justice" impartially, and limit its action in accordance with the civil laws enacted by the consent of the major part.

In discussing the limits of the state, Williams frequently repeated that "the *Government* of the *civill Magistrate* extendeth no further than over the *bodies* and *goods* of the Subject."[81] Furthermore, he placed limits on what can be done with and to these *"bodies* and *goods"* in the form of a commission or constitution. The civil government acts "as *Derivatives* and *Agents* immediately derived from" the whole; therefore it has no more power than the *"Bodies* or *Fountaines* themselves, which Power, Might, or Authority, is . . . but natural, humane, civill," nor than "the common weale derive unto, and betrust it with."[82] State powers and activities may not at any time transgress the "bounds of

---

[78] *Ibid,* pp. 249 f.

[79] *Ibid,* pp. 355, 418, 96, 365, 415, 419, 297. N C P., Vols. IV, p. 300; and VI, pp. 4 ff, 267. This does not deny the state's right to resist rebellion.

[80] *Queries,* N C P., Vol. II, p. 254; N C P., Vols. II, IV, and I, Williams' *Prefaces.*

[81] N C P., Vols. III, pp. 228, 252; IV, p. 409; and II, p. 254.

[82] *Bloudy Tenent of Persecution,* N C P., Vol. III, p. 398. *Queries,* N C P., Vol. II, pp. 253, 266.

civility,"[83] and require an oath on any occasion; "for an *oath,* being an *invocation* of a true or false *God* to judge in a case, is an action of a *spirituall* and *religious* nature."[84] And so the state ought to limit its actions to civil activities.

The functions of the state are so limited that the government may receive only "*politicall* and *state abilities* to *make* and *execute* such *Civill Lawes* which may concern the common rights, peace and safety." But it may not be arbitrary in its civil exercise.[85] Yet it has sufficient power to keep the civil peace and order. "In the *Civill State* from the beginning of the World, God hath Armed *Fathers, Masters, Magistrates,* to punish evill doers, that is, such of whose action [they] are to judge, and accordingly to punish such . . . as transgresse against the good and peace of their Civill State, *Families, Townes, Cities, Kingdomes;* their *States, Governments, Governors, Lawes, Punishments,* and *weapons* being all of a *Civill Nature*" and therefore all forms of disobedience, resistance, and social evils forbidden by civil laws are to be "supprest, as may best conduce to the *pulicke safety.*" The sword "of *Civill Justice* [is] of a *material civill Nature,* for the *defense* of *Persons, Estates, Families, Liberties* of a *City* or *Civill State;*" in fact, "*Civil rights* . . . ought justly to be *preserved* by a *civil State.*"[86] And in case of rightful activities and of urgent need, the state can also "require the help of any of her members"[87] to help preserve the civil peace.

In its powers and activities the state is limited to securing to each member of society his common rights, peace and safety. To protect the individual from social and civil oppression is the essential duty of the state. It must refrain from any partial or unequal action in relation to any group or portion of the people.[88] And at all times it must distribute and divide the agencies of administration according to the agreement or instructions creating

---

[83] *Bloody Tenent Yet More Bloody,* N C P., Vol. IV, p. 203. See also R I C R., Vol. I, p. 441, (1658). An act of the Assembly declares that to secure "wholesome liberty for the whole or major part" no law is to go into effect until twenty days after the dissolution of the Assembly to allow for a referendum in case of dissatisfaction.
[84] N C P., Vol. III, p. 253; Vol. II, pp. 48 ff. Winthrop: *Journal,* Vol. I, pp. 123 ff. Straus: *Roger Williams,* p. 46.
[85] *Bloody Tenent of Persecution,* N C P., Vol. III, pp. 366, 394. N C P., Vol. IV, p. 360.
[86] *Ibid,* pp. 108 f, 384, 160. N C P., Vol. II, p. 266; Vol. IV, p. 74.
[87] *Letters,* N C P., Vol. VI, p. 150.
[88] *Bloody Tenent of Persecution,* N C P., Vol. III, pp. 389, 395, 401 f.

the administrative machinery. It must guarantee to its people publicity of all government action and freedom of opinion in speech and press. "The magistrates power and weapons being essentially civill, and so" do not reach "to the impiety or ungodliness, but the incivility and unrighteousness of tongue and hand."[89] The state must not interfere with faith and the religious functions of the church; it is confined to the adjudication of such questions as involve the rights of property and civil corporations voluntarily formed under the statute laws. The government is merely the servant of the people to look after the general welfare of society. To do either more or less than is conducive to the general welfare of the people is to have missed its ultimate purpose and its highest ends.

The limits which Williams placed upon the powers and activities of the civil state are in harmony with and a logical outgrowth of his concept of state, its sovereignty, purpose and functions. The entire machinery of the new social structure erected by Williams and his fellow-colonists is shaped and conditioned to allow for the greatest possible amount of individuality to its members. The state is limited in its functions to allow (1) for religious liberty and liberty of consciences; (2) for the expression of an individualism modified by reciprocal social and civil duties and obligations, and influenced by reason, will, and obedience through law; (3) for the full play of man's natural and civil rights and liberties in civil society. The state is further limited (4) to natural, humane and civil power over the bodies and goods in accordance with a commission, (5) to the impartial enforcement of civil laws, and (6) to look after the general welfare of its individual members. The state has most perfectly fulfilled its purpose and has been most thoroughly cognizant of its ideal limits when it has maintained for each individual the *"Civil right and Priviledge* due to him as a Man, a Subject, a Citizen."[90]

---

[89] *Ibid*, p. 270.
[90] *Bloody Tenent Yet More Bloody*, N C P., Vol. IV, p. 414.

PART 3

INDIVIDUALISM AND THE CIVIL POWER

The success of Williams' venture to establish a state on the basis of religious and political freedom was due in some measure to the place and age. "There were many fostering circumstances. The conditions of life and society in the new world, where men had to found *de novo* their institutions, at great distance from the straitening influence of age-long prescription and custom, had much in them to abet impatience with whatever should seek to fetter free expansion. The character of much of the immigration went for the issue of liberty. The adventurous spirit out of which came, first, more or less of dissatisfaction with home conditions; and second, voluntary exile into new climes to meet hardness and danger, insensibly fitted the mind to the propositions of liberty. Almost from the very beginning the colonists assumed a larger political liberty than they had known, as the plain necessity of their colonial life. It is not strange that, in harmony with this new spirit, the conscience should presently seek to free itself from all bonds of human authority. To this was added a natural resentment towards the foolish and arbitrary actions of the civil authorities in many questions of religious import. The unwise severity of theocratic Massachusetts revolted many of her own citizens[;] . . . by reason of'. . . general and many minor influences, the education of the people in the principle of religious liberty was equal-paced with that which issued in"[91] political and civil liberty.

Because of the difficulties encountered in trying to adjust state action to the concept of individual liberty, the limits of state action are not susceptible to a clear indication in general terms. That natural and imperative limits actually operate, no one who seriously studies the structure of society can doubt. But beyond the limit of necessary cooperation imperative for public good, state action becomes merely convenient for industrial and social enterprise. To maintain such limits of action that man may be assured of even a tolerable existence, some universal authority is needed to make opportunity equal between man and man. And that authority is what is generally recognized as the civil state.

---

[91] Cobb: *Rise of Religious Liberty*, pp. 14 f.

200

The ancient state directed all things, civil and religious, and reserved to itself the right to interfere in every relation of life. Every sphere of human activity—including religion, law, morals, art, culture and science—was subject to state interference. No recognition was given to the personal rights of man. He was born and lived for the state, and it was the duty of the state to determine his life.[92]

In the Middle Ages, church and state were considered undisputed masters over man's entire existence. Neither political nor individual liberty was recognized.[93] The Church of Rome declared the state subservient to the church and obliged to obedience. In actual practice the man who differed with the dogma of the church was excommunicated, and was without the privileges and protection of the state. With the loss of standing in the church, his claim to civil privileges ceased to exist. "His faith, his thought, his speech, his writings, his very conscience, were alike to be determined by ecclesiastical authority."[94] In opposition to dictation of the church, neither thought nor action was permissible. The Middle Ages tolerated no freedom of religious belief, at least outside the pale of academic discussions. The state was, in fact, a mere tool of the church; it was nothing more than the secular arm of the church to administer its decree and carry out its will.[95]

But underneath this apparent acceptance of the universal superiority of the Church of Rome, the disintegrating forces were silently but none the less surely at work. The sovereignty of state and sovereignty of the individual were steadily on their way toward becoming the two central axioms from which all theories of social structure would proceed, and whose relationship to each other would be the focus of all theoretical controversy. "And soon we may see that combination which is characteristic of the 'nature-rightly' doctrines of a later time: namely, a combination of the Absolutism which is due to the renaissance of the antique idea of the State, with the modern Individualism which unfolds itself from out the Christiano-Germanic

[92] Sherger: *The Evolution of Modern Liberty*, p. 1. Bluntschli: *The Theory of the State*, p. 58.
[93] Cobb: *Rise of Religious Liberty*, p. 32.
[94] Waring: *Political Theories of Martin Luther*, p. 233.
[95] MacKinnon: *A History of Modern Liberty*, Vol. I; Vedder: *The Reformation in Germany, Introduction*, pp. XXV-IXL.

thought of Liberty." During the Reformation and the centuries following, the state and individual have fiercely contended over "the delimitation of the provinces assigned to them by Natural Law, and in the course of the struggle all intermediate groups have been first degraded into the position of the more or less arbitrary fashioned creatures of mere positive Law, and in the end obliterated."[96] Throughout the last four centuries, the two forces have been struggling for supremacy in the forms of nationalism and individualism.

With the beginning of the Reformation, the combat between state and individual for authority in civil life came into prominence. Luther was the chief mouthpiece of the movement both in church and state. The Church of Rome was soon entirely eliminated from the controversy, and relegated to spiritual things alone. Luther declared the sphere of action of church and state to be separated and distinct. The church can act only in matters of doctrines, morals, and within its own organization—that is, only as a spiritual authority. All temporal affairs are exclusively of secular interest. To man he granted the right of self-defense against tyranny, and of religious and civil liberty. In civil things, he declared the church subject of state control.[97] "Religious and Civil liberty—of conscience, speech, and press—are inalienable rights belonging alike to every individual, subject only to equal rights to others, the maintenance of public peace and order, and the sovereign power of the state over the external life, where it touches the lives of others."[98] But Luther, in trying to charter the sphere of action of church and state, was after all only setting forth in theory the ideal state activity. It remained for Williams and his followers in Rhode Island to establish as constitutional principles recognized limits of interference and relationships between church and state and individual. But the majority of the settlers seem to have had little sympathy with Williams' theory of social life, except "as to what the state should *not* do."

In the founding of Providence the "Christiano-Germanic thought of liberty" becomes for a time supreme over the ancient idea of the absolute state of the Renaissance. Williams laid down

---

[96] Gierke: *Political Theories of the Middle Ages*, pp. 87, 100.
[97] Luther: *On the Liberty of the Christian Man; To the German Nobility; On Civil Magistracy; On the Babylonian Captivity.*
[98] Waring: *Political Theories of Martin Luther*, pp. 277, 232-261.

a definite sphere of action for both the church and state, making each supreme in its particular sphere, and made the state a servant to the individual man. Liberty of conscience and religious liberty is made a recognized principle of constitutional law. The church and state are held separate and distinct in the essential nature and object of each. And the church is made a civil corporation with only corporation rights and subject to state control in its civil corporate activities which the state is required to protect and regulate. Membership in the church body, like that of any other civil corporation, neither increases nor diminishes any of the rights and privileges of a citizen. The church can act only in matters of doctrine, morals, worship and affairs within its own body, with definite limits of action between civil and religious affairs. "Where civil liberty is entire," writes Williams, "it includes liberty of conscience, and where liberty of conscience is entire, it includes civil liberty."

A written constitution for this modern society limits the state powers in civil affairs and creates the government machinery with a prescribed sphere of civil action. The civil powers of the government extend only over the bodies and goods of the citizens and inhabitants. Just what can be done with these bodies and goods is established by the people in variable fundamental laws. In general it may be said that the essential duty of the government is the protection of the individual from social and civil oppression. At the same time that it upholds individual rights, the government also uses its authority to encourage the individual in carrying out his duties and obligations in society, in order to guarantee mutual humane and civil rights and liberties. But in all civil things the government merely looks after the general moral and civil welfare of society.

The individualism of Williams finds its clearest expression in his attempt to adjust state authority to the concept of individual liberty. This adjustment is made by postulating individual liberty as possible only through equitable civil laws. Since individual action in this new society is guided by common interests and welfare, certain "natural rights" are replaced by mutual civil rights and liberties. The individual acquires duties as well as rights in this new social arrangement. Of the chief duties acquired are those of obedience to lawful government as equitable, fair, reasonable and expedient; those of service to the state in "person and purse," in the form of official tasks and defense, and of taxes, tolls, customs for the maintenance of the civil machinery; those of arbitration and adjudication of differences and interests; and those of individual responsibility for the rights, liberties and welfare of the other members. Among the natural and civil rights and liberties, Williams considered: liberty of conscience, person, speech, writing, printing, debates, disputes, etc.; rights of property, corporation, self-government, referendum and recall, communion and organization with regard to indifferent civil things without the consent of the state; and rights of rebellion, assembly, civil reform, petition, equal justice, impartial treatment and enforcement of all civil laws, and equal taxation for the support of the government. These duties, rights and liberties, he contended, are an essential part of the fundamental laws, but always subject to the nature, conditions and circumstances of time and place. With the founding of Rhode Island by Roger Williams, the combat between the Renaissance ideal of the ancient absolute state and Christiano-Germanic individualism resulted in enthroning the individual man as the master of the state in a new society developing in the American wilderness.

PART 4
CONCLUDING REMARKS ON WILLIAMS' POLITICAL THOUGHT

Roger Williams has been considered in this study primarily as a political philosopher—a forerunner of Locke and the "nature-rightly" school of the eighteenth and nineteenth centuries, and the pioneer of modern individualism and modern federalism. There is no intention to obscure his significance as a theologian, for in this field he also ranks with the foremost liberals of his day, with Milton and Sir Henry Vane, Jr. But our chief task here is with him as a political thinker and statesman. His true place in American thought has been too long obscured by the ecclesiastical historians, who in emphasizing his defense of liberty of conscience, failed to recognize that his principles of religious liberty and liberty of conscience were naturally deduced from the major premises of his political theory. In his whole-hearted devotion to discovering a new basis for social life, he left no system or theory of state unchallenged. Although the cast of his thought was social rather than theological, he eventually realized that the establishment of a new system of relationship between church and state and individual was the only key to a new social order.

In the new social order outlined by Williams, the abstract theories of state were rejected for a more idealistic and more realistic concept of the nature, origin and necessity of the state and its sovereignty. The state originates, as a social necessity, in a community consciousness of a common will and purpose for mutual protection, peace, order and welfare. By nature it is civil, humane, and political, being both objective and subjective in its manifestations. In the body of citizens representing the community consciousness in a political capacity is located, originally and perpetually, the sovereignty which is absolute, indivisible, competent, and independent. This sovereignty delegates its powers through a variable civil agreement to the civil government and the local territorial administrative units, both of which are limited in their capacity by the powers conferred by this commision. Externally this sovereignty is independent of the authority of any foreign power, ecclesiastical and civil, and the equal of every other state in international affairs.

The civil government is the civil state functioning as the agent and instrument of the sovereign people to achieve the desired end. In its functions the government is strictly limited with regard to the local units, church, and individual members. The chief end of the state is to secure for each individual citizen the largest measure of freedom and well-being. To effect this end, the state is further limited in its use of force, and can subsist only by endeavoring to make proselytes through reason and will and law, by compromise, arbitration and adjudication of differences and interests between the state and individual and between man and man.

In his theory of individualism Roger Williams carried toward a logical conclusion the principles of the rights and liberties of man inherent in the Reformation movement and the Renaissance. The civil constitution which forms the basis for the functions of state is a mutual civil agreement, responsive to changing conditions and capable of modifications to meet present needs, entered into by the joint and free consent of individuals, orderly assembled, in a political organization in accordance with nature, experience, equity, reason and expediency. By an application of the medieval theory of corporation to the social structure in two distinct spheres of activity, Williams cemented the machinery of the federal state with the principle of self-government, and demonstrated that the origin, nature, functions and ends of the church are distinct from those of the state, giving the church only civil corporation privileges.

The rights and liberties of the individual in this new social experiment were guarded in numerous ways. A bill of rights protected him from interference from the state and fellow-citizens. He was guaranteed liberty and equality "both in land and government." By means of frequent elections, joint and individual initiative of laws, compulsory referendum, the right of recall of all laws including the constitution, and appeal to arbitration, and a single legislative body, the government was continually held in check by the sovereignty of the people. The civil laws and constitution could be interpreted only by the same power that created them originally, the sovereignty of the people represented in the legislature. The civil government in Rhode Island was conceived by Williams as a corporation for public service, the agent of the people to maintain for each individual the "*Civill rights* and *Priviledges* due to him as a Man, a Subject, a Citizen."

"If we follow the development," ventures Borgeaud in his *Rise of Modern Democracy*, "of the principles of the Reformation in Europe, first on the Continent, then in England and Scotland, and finally in America, we for our part shall have no difficulty in admitting that there was a process of evolution in which the whole Western World took part. Anglo-Saxon democracy failed in the seventeenth century in Europe in its struggle against ancient laws and institutions. It began afresh beyond the ocean, in a new society which had been born again. It was there that the movement of the eighteenth century began; New England was the country in which it burst its bark, and every one of the colonies of the refugees has had its share, a large or small part, but none the less real, in giving birth to what has become the mighty American democracy. . . . Democracy is not the heritage of the single State of Rhode Island." While Connecticut, Plymouth, and in a lesser degree Massachusetts, contributed to the development of the modern democratic state, it was, however, in Rhode Island where the idea had its completest and fullest expression in the seventeenth century.

The controlling spirits of Rhode Island were simply in advance of the age, and her people were necessarily misunderstood; and they suffered as such reformers and pioneers usually have suffered. But in extenuation of Puritan bigotry, no need arises for any denial of historical facts. The magistrates and leaders of the other New England colonies were mostly honest, sincere and conscientious men. Their course was consistent with their theory of government. If that course was ill-judged and narrow, the fault may not have been so much in the leaders as in the times. The leaders of Massachusetts, Plymouth, and Connecticut and New Haven, had breathed the same political atmosphere as had Roger Williams. Many had gone to the same university, and read many of the same books. If few of them traveled or lived on the continent, they nevertheless came in contact with men who had been there, heard praises of Italian Republics, had taken part in the government of their towns at home, and some of them had a knowledge of the democratic government of gild or trading company. Their experiences were in many ways similar to those of Roger Williams.

But in Williams, more thoroughly and completely than in any other of the New England leaders, we see the blending of English, Dutch, Italian, Greek, Roman, and Jewish ideas with the influence of town, gild, company, college and church. With the fullest realization of how many factors went into the conception of the new social and democratic experiment, there will come a greater appreciation of the significance of his achievement—and a realization that the American conception of the federal state with its constitution was not entirely thought out in Independence Hall, Philadelphia. The fundamental doctrines of the American democracy had been implicit in America for over a century, and many of them had been tested in countries and institutions before they were applied in America. The ideas that formed the basis of the federal state were originally independent of federalism—but all of them synthesized under a form of government laid the basis for the modern federal state.

To Roger Williams, the state of Rhode Island with its constitution and government was an experiment, as all life is an experiment. He had a definite realistic strain in his thinking, expressed in his refusal to take words and formulae for facts, in his belief that intelligent morals consist in making clear what we want and that we must pay to get it, and in the idea of rule by law and reason where social force will eventually impinge in the case of any adopted course of conduct. He very often almost suggested in his realism that whatever wins out in fair conflict of the struggle for existence is the fit and the good. His social attitude suggested that liberalism is a method of intelligence prior to being a method of action; it signifies the adoption of a method of inquiry to social affairs, combining in the conclusion reached insight, social desire, and actual conditions under observation. Within the limits set by the social structure, the organized community has a right to try experiments, and Williams set as his task the continual urging and prodding of his fellowmen to follow him in his seeking and searching and experimenting to find a nobler social conception than Europe had vouchsafed them.

Williams had no social panacea to dole out, no fixed social programs, no code of fixed ends to be realized. He did not idealize popular government; and to him the voice of the people instead of being the voice of God merely represents their social desire at that particular time. He repudiated the false logic which applies the classic system of fictitious fixed concepts to social issues which arise out of the conflicts of daily life. He met the requirements of a scientific attitude toward social problems by applying the method of comparison by means of measuring and weighing in his advocacy of compromise and adjudication of public and common interests. In his belief in freedom of thought and expression as the necessary directive for an equitable social structure and in his belief in the experimental character of life and thought, Williams takes a foremost place as the colonial representative of the liberal mind.

Williams was conscious of the great work he was doing. Although harassed by trials and dissensions, he never despaired of ultimate success. In this new social structure, he avoided the prevalent error of overestimating the intelligence and underestimating the instinct of man, an error found in all the writers —as Grotius, Hobbes, Spinoza, Pufendorf, Locke and Rousseau— vho explain the origin of state by the hypothesis of an original ocial compact based on an element of intelligent selection.[99] Villiams adopted the safer view of regarding the state and government as the product of the natural growth of society. Numrous so-called inconsistencies and faults of his, so much harped pon, such as procuring a charter from England, debate with ie Quakers, and arrest of Harris; do not show a lapse in his inciples, but rather substantiate them. For it was only by overming all opposition dangerous and subversive to the structural velopment of his new social experiment, by means of reason, bate, disputes and expediency, that he could hope to achieve ideal of complete civil liberty.

That Williams correctly estimated the psychological, econic, social and political aspects underlying the free state of a rty-loving people, is fully attested by Channing in referring he characteristics of the colony: "Foremost among the pearities may be mentioned a spirit of intense local patriotism :h has no parallel elsewhere; the people of each town seem to ealous for their local rights and distinctions, and the people ll towns of the state seem to combine together only in op-

Stevens: *Sources of the Constitution of the United States*, p. 1.
 and Crane: *Politics*, p. 68.

position to other colonies and states. In Rhode Island, individualism always had its highest development. . . . Everywhere in
the colony men held strong opinions, and everywhere there was
extreme toleration of the ideas of others. In such a community,
men of power would profoundly influence the thoughts, lives,
souls, and doings of others."[100] Williams himself stated that he
founded a society possessing an unprecedented measure of "such
unheard of liberties." "A human and liberal spirit," say Parrington, "he was groping for a social order more generous than
any theocracy—that should satisfy the aspirations of men for a
catholic fellowship, greater than sect or church, village or nation, embracing all races and creeds, bringing together the
sundered societies of men in a common spirit of good will."[101]

The founding of Rhode Island was not accomplished without
violent expressions of discontent among its members, and oc-
casional civil disorders. But all these things marked the ferment
caused by a new and vital spirit. The principle had to be learned
by degrees in its practical application. The "lively experiment"
had to be put upon its trial, until men should discover that liberty and law must go hand in hand; "that faith, freedom, and
union are needful to the 'civil' and spiritual man. . . . This lesson Rhode Island was the first of all the States in the world to
set herself to learn. She learned and gave it as an object lesson to her sisters and the earth at large. Her experiment was
a success. . . . Thus was constituted . . . a genuine republic—
the first thoroughly free government in the world, where the
state was left plastic to the moulding will of the citizen; the conscience at liberty to express itself in any way of doctrine and
worship; the church untrammelled by any prescription or prefer-
ence of the civil law. In this little colony of Rhode Island was
first set up this 'ensign of the people,' the model for the sister-
hood of states which was yet to possess the continent."[102]

---
[100] Channing: *History of the United States*, Vol. I, pp. 347 f.
[101] Parrington: *Main Currents in American Thought*, Vol. I, p. 63.
[102] Cobb: *Rise of Religious Liberty*, pp. 439 f, 436.

BIBLIOGRAPHY

I. COLLECTED AND SEPARATE WRITINGS

Williams (Roger), *Collected Works*,[1] (Ed. members of the Narragansett Club.) 6 volumes. The only collected edition, but several of his shorter treatises have not been included. Contains also *John Cottons Answer to Roger Williams*, together with a list of his separate works and an incomplete bibliography. Providence, 1866-1874.

A Key into the Language of America: or, an Help to the Language of the Natives of America called New England. Together with briefe observations of the Customes, Manners and Worships, etc. of the aforesaid Natives,[2] etc. London, 1643. Reprinted in Colonial Rhode Island Historical Society, Vol. I; and in greater part, in Colonial Massachusetts Historical Society, First Series, Vols. III and V. Reprinted from a manuscript copy by Z. Allen, 1827. Ed. in Narragansett Club Publications, Vol. I, by J. H. Trumbull, 1866.

Mr. Cottons Letter Lately Printed, Examined and Answered. London, 1644.

The Bloudy Tenent, of Persecution, for the Cause of Conscience, discussed, in a Conference between Truth and Peace, who, in all tender Affection, present to the High Court of Parliament, (as the Result of their Discussion,) these, (amongst other Passages) of highest Consideration. [London], 1644. Reprinted by the Hanserd Knollys Society, 1848. Printed in the Narragansett Club Publications, Vol. III, 1867. (Ed. Samuel Caldwell.)

---

[1] Bibliography of the writings of Roger Williams unpublished at the time of his death listed chronologically with references to where the writings have been printed and the present location of the originals has been published in Rhode Island Historical Society Collections, Vol. XI, pp. 11-17. Providence, 1918.

[2] An unknown pamphlet attributed to Williams is entitled a *Discourse of the Name Heathen*. According to the table appended to the *Key*, this "little additional *discourse*" on "that great point of their *Conversion*" was sent to press about the same time. Referred to as from Roger Williams' hands by Baillie in *A Dissvasive from the Errour of the Times*, London, 1645, pp. 60, 69. John Cotton in the first part of *The Way of Congregational Churches Cleared*, etc., in reply to Baillie's *Dissvasive*, upholds Baillie's testimony.

A Paroenetick, or Humble Address to the Parliament and Assembly for (not loose but) Christian Libertie. Second Impression, 1644. [Attributed by J. Carter Brown catalogue to R.W.]

Queries of highest consideration Proposed to Mr. Tho. Goodwin, Mr. Phillip Nye, Mr. Wil. Bridges, Mr. Jer. Burroughs, Mr. Sidr. Simpson, all Independents; and to the Commissioners from the General Assembly (so called) of the Church of Scotland upon the occasion of their late printed Apologies for themselves and their Churches. In all Humble Reverence presented to the view of the Right Honourable the Houses of the High Court of Parliament. London, 1644. Reprinted from the only known copy in the British Museum, by the Narragansett Club. (Ed. Reuben Guild, 1867.) Narragansett Club Publications, Vol. II, 1867.

Christenings make no Christians, R. W. London, 1645. Found by Dexter in the British Museum. Ed. with introductory comments by Sidney Rider in The Rhode Island Historical Tracts, No. 14. Providence, 1881.

The Bloody Tenent yet more Bloody: by Mr. Cottons endeavour to wash it white in the Blood of the Lambe; of whose precious Blood spilt in the Blood of his Servants; and of the Blood of Millions spilt in former and later Wars for Conscience Sake, that most Bloody Tenent of Persecution for the cause of Conscience, upon a second Tryal, is found now more apparently and more notoriously guilty. In this Rejoynder to Mr. Cotton, are principally *I The Nature of Persecution; II The Power of the Civill Sword in Spiritualls Examined: III The Parliaments permission of Dissenting Consciences* Justified. Also (as a Testimony to Mr. Clarks Narrative) is added a Letter to Mr. Endicot Governor of Massachusetts in N.E. London, 1652. Reprinted in Narragansett Club Publications, Vol. IV. (Ed. Samuel Caldwell, 1870.)

The Fourth Paper, Presented by Major Butler to the Honourable Committee of Parliament, for the Propagating of the Gospel of Christ Jesus. Which Paper was humbly owned, and was, and is attended to be made good by Major Butler, Mr. Charles Vane, Col. Danvers, Mr. Jackson, Mr. VVall and Mr. Turner. Also a Letter from Mr. Goad, to Major Butler upon occasion of the said fourth Paper, By way of Explanation upon the Four Proposalls of it, By R. W. etc. [London, 1652.] (Ed. Clarence S. Brigham for the Club of Colonial Reprints. Providence, 1903).

The Hireling Ministry None of Christs, or a Discourse touching the Propagating the Gospel of Christ Jesus. Humbly Presented to such Pious and Honourable Hands, whom the present Debate thereof concerns. London, 1652.

Experiments of Spiritual Life and Health, and their Preservationes in the Weakest Child of God may get Assurance of his Spirituall Life and Blessednesse, of his Christian Growth, and the means of it. London, 1652.

George Fox Digg'd out of his burrowes, or an Offer of Disputation on fourteen Proposalls made this last summer 1672 (so call'd) unto G. Fox than present on Rhode-Island in New-England, by R. W. As also how (G. Fox slily departing) the Disputation went on being managed three dayes at Newport on Rhode-Island, and one at Providence, between John Stubs, John Burnet, and William Edmundson on the one part, and R. W. on the other. In which many Quotations out of G. Fox and Ed. Burrowes Book in Folio are alledged. With an Appendix in some scores of G. F. his simple lame Answers to his Opposites in that Book, quoted and replyed to. Boston, 1776. Reprinted in Narragansett Club Publications, Vol. V. (Ed. J. L. Diman, 1872.)

Letters. From the year 1632 to 1675. In part reprinted in Massachusetts Historical Society Collections, Fourth Series, Vol. VI. Collected for the first time in Narragansett Club Publications, Vol. VI. (Ed. J. R. Bartlett, 1774.) Eight letters to Winthrop, reprinted in Old South Leaflets, No. 54, Vol. III.

Ten Letters. Rhode Island Historical Society Publications, New Series, Vol. VIII.

Manuscript of *Esau and Jacob's Mystical Harmony.* Copy in Massachusetts Historical Society Library.

Letters of Roger Williams to Lady Masham. Photostats in Rhode Island Historical Society Library. Printed in New England Historical and Genealogical Register, Vol. XLIII, p. 315, and in Rhode Island Historical Society Collections, Vol. XI, p. 132.

II. LIFE AND CRITICISM

Angell (Walter), *Williams vs. Williams Suit in Chancery,* 1644. Given to Rhode Isand Hist. Soc.

Arnold (Samuel G.), *History of Rhode Island* 1636-1790. Two volumes. New York, 1859-60. Chronological Record.

Carpenter (Edmund J.), *Roger Williams; a Study of the Life, Times and Character of a Political Pioneer.* Grafton Hist. Series. New York, 1909.

Dean (John W.), *Early Statements Relative to the Early Life of Roger Williams.* N. E. Hist. and Gen. Reg. Vol. L.

Deane (Charles), *Roger Williams and the Massachusetts Charter.* Mass. Hist. Soc. Proc. Feb., 1873.

Dexter (Henry M.), *As to Roger Williams and his "Banishment" from the Massachusetts Plantation.* Boston, 1876.

Durfee (Thomas), *Two Hundred and Fiftieth Anniversary of the Planting of Providence.* June 24, 1886.

Eddy (D. C.), *Roger Williams and the Baptists.* Boston, 1861.

Elton (Romeo), *Life of Roger Williams.* London and Providence, 1873.

Gammel (William), *Roger Williams.* Sparks Lib. Am. Bio., 2nd Series. Vol. IV. New York, 1844-8.

Guild (R. A.), *An Account of the Writings of Roger Williams.* Providence, 1862.
  Footprints of Roger Williams. Providence, 1886.
  Roger Williams, Freeman of Massachusetts. Am. Antiques Soc., New Series, Vol. V. Worcester, 1888.

Hall (Mary E.), *Roger Williams.* Boston, 1917.

Johnson (L. D.), *The Spirit of Roger Williams.* Boston, 1839.

Knowles (James D.), *Memoirs of Roger Williams.* Boston, 1834.

Matthews (A. R.), *Roger Williams and Sir Thomas Urquhart.* N. Y. Nation, Vol. LXX, p. 435.

Merriman (Titus M.), *Pilgrims, Puritans, and Roger Williams Vindicated, etc.* Boston, 1892.

Straus (Oscar S.), *Roger Williams, the Pioneer of Religious Liberty.* Boston, 1894.

Tuckerman (H. T.), *Roger Williams, The Tolerant Colonist.* In Essays, Biographical and Critical. Boston, 1857.

III. HISTORICAL BACKGROUND

Acts of the United Colonies of New England, Vols. IX-X, Plymouth Colony Records. (Ed. Hazard) Vol. II, Historical Collection. Philadelphia, 1792-4.

Adams (Brooks), *The Emancipation of Massachusetts.* Boston, 1887.

Adams (Charles Francis), *Massachusetts, Its Historians and History.* Boston and New York, 1893.
  Three Episodes of Massachusetts History. Boston and New York, 1903.

Adams (James T.), *The Founding of New England.* Boston, 1921.

Backus (Isaac), *History of New England.* Two volumes, 2nd ed. Backus Historical Society. Newton, Massachusetts. 1871.

Baillie (Robert), *Dissvasive from the Errour of the Times.* London, 1645.

Bancroft (George), *History of the United States,* Vol. I. New York, 1895.

Barry (John S.), *The History of Massachusetts.* Boston, 1855-57.

Bax (Ernest B.), *Rise and Fall of the Anabaptists.* New York, 1903.

Beard (Charles A.), *The Reformation of the Sixteenth Century in its Relation to Modern Thought and Knowledge.* In Hibbert's Lectures. 5th ed., 1906.

Bowen (C. W.), *Boundary Disputes of Connecticut.* Boston, 1882.

Bradford (William), *History of Plymouth Plantation.* Printed from original Mss. for the Massachusetts Historical Society, 1856.

Bryce (James), *The Relation of the Advanced and Backward Races of Mankind.* Romanes Lecture. Oxford, 1902.

Bull (Henry), *Sketches of the History of the State of Rhode Island.* Published by Rhode Island Republican at Newport. 1832.

Byington (Ezra), *The Puritan in England and New England.* Boston, 1900.

Calendars of State Papers, Colonial Series, America and West Indies, 1574-1696. 9 volumes, 1860-1903.

Callender (John), *An Historical Discourse on the Civil and Religious Affairs of the Colony of Rhode Island, etc.* Boston, 1739. Reprinted, 1838.

Campbell (Douglas), *The Puritans in Holland, England and America.* New York, 1892.

Chalmers (George), *Political Annals of the Present United Colonies from their Settlement to the Peace of* 1763. London, 1780.

Channing (Edward), *History of the United States.* 6 volumes. See Vol. I. New York, 1907-1921.

Clarke (John), *Ill Newes from New England: or a Narrative of New England's Persecution.* London, 1652.

Connecticut Colonial Records. (Ed. Dr. J. H. Trumbull.) 12 volumes. 1850-82. Hartford.

Connecticut Historical Society Collection. 1860-70.

Constitution of the United States.

Cotton (John), *The Way of the Churches of New England.* London, 1645.
The Way of the Congregational Churches Cleared. London, 1648.

Crosby (Thomas), *History of the English Baptists.* 4 volumes. London, 1738-1740.

Daly (Charles P.), *The Settlement of the Jews in North America.* (Ed. Max Kohler.) New York, 1893.

Dexter (Henry M.), *The Congregationalism of the Last Three Hundred Years as Seen in its Literature.* New York, 1880.

Doyle (John A.), *English Colonies in America.* 3 volumes. See Vols. II-III, "Puritan Colonies." New York, 1889.

Drake (Samuel G.), *History and Antiquity of Boston.* Boston, 1856.

Drake (Samuel A.), *The Making of New England.* New York 1900.

Edwards (Morgan), *History of the Baptists of Rhode Island,* Rhode Island Hist. Soc. Coll., Vol. VI, 1885. Providence, 1885.

Edwards (Thomas), *Antapologia*. London, 1644.
Gangroena. London, 1647.

Ellis (George E.), *Puritan Age and Rule in Massachusetts.* (1629-1685.) New York, 1888.

Felt (Joseph B.), *The Ecclesiastical History of New England.* 2 volumes. Boston, 1862.

Field (Edward), *State of Rhode Island and Providence Plantation*. Boston, 1902.

Fisher (George P.), *The Reformation*. New York, 1907.

Fiske (John), *The Beginnings of New England*. Boston, 1889.

Gardiner (Samuel R.), *History of the Commonwealth and Protectorate* 1649-1656. New ed. London, 1903.
History of England . . . 1603-1642. 10 volumes. London, 1883-84.

Gardiner (James W.), *A History of the Great Civil War.* 1642-1649. 2nd ed. 3 volumes. London, 1888-91.

Goodwin (John A.), *The Pilgrim Republic*. Boston, 1887.

Gorton (Samuel), *Simplicity's Defence Against Seven-Headed Policy*. London, 1646. Republished in Coll. of Rhode Island Hist. Soc., Vol. III. Narrative centers around Warwick.

Hallam (Henry), *View of the State of Europe, During the Middle Ages*. New York, 1872.

Hart (Albert B.), *American History Told by Contemporaries.* Vol. I. "Era of Colonization, 1492-1689." New York, 1898-1901.

Hazard (E.), *Collection of State Papers.* 2 volumes. Philadelphia, 1792, 1794.

Holmes (Abiel), *American Annals*—1492 to 1806. Cambridge, Mass., 1813.

Hopkins (Stephen), *History of Providence*. Appeared in *Providence Gazette*—1762. Republished collection of the Mass. Hist. Soc. History of Town of Providence to 1645.

Hosmer (James K.), *The Life of Young Sir Henry Vane, Governor of Massachusetts Bay, and Leader of the Long Parliament*. New York, 1889.

Howard (George E.), *An Introduction to Local Constitutional History of the United States*. Baltimore, 1889.

Hubbard (William), *A General History of New England from the Discovery to MDCLXXX.* Mass. Hist. Soc., Cambridge, 1815.

   The History of the Indian Wars in New England from the first Settlement to the Termination of the War with King Philip, in 1677. (Woodward Hist. Series.) Roxbury, Mass., 1865.

Hutchinson (Thomas), *The History of . . . Massachusetts Bay.* Boston, 1764-1828.

Johnston (Alexander), *History of Connecticut.* New York, 1887.

Kimball (Gertrude S.), *Providence in Colonial Times.* New York, 1912.

King (Henry), *Sir Henry Vane, Jr., Governor of Massachusetts and Friend of Roger Williams and Rhode Island.* Providence, 1909.

Lechford (Thomas), *Plain Dealing.* London, 1642.

Lecky (W. E. H.), *History of the Rise and Influence of the Spirit of Rationalism in Europe.* 2 volumes. 2nd ed. London, 1865.

Lindsay (Thomas M.), *A History of the Reformation.* 2 volumes. New York, 1906-07.

   Luther and the German Reformation. Edinburgh, 1913.

Lowell (James R.), *New England Two Centuries Ago.* (In *Among My Books*). New York, 1871.

Massachusetts Historical Society Proceedings, Vols. I-LVIII. Boston, 1791-1925.

Massachusetts Historical Society Collections. Boston, 1794-1923.

Masson (David), *Life of Milton.* London, 1859-1880. Especially Vols. II-III.

Mather (Cotton), *Magnalia Christi Americana.* VII, 2. Hartford, 1855.

Morton (John), *The Heart of New England Rent at the Blasphemies of the Present Generation.* London, 1660.

Morton (Nathaniel), *New England's Memorial: or A Brief Relation, etc.* Boston, 1855.

Narragansett Historical Register. Providence, 1882-1890.

Neal, (Daniel), *The History of the Puritans, or Protestant Non-conformists.* Vols. I, II. New York, 1848-49.

Newman (Albert H.), *A History of the Baptist Churches in the United States.* Philadelphia, 1898.

Nuelsen (John L.), *Luther the Leader.* Cincinnati, 1906.

Osgood (Herbert L.), *American Colonies in the Eighteenth Century.* New York, 1924.

Painter (F. V. N.), *Luther on Education.* Philadelphia, 1889.

Palfrey (John G.), *History of New England.* New York, 1866.

Parrington (Vernon L.), *Main Currents in American Thought,* Vol. I. New York, 1927.

Potter (Elisha R.), *The Early History of Narragansett.* Providence, 1835.

Prince (Thomas), *A Chronological History of New England in the Form of Annals.* (Ed. Drake, 1736.)

Providence Records, 17 volumes. 1892-1905.

Ranke (Leopold), *History of the Reformation in Germany.* 2nd ed., translated by Sorel Austin. New York, 1905.

Rhode Island Historical Society Collections. 1872-1897. 9 volumes; 1918-1925, Vols. XI-XVIII.

Rhode Island Historical Society Publications. New Series. Vols. I-VIII. 1893. Jan., 1901. Providence Society, 1893-1901.

Rhode Island Historical Society Proceedings, 1872-1892. 21 numbers. Providence.

Rhode Island and Providence Plantations in New England, Records of the Colony of, Vols. I and II. Providence, 1856.

Richman (Irving Berdine), *Rhode Island: Its Making and Its Meaning.* 1636-1683. 2 volumes. New York and London. 1902.

Rhode Island: A Study in Separatism. Boston and New York, 1905.

Rider (Sidney S.), *Rhode Island Historical Tracts.* Series 1, 1877-1895, Nos. 1-20; Series 2, 1889-1896, Nos. 1-5. Providence.

Scottow (Joshua), *A Narrative of the Planting of Massachusetts Colony, etc.* Mass. Hist. Coll., Vol. IV.

Smith (Helen A.), *The Thirteen Colonies*. New York and London, 1901.

Sprague (William B.), *Annals of the American Pulpit*. Vols. I-II. New York, 1857.

Staples (William R.), *Annals of the Town of Providence from its Settlement to the Organization of the City Government*. June, 1832. Providence, 1843.

Steffens (Joseph L.), *The Struggle of Self-Government*. New York, 1906. "Rhode Island: a corrupted people."

Tyler (Moses C.), *History of American Literature During the Colonial Period* . 1607-1765. New York, 1898.

Updike (Wilkins), *History of Episcopal Church in Narragansett, R. I., etc.* New York, 1907.

Upham (Charles W.), *Life of Sir Henry Vane, Fourth Governor of Massachusetts*. Spark Libr. of Am. Bio. Vol. IV, pp. 85-403. 1854-72.

Vedder (Henry C.), *The Reformation in Germany*. New York, 1914.

Ward (Nathaniel), *Simple Cobbler of Agawan*. 1647.

Waters (Henry F.), *Genealogical Gleanings in England*. N. E. Hist. and Gen. Reg., Vol. XLIII, 290ff.

Weeden (William B.), *Early Rhode Island; A Social History of the People*. (Grafton Historical Series.) New York, 1910.

Welde (Thomas), *A Short Story of the Rise, Reign and Ruin of Antinomians, Familists, and Libertines that Infected the Churches of New England*. London, 1644.

Willcock (John), *Life of Sir Henry Vane, The Younger, Statesman and Mystic*. London, 1913.

Winslow (Edward), *Hypocrisie Unmasked*. 1646.

Winsor (Justin), *Narrative and Critical History of New England*. New York, 1884.

Winthrop (John), *Journal, "History of New England."* 2 volumes. (Ed. J. K. Hosmer.) New York, 1908.

IV. POLITICAL THEORIES

A. AMERICAN

Adams (Brooks), *The Theory of Social Revolutions.* New York, 1913.

Adams (John), *Works.* 10 volumes. (Ed. C. F. Adams.) Boston, 1856.

Adlam (Samuel), *Origin of the Institutions of Rhode Island.* Providence, 1871.

Beard (Charles A.), *The Economic Basis of Politics.* New York, 1922.

Bentley (Arthur), *The Process of Government.* Chicago, 1908.

Bourgeaud (Charles). *The Rise of Modern Democracy in Old and New England.* London, 1894.

Burgess (John W.), *Political Science and Comparative Constitutional Law.* 2 volumes. Boston and London, 1890.

Calhoun (John), *Works.* 6 volumes. New York, 1888.

Cambridge Platform of Church Discipline. 1648.

Coker (Francis W.), *Readings in Political Philosophy.* New York, 1914.

Constitutional History of Rhode Island. 1636-1792. (Ed. Arnold Green.) Providence, 1885.

Chamberlain (L. T.), *The State, its Nature, Origin and Functions.* New York, 1898.

Chipman (Nathaniel), *Principles of Government: a Treatise on Free Institutions.* Burlington, Vt., 1833.

Dickinson (Edwin De W.), *The Equality of States in International Law.* Cambridge, Mass., 1920.

Dodd (Walter F.), *Modern Constitutions.* 2 volumes. Chicago, 1909.

Federalist, The: Philadelphia, 1892.

Fenwick (Charles G.), *International Law.* New York and London, 1924.

Fiske (John), *Civil Government in the United States Considered with Some Reference to its Origin.* New ed. Boston, 1898.

Fundamental Orders of Connecticut. (1639).

Garner (James W.), *Introduction to Political Science.* Chicago, 1910.

Gettell (Raymond G.), *Introduction to Political Science.* Boston, New York, 1910.
History of Political Thought. New York and London, 1924.

Goodnow (Frank J.), *Principles of Constitutional History.* New York and London, 1916.

Hart (Albert B.), *Actual Government as Applied under American Conditions.* New York, 1903.

Holcombe (Arthur N.), *Foundations of the Modern Commonwealth.* New York, 1923.

Hooker (Thomas), *The Saints Dignitie and Dutie.*
A Survey of the Summe of Church Discipline. London, 1648.

Innes (A. Taylor), *Church and State.* 2nd ed. No date. New York.

Kentucky and Virginia Resolutions. (1798-9.) Documentary Source Book of American History. Macdonald. New York, 1926.

Lieber (Francis), *On Civil Liberty and Self-Government.* (4th ed. rev. by Theodore Woolsey.) Philadelphia, 1901.

Madison (James), *Notes on Jonathan Debates.* Works, Vol. V. New York, 1900-05.

McIlwain (Charles H.), *The Political Works of James I.* Printed from the ed. 1616. Camb. Univ. Press, 1918.

Merriam (Charles E., Jr.), *History of the Theory of Sovereignty since Rousseau.* New York, 1900.
American Political Theories. New York, 1920.

McKechnie (William S.), *The State and the Individual.* New York, 1896.

Model of Church and Civil Power, by the Ministers of Massachusetts Bay. Quoted in part by Roger Williams in the *Bloudy Tenent of Persecution,* Narr. Cl. Pub., Vol. III, pp. 221 ff.

Moriarty (Andrew, Jr.), *Manuscript Abstracts,* in Rhode Island Hist. Soc. Pub., 1892-1901. Providence.

Moulton (Augustus F.), *Church and State in New England.* Portland, Me., 1901.

Munro (William B.), *The Government of the United States.* New York, 1919.

Osgood (Herbert L.), *The Political Theories of the Puritans.* Political Science Quarterly, 1891.

Poore (Benjamin P.), *The Federal and State Constitutions, Colonial Charters, and Other Organic Laws of the United States.* 2 volumes. Washington, 1878.

Pound (Roscoe), *The End of Law.* Harvard Law Review, 226. *An Introduction to the Philosophy of Law.* New Haven, 1922.

Prall (William), *The State and the Church.* San Francisco, 1900.

Scott (Ebers G.), *Development of Constitutional Liberty in the English Colonies of America.* New York, 1882.

Sherger (George L.), *The Evolution of Modern Liberty.* New York, 1904.

Sheldon (Henry C.), *History of Christian Doctrine.* 4th ed. New York, 1906.

Stevens (Charles E.), *Sources of the Constitution of the United States.* 2nd ed. New York, 1894.

Story (Joseph), *Commentaries on the Constitution of the United States.* 2 volumes. Book I, Chapter I. Boston, 1891.

Straus (Oscar), *The Origin of Republican Form of Government in the United States of America.* New York, 1900.

Sullivan (James), *The Antecedents of the Declaration of Independence.* Am. Hist. Ass'n. Annual Report for 1900. Vol. I, pp. 65-85.

Taylor (Thomas W., Jr.), *The Individual and the State.* Boston, 1895.

Tucker (H. St. George), *Blackstone's Commentaries: with Notes of Reference to the Constitution and Laws of the . . . United States and of . . . Virginia.* n.p. 1803.

Walker (Thomas A.), *History of the Law of Nations.* 2 volumes. New York, 1899-1900.

Webster (Daniel), *Works.* 16th ed. Boston, 1872.

Willoughby (William F.), *The Government of the Modern State.* New York, 1919.

Willoughby (Westel W.), *An Examination of the Nature of the State.* New York, 1896.
The American Constitutional System. New York, 1904.

Wilson (Woodrow), *Old Master and Other Essays.* New York. 1893.

The Real Idea of Democracy. Chapter on "Problems of Modern Democracy." Philadelphia, 1901.

The State. Revised Edition. Boston, 1902.

Constitutional Government in the United States. New York, 1911.

Address at Independence Hall, July 4, 1914. New York, 1918.

Woolsey (Theodore D.), *Political Science, or the State.* 2 volumes. New York, 1900.

B. Ancient and Medieval

Ante-Nicene and Post-Nicene Fathers. New York, 1885-1896.

Aquinas (Thomas), *Opuscula Contra errores Croetorum; Summa Theologia: De Regimine Principium; Summa Contra Gentiles. (Opera Omnia.* Antwerp 1612, and Parma, 1852-72.)

Aristotle, *Ethics and Politics.* A translation from the Greek. London, 1813.

Augustine (St.), *Works.* New York, 1901-05. Vol. I, *Confessions.* Vol. II, *De Civitate Dei.* Sermons in *Ante-Nicene and Post-Nicene Fathers.*

Cicero, *De Republica.* Milano, 1916.

Dante (Alighieri), *Monarchia.* Translation and notes by Aurelia Henry. Boston and New York, 1904.

Dunning (William A.), *A History of Political Theories: Ancient and Medieval.* New York, 1902.

Engelbert von Volkersdorf: *De Ortu.* Basle, 1553.

Eusebius (Pamplitus), *Ecclesiastical History.* Translated from the Greek by C. E. Cruse. London, 1908.

Gerson (Johannes), *Opera Omnia,* (Ed. Goldast). Vol. II, 1384 *et seq.* Antwerp, 1706.

Gierke (Otto), *Political Theories of the Middle Ages.* Translated by F. W. Maitland. Cambridge, 1900.

Giles of Rome, *De Potestate ecclesiastica.* Vienna, 1862.

Gratianus (Franciscus), *Decretium Gratiani.* Leipzig, 1879.

Jenks (Edward), *Law and Politics in the Middle Ages.* New York, 1898.

Machiavelli (Niccolo), *The Prince.* New York, 1908 (Everyman).

Manegold von Lautenbach, *Works in Monumenta Historica Libelli de Lite.* Vol. I, 308 *et seq.*

Marsiglio of Padua, *Defensor Pacis.* Frankfort, 1612. *De Concordia Catholica.*

Occam, William of, *Octo Quaestiones: Dialogues.* Strassburg, 1491.

Plato, *Republic.* Translated by Benjamin Jewett. Oxford, 1908. *Dialogues.* New York, 1875.

Polybius, *Histories.* Translated by Evelyn S. Schuckburgh. 2 volumes. New York, 1889.

Poole (Reginald L.), *Illustrations of Medieval Thought.* London, 1884.

John of Salisbury (Saresberiensis), *Opera Omnia in Migne.* Tom. 199. Liepzig, 1862.

Smith (Arthur L.), *Church and State in the Middle Ages.* Oxford, 1913.

Thomas of Canterbury, *Opera Omnia in Migne,* l. c., Tom. 190.

Ulpianus (Domitius), *Domiti Ulpiani Fragmento.* Bonn, 1836.

Wycliff (Johannes), *Trialogus et Supplementum.* "Trialogi." (Ed. Oxon.) 1869.
De Civili Dominio. London, 1885.
De Dominio Divino, London, 1890.

C. Reformation and Post-Reformation

Agreement of the Army, 1649. [London.]

Agreement of the People, 1647. [London.]

Augsburg Confession. Philadelphia, 1892.

Bacon (Francis), *Novum Organum.* Translated. London, 1900.

Bodin (Jean), *De la République.* Paris, 1577.

Brown, *A Book which Sheweth,* 1582.
True and Short Declaration, 1584.

Barclay (Robert), *Inner Life of the Religious Societies of the Commonwealth.* London, 1876.

Calvin (John), *Institutes of the Christian Religion.* Translation by Henry Beveridge. Edinburgh, 1845-6.

Duff (Robert A.), *Spinoza's Political and Ethical Philosophy.* Glasgow, 1903.

Dunning (William Archibald), *A History of Political Theories, from Luther to Montesquieu.* New York, 1905.

Filmer (Robert), *Patriarcha.* In John Locke, *Two Treatises on Civil Government.* London, 1751.

Gardiner (Samuel R.), *Constitutional Documents of the Puritan Revolution.* 1625-1660.. Oxford, 1899.

Grotius (Hugo), *De Jure Belli ac Pacis.* In the Classics of International Law, Carnegie Institute, Vol. I. Reproduction of Edition of 1646. Vol. II, Translation of the Text. Washington, D. C., 1913.

Harrington (James), *The Commonwealth of Oceana.* (1656). London, 1737.

Hobbes (Thomas), *Leviathan:* or the Matter, Force & Power of a Commonwealth, ecclesiastical and civill. Cambridge, 1904.

Hooker (Richard), *Ecclesiastical Polity.* London, 1705.

Locke (John), *Two Treatises on Civil Government.* Works, Vol. II. London, 1751.

Luther (Martin), *D. Martin Luther's Werke. Kritische Gesammatus-Gabe.* Herman Bohlau, Weimar, 1883-91. 33 volumes. *Works of.* 2 volumes. Philadelphia, 1915.

Milton (John), *The Prose Works of.* Vol. II. London, 1909. *The Tenure of Kings and Magistrates,* 1649. *Areopagitica.*

More (Sir Thomas), *Utopia.* New York, 1887.

Murray (Robert H.), *The Political Consequences of the Reformation.* London, 1926.

Pufendorf (Samuel von), *De Jure Naturae et Gentium.* In the Classics of International Law, Carnegie Institute. Vol. I. Original Text of 1676. Vol. II, a Translation. Washington, D. C., 1916.

Robinson (John), *Justification of Separation: A Just and Necessary Apology,* 1610. *Essays of Observations Divine and Moral.* 1625.

Spinoza (Benedictus de), *Tractus Politicus: Ethica.* 2 volumes. London, 1900-1.

Suarez (F.), *Tractatus de Legibus ac Deo Legislatore.* 2 volumes. Porsius, 1841.

Tracts on Liberty of Conscience and Persecution; 1614-1661. By the Hanserd Knollys Society, with an Historical Introduction by Edward Bean Underhill. London, 1846.

Waring (Luther H.), *The Political Theories of Martin Luther.* New York and London, 1910.

D. MODERN EUROPEAN

Austin (John), *Lectures on Jurisprudence, or the Philosophy of Positive Law.* 2 volumes. London, 1873.

Barker (Ernest, *Political Thought in England from Herbert Spencer to the Present Day.* (Home University Library Series) New York and London, 1906.

Bentham (James), *Fragments on Government.* Oxford, 1776.

Bluntschli (J. K.), *The Theory of State.* Authorized English translation from the 6th German edition, 1885.

Brett (Oliver), *A Defence of Liberty.* New York, 1921.

Bryce (James), *Studies in History and Jurisprudence.* New York, 1901.
Modern Democracies. New York, 1921.

Bullowa (Ferdinand), *The History of the Theory of Sovereignty.* New York, 1895.

Carlyle (Thomas), *The French Revolution, A History.* New York and London, 1902.

Cobb (Sanford H.), *Rise of Religious Liberty in America.* New York and London, 1902.

Cole (G. D. H.), *Chaos and Order in Industry.* London, 1920.
Social Theory. London, 1920.
Guild Socialism. In Hague, *British Labour Speaks.* New York, 1924.

Dicey (Albert V.), *Lectures on the Relation Between Law and Public Opinion in England During the Nineteenth Century.* London, 1905.

Duguit (Leon), *Law in the Modern State.* New York, 1919.

Figgis (John N.), *Studies of Political Thought from Gerson to Grotius*, 1414-1625. 2nd ed. Cambridge, 1907.
Church in the Modern State. New York, 1913.
The Divine Right of Kings. Cambridge, 1914.

Geffcken (Heinrich), *Church and State; their Relations Historically Developed.* 2 volumes. Translated by Edward Fairfax Taylor. London, 1877.

Gervinus (George G.), *Einleitung in die Geschichte des Neunzehnten Jahrhunderts.* Leipzig, 1853.

Gilchrist (Robert), *Principles of Political Science.* New York, 1921.

Gooch (George P.), *History of Democratic Ideas of the Seventeenth Century.* Cambridge, 1898.
Political Thought in England from Bacon to Halifax. London, 1914-15.

Harnack (Adolph), *History of Dogma.* Translation published by Williams and Norgate. London, 1899.

Hoffmann (Frank S.), *The Sphere of the State; or, the People as a Body Politic.* Edition Revised. New York, 1898.

Holtzendorf (Franz J. W. P. von), *Die Principien der Politik.* Berlin, 1869.

Humboldt (William von), *Sphere and Duties of Government.* Translated by Joseph Coulthard, Jr. London, 1854.

Huxley (Thomas H.), *Methods and Results.* In Essays, London, 1912.

Jellinek (Georg), *The Declaration of the Rights of Man and of Citizens.* Translated by Max Farrand. New York, 1901.

Jenks (Edward), *Government of Victoria.* London and New York, 1891.

Kant (Emmanuel), *Richtlehre.* In his Sämmtliche Werke. Leipzig, 1867-68.

Krabbe (Hugo), *The Modern Idea of the State.* New York, 1922.

Laski (Harold J.), *Studies in the Problem of Sovereignty.* New Haven, 1917.
Authority in the Modern State. New Haven, 1919.
The Foundations of Sovereignty. New York, 1921.
A Grammar of Politics. London, 1925.

Lasson, *System der Rechtsphilosophie.* Berlin, 1882.

Mackinnon (James), *A History of Modern Liberty.* 2 volumes. London, 1906.

Maine (Henry S.), *Ancient Law.* 3rd American and 6th London ed. New York, 1885.

Marx (Karl), *Kapital.* Chicago, 1906-09.

Maurice (Frederick D.), *The Workingman and the Franchise.* London and New York, 1866.

Montesquieu, *Spirit of the Laws.* (Bohn Library) New York, 1902.

Morris (William), *Socialism, Its Growth and Outcome.* London and New York, 1893.

Oppenheimer (Franz), *The State; Its History and Development Viewed Sociologically.* Indianapolis, 1914.

Owen (Robert), *A New View of Society.* Edinburgh, 1812. *Outline of the Rational System of Society.* London, 1830.

Paine (Tom), *The Rights of Man. The writings of Thomas Paine,* Vol. II. New York, 1894-96. (Ed. M. D. Conway.)

Pollock (Sir Frederick), *An Introduction to the History of the Science of Politics.* London, 1890.

Ritchie (David G.), *Natural Rights.* London, 1895. *Principles of State Interference.* New York, no date. *Studies in Political and Social Ethics.* New York, 1902.

Rousseau (Jean Jacques), *Social Contract.* New York, 1893.

Russell (Bertrand), *Political Ideals.* New York, 1917. *Proposed Roads to Freedom.* London, 1919.

Sidgwick (Henry), *The Development of European Polity.* New York, 1903.

Sorel, (Georges), *Le Décomposition du Marxisme.* Paris, 1910.

Stahl (F. J.), *Die Philosophie des Rechts.* 2 volumes in 3 parts. Heidelberg, 1854-56.

Stubbs (William), *The Constitutional History of England in its Origin and Development.* 3 volumes. Oxford, 1896.

Tocqueville (Alexis de), *Democracy in America.* Translated by Henry Reeve. New York, 1904.